THE
HIDDEN
CAMPAIGN

THE
HIDDEN
CAMPAIGN

FDR'S HEALTH AND
THE 1944 ELECTION

HUGH E. EVANS, M.D.

M.E. Sharpe
Armonk, New York
London, England

Library of Congress Cataloging-in-Publication Data

Evans, Hugh E., 1934-
   The hidden campaign : FDR's health and the 1944 election / Hugh E. Evans.
      p. cm.
   Includes bibliographical references and index.
   ISBN 0-7656-0855-3 (alk. paper)
   1. Presidents—United States—Election—1944. 2. Roosevelt, Franklin D. (Franklin
Delano), 1882-1945—Health. 3. United States—Politics and government—1933-1945.
4. Presidents—United States—Biography. I. Title

E812 .E93 2002   2002021020
973′.09′9—dc21

Printed in the United States of America

The paper used in this publication meets the minimum requirements of
American National Standard for Information Sciences
Permanence of Paper for Printed Library Materials,
ANSI Z 39.48-1984.

MV (c)   10   9   8   7   6   5   4   3   2   1

Contents

List of Tables   vii
Preface   ix
Acknowledgments   xi
Introduction   xiii
Photographs follow page 42

1. The Twentieth-Century Presidency: A High-Risk Occupation   3
2. Pre-Presidential Years: The Defining Experiences   14
3. Presidential Years 1933–1943: The Picture of Health   26
4. Presidential Years 1943–1944: Decline and Deception   43
5. Presidential Years 1944–1945: The Last Campaign   62
6. "The Day of the Lord, April 12, 1945"   96
7. Lessons for the Twenty-First Century   118

Appendixes:
   A. Death Certificate of Franklin D. Roosevelt   135
   B. "Clinical Notes on the Illness and Death of President
      Franklin D. Roosevelt," *Howard G. Bruenn*   137
   C. Interviews   159
   D. Wartime Conferences   163

Notes   165
Bibliography   187
Index   193
About the Author   203

List of Tables

1.1 Longevity of Presidents Compared with Longevity
of Their Parents   5

1.2 Longevity of Presidents Compared with Longevity
of Cabinet Officers   5

1.3 Longevity of Presidents Compared with Longevity
of Supreme Court Justice Appointments   6

1.4 Presidential Life Expectancy   7

1.5 Twentieth-Century Mortality and Morbidity in Presidents
of the United States   9

1.6 Longevity of FDR's Vice Presidents and Cabinet Members   12

1.7 Longevity of World Leaders During Roosevelt's Presidency   12

3.1 FDR's Blood Pressure   40

3.2 Longevity in FDR's Family   40

4.1 Presidential White House Appointments Daily Average
for March 1934, 1937, 1939, 1941–45   49

4.2 *New York Times*: Number of References to FDR's Health   51

5.1 FDR's Survival Probability—Central Nervous System/Vascular
Lesion   68

5.2 FDR's Survival Probability—With Addition of Nephritis   68

5.3 FDR's Survival Probabilities—Cardiac Disease   68

6.1 Succession to the Presidency   107

Preface

The second Thursday in April 1945 was a warm and golden spring day. Hope was everywhere. The long and costly war in Europe was ending and victory seemed assured in the Pacific. The secular trinity—the Dodgers, Giants, and Yankees—had resumed playing baseball to crowds of admiring fans, including a growing number of returning servicemen. Lamb chops, always a treat for me as a child, were the main course at dinner that evening as they were every Thursday. Then came Captain Midnight's latest radio adventures. Spellbound, I listened—and then the world changed. Suddenly, the narrative stopped. Without preface or explanation, a voice intruded. "The president is dead," it announced. That was all.

To a child of that era, this was inconceivable. Franklin D. Roosevelt was the president. He had always been the president and would always be, or so it had seemed. I thought the announcement could be a mistake. There had been a premature announcement of V-E day a few weeks before. Some radio stations resumed their original broadcast, reinforcing that hopeful possibility. But finally every station on the band reiterated the shocking news. It was 5:47 P.M., Eastern War Time. To a ten–year-old's ears, the only clinical detail, a massive cerebral hemorrhage, sounded both grave and impressive, though of course I did not understand the terminology.

For three days following the death of the president, a kaleidoscope of eulogies, some from improbable sources like the newly installed Japanese government, cascaded over the airwaves. Intermixed were reminiscences and excerpts from Roosevelt's speeches, from "The only thing we have to fear . . ." through ". . . a date which will live in infamy" to "I see one-third of a nation. . . ." It was as if the country was trying to encapsulate in three days a tumultuous twelve-year period. Then came the ceremonies: a Lincolnesque funeral train from the Little White House in Warm Springs, Georgia; a procession in Washington; services in the East Room of the White House; and burial at Hyde Park, New York on Sunday, April 15. Amidst all this, Harry S. Truman, a stranger to most Americans after serving as vice president for only eighty-three days, was sworn in as Franklin D. Roosevelt's successor. Eventually, the pulse of government and life resumed.

Over my forty years as a physician I have assumed teaching, research, and administrative responsibilities in several large teaching hospitals. The interplay of medicine and politics has been for me a subject of study and daily concern. That interplay shaped the arc of Roosevelt's career and his life. Thus, it also shaped the course of world history. I have read many biographies of Roosevelt, and have poured over documents at the Roosevelt library at Hyde Park, reviewed papers from the Truman library, and interviewed friends, family members, professional associates, Secret Service agents, political scientists, historians, and even airplane pilots. Especially informative was the late Dr. Howard G. Bruenn, Roosevelt's cardiologist in the last year of the president's life. I have come to believe that the president's clinical history epitomizes the limitations of medicine when practiced in the context of extraordinary celebrity and intense political pressure.

The issues raised by Roosevelt's disabilities cast shadows over his presidency, shadows that persist over the half-century since his death. They also foreshadowed the future. Many health care issues of the 1990s and the new millennium were augured in the twelve years of his administration. Roosevelt's illnesses also shaped his style and the substance of his agenda. He assumed a leading advocacy role for the disabled. His paralysis notwithstanding, he endured the physical, intellectual, and emotional demands imposed by the two most threatening crises of the century, the Great Depression and World War II. He became a bold, seemingly indispensable leader. Political considerations ultimately compromised his health care. His years as president form the DNA of modern world politics and government, for better or worse.

I have sought objectivity throughout my study, but inevitably one's own biases and judgments intrude. Eleanor Roosevelt's pronouncement in late April 1945 that "the story is over"[1] is contradicted by events. The story, and its significance for the presidency, is still far from over. It will invite, if not demand, analysis and interpretation for generations to come.

Acknowledgments

This volume was prepared over the course of the past decade. Numerous people have contributed their recollections as cited. Others have advised me as a novice in this area. Doris Kearns Goodwin, Gerald Pomper, James MacGregor Burns, Stephen Ambrose, Robert Gilbert, Jerrold Post, Herbert Abrams, Geoffrey Ward, and Jan Herman made useful suggestions and identified many of the sources.

Dr. F. Kennon Moody whose PhD dissertation examined the relationship of Roosevelt to the people of Dutchess County, New York, and who for many years has been a recognized scholar and independent researcher of material in the Franklin D. Roosevelt Library, helped reorganize earlier editions and revise the citations, tables, and illustrations. He located the death certificate and provided the reference of Rabbi Edwin H. Friedman.

Mrs. Nancy Deegan, my secretary, has not only typed, and retyped the manuscript, research notes, and memoranda all too often, but has offered suggestions which have helped to clarify difficult areas. Even with modern technology this has been, at times, onerous for her, but she has worked with enthusiasm and humor. Ms. Pat Peluso, departmental secretary, completed this chore with dedication and skill, following Mrs. Deegan's retirement.

The Department of Pediatrics at New Jersey Medical School has been supportive of these efforts.

Scholars and archivists at the Franklin D. Roosevelt Library, Hyde Park, New York, and the Harry S. Truman Library, Independence, Missouri, have provided guidance and have offered useful advice.

Finally, I would like to dedicate this volume to the memory of Mrs. Ruth Evans (1940–1999), my wife of four decades. Her rare intelligence, wit, and charm were undimmed by the inexorable effects of end-stage renal disease. She discussed this project with me on many occasions, and was always constructive and insightful in her comments. I hope that these efforts will prove worthy of her.

Introduction

The death of President Franklin D. Roosevelt on April 12, 1945, came as a shocking surprise to a nation and world still engaged in war. The magnitude of shock and surprise at word of his death is a testimony to the success achieved in covering up his lethal illness from nearly everyone: the general public, leaders in government, family members, his successor, and the "patient" himself.[1]

A mortally ill chief executive, the commander-in-chief during the most significant war of the century, was repeatedly depicted to the public as healthy for over a year, the last of his life. In reality, he suffered from severe hypertension (elevated blood pressure) for several years. This had caused congestive heart failure,[2] and led to his fatal massive cerebral hemorrhage eighty-three days into his fourth term.[3] Death was described on the front page of the *New York Times* as "sudden and unexpected."[4]

His death was clearly predictable because of the severe hypertension sustained for several years. The resulting congestive heart failure was belatedly diagnosed on March 28, 1944, thirteen months prior to his death.

The 1944 presidential campaign included a "whispering campaign" and intimations by both friend and foe of grave illness.[5] The repeated reassurances of his official physician, Vice Admiral Ross T. McIntire, were entirely baseless and contrary to his known but closely guarded medical realities. There were no leaks prior to Roosevelt's death, but even at the moment of his death and for some time thereafter, the deception was reiterated by McIntire.[6] Roosevelt's clear physical deterioration, readily observed in newsreels and photographs, was rationalized in many ways. It was pointed out, with humor, that he was inevitably four years older than in his previous campaign in 1940, when he ran for an unprecedented third term. He must be assumed to be healthier than Stalin and Churchill, since he was younger. Fatigue, chronic bronchitis, episodes of influenza, colds, and intentional weight loss were invoked as explanations for his deteriorating appearance. Not a hint of even mild elevation in blood pressure, much less congestive heart failure and its ongoing treatment, was revealed to his staff.

Rationalizations aside, the voting public had a right to know that one candidate in the presidential election of 1944 was mortally ill with no realistic expectation of surviving a fourth four-year term. Indeed, Roosevelt's death occurred prior to the life expectancy of presidents generally, as expressed by actuarial information of that day. Mortality data forecast that he could have lived 21.4 years after being first inaugurated, but due to complications of severe hypertension he lived only 12.1 years of that interval.[7]

Misleading statements by both the physician and the patient constituted a positive spin on his physical condition. This was reinforced by his selective, but vigorous campaigning. His appearance in the fall campaign of 1944 in New York City in a driving rainstorm while in an open car, his ironic "Fala" speech, his address to the Foreign Policy Association, all enhanced the illusion of reasonable health.

Harry S. Truman, as senator, reluctant vice presidential nominee, vice president elect, and for eighty-three days vice president was not advised, even in deepest confidence, of the inevitable, fatal outcome of Roosevelt's deteriorating health.

The cover-up of Roosevelt's illness had been so effective that even his increasingly fatigued, haggard appearance at the Yalta conference did not trigger general alarms. No disclosure was made of an abnormality in his pulse, strongly associated with congestive heart failure, for twenty-five years. His final public address, delivered to a joint session of Congress, March 1, 1945 was generally well received. His excessive ad-libs and momentary lapses when he lost his place in the text were not attributed to his rapidly deteriorating health.

"Don't you know there is a war on?" was the most frequent question of the era. All other concerns faded into the background. War news saturated the consciousness of the public, on a controlled and censored basis. The domestic and foreign travels of the commander-in-chief were military secrets—including foreign travel to an unprecedented extent in the history of the presidency. Roosevelt could, and did, disappear from public view for days, weeks, and even a month without inquiry, much less concern for his health. A "vacation" was the explanation given for his one-month stay in April 1944 at Hobcaw, the home of Bernard Baruch in South Carolina. This was immediately following the initial belated diagnosis on March 28, 1944 of congestive heart failure by his new physician, Dr. Howard G. Bruenn who was sworn to secrecy.[8] The global struggle commanded the attention of the entire nation. With it were the inevitable casualty lists published each day, ultimately including 500,000 fatalities. Nothing less than complete dedication was demanded of a wartime commander-in-chief. He could not leave his post any more readily than those in actual combat.

Mass media was technologically sophisticated and in frequent contact with the president. Indeed, 998 press conferences were held by Roosevelt, the last only a few days before his death. However, the style of that era precluded detailed discussion of health issues. They were, simply, personal. Presidents were accorded a wide perimeter of privacy, extending to both their health and sexual activities. The media, operating under wartime restrictions would not penetrate the curtain of misleading medical information that related to Roosevelt. Even the *New York Times* accepted reassuring reiterations by Roosevelt's official physician (McIntire), plainly at variance with his progressively haggard appearance, without question. A decade would elapse before presidential illness would be presented in clinical detail. The front-page mention, in the *New York Times*, of President Eisenhower's bowel movements created controversy even in 1955.

Roosevelt was shielded by his iconic status. More than any other twentieth-century president he was either deified or demonized, with little space between these polarities. This status created an illusion. Having survived so much, medically and politically, there was the general presumption, indeed illusion, of indefinite survival regardless of obvious deterioration.

Roosevelt's overall wartime leadership largely transcended partisanship. Continuity of direction was considered essential by most even if long-term survival was not realistic. An ideologically divergent pair of observers, Douglas MacArthur II and Professor Richard Neustadt, said that they probably would have voted for Roosevelt, and would have encouraged others to do so, even if they had known that his fourth term could end in eighty-three days because his role was, in their view, absolutely vital.[9]

The eighty-three days, January 20 to April 12, 1945, were critical in shaping the world for generations to come. National boundaries in Europe and Asia were being determined. The United Nations was in active early formation. The final scientific and military efforts were being completed to launch the nuclear era. The deft touch of Roosevelt was vital in maintaining the alliance in spite of ever increasing strains as victory neared.

The presidency and personality of Roosevelt had achieved an unparalleled level of indispensability in the conduct of the Allied cause. The cover-up of Roosevelt's medical condition was the first at a presidential level in the modern mass media era. It contrasts sharply with the more recent presidential cover-ups. Roosevelt's cover-up was successful at the time and for years thereafter. The issue was only medical and because it was never uncovered had no immediate political impact. The consequence of this cover-up was the sacrifice of Roosevelt's health. At present the perimeter of privacy accorded national politicians is narrower and the president today receives far greater scrutiny from the press. This change in coverage began in the 1970s as a result of the Watergate scandal during the presidency of Richard M. Nixon.

Months of White House deception and misinformation obstructed justice and ultimately led to Nixon's resignation from the office in August of 1974.[10] "Twelve years later, during the administration of Ronald Reagan, the United States Senate and the Tower Board revealed deception by the executive branch regarding diversion of revenues from the sale of missiles to Iran and to the Contras in Nicaragua.[11] The cover-up led to numerous resignations and indictments and damaged the reputation of President Reagan. In the 1990s, President Bill Clinton became embroiled in numerous scandals, some of which also involved deception and the effort to cover up information. His misleading statements to a grand jury led to his impeachment in 1999.[12] All of these scandals had serious repercussions and revealed the dire consequences presidents face when they lie to or attempt to conceal information from the American public.

The presidential scandals and cover-ups of the late twentieth century eroded the stature of the office, the respect usually accorded its occupants, and their credibility. Crisis management is undermined by suspicions of presidential motives. These cover-ups of presidential behavior have caused the words and deeds of the chief executive in many instances to be dimly viewed through the murky lens of scandal.

The central focus in American political life from 1933 to 1945 was the president himself. All radio networks carried his speeches, preempting all other programs. Follow-ups in the newspapers, magazines, newsreels, and photographs amplified his message. The saturated coverage of the death of Roosevelt was a reflection of the respect and honor accorded him in his presidential lifetime. The medical cover-up allowed Roosevelt to serve during wartime emergency at the risk of his health and ultimately his life.

The character and capability of future presidents, together with their responses to future crises, will determine whether, or if, the office will regain its earlier luster.

This study considers the medical consequences, even the hazards, inherent in the twentieth-century presidency. It seeks to understand how the medical cover-up of Roosevelt actually occurred, why participants thought it necessary, what questions it raises regarding succession to the presidency, and an analysis of issues raised and their relevance to current controversies.

Chapter 1 offers a framework for considering Roosevelt's clinical course in office. It describes the adverse effects of the office of the presidency on many other chief executives of the twentieth century. Chapter 2 highlights the influence of events in Roosevelt's early life and career, including his polio and subsequent election as governor of New York. Chapter 3 shows that he was in relatively good health for the first ten years of his administration, although the silent threat of chronic high blood pressure started as early as 1937 and progressed inexorably, compounded by wartime stresses. Chapter 4 shows that a marked decline in Roosevelt's health occurred in 1944, accompanied by a White House cover-up of his condition that deepened into 1945. Chapter 5 covers the politics and wartime pressures that led to a fourth campaign and ultimately, by compromising his health, to death. Chapter 6 describes the day of Roosevelt's death, April 12, 1945, and the shock of this unexpected event for the nation and the world. Only in retrospect did his passing seem almost inevitable, so successful had the cover-up been. Chapter 7 explores the questions raised by Roosevelt's medical history and his death. Should this have been anticipated? What plans for succession should have been made? The study concludes with an analysis of issues raised and their relevance to current controversy.

THE
HIDDEN
CAMPAIGN

~ 1 ~

The Twentieth-Century Presidency: A High-Risk Occupation

The office of the president of the United States proved to be a high-risk occupation in the twentieth century. There were seventeen presidents from William McKinley (1897–1901) through Bill Clinton (1993–2001). Only five—Theodore Roosevelt, William Howard Taft, Calvin Coolidge, Jimmy Carter, and Clinton—survived their terms without serious assassination attempts or significant illnesses. It is not a good record.

Possible assassination has been the most obvious risk in the presidency. Two presidents in the twentieth century, William McKinley and John F. Kennedy, were fatally wounded. One, Ronald Reagan, was seriously wounded. Two presidents narrowly escaped injury in assassination attempts: Harry S. Truman once and Gerald Ford twice. If the time beyond the actual presidential terms is considered, other names can be added to the list. Theodore Roosevelt had served out McKinley's term and completed his own first term. While campaigning for the presidency as a third-party candidate in 1912, he was wounded in an assassination attempt. As president-elect Franklin D. Roosevelt escaped injury in an assassination attempt in Miami, Florida, in February 1933.

As dramatic as assassination attempts may be, illness may contribute in a greater manner to the presidency as a high-risk occupation. Two twentieth-century presidents, Warren G. Harding and Franklin D. Roosevelt, died of illness while in office. Woodrow Wilson, Lyndon B. Johnson, and Richard Nixon may have suffered occupationally related illnesses, both physical and

3

emotional[1] The life spans of Woodrow Wilson and Lyndon B. Johnson were probably shortened by these illnesses. Herbert Hoover, Dwight Eisenhower, and George H. Bush suffered marked declines in health while in office. Hoover probably suffered from exhaustion. Eisenhower's heart problems and Bush's hyperthyroidism, an excessive activity of the thyroid gland causing nervousness and rapid pulse, may also have reflected the stresses of office, but these associations are less clear-cut.[2]

Although two presidents lived to advanced age—Herbert Hoover to ninety, and Harry S. Truman to eighty-eight—and while Jimmy Carter, Gerald Ford, Ronald Reagan, and Bill Clinton ended their terms in apparent good health, the clinical outcomes of the eighteen chief executives serving in the twentieth century appear unfavorable. Although the "patient population" is small, the frequency of death and disability is inordinate. In view of this, it is important to achieve some understanding of presidential health and longevity even though there are no clearly valid control groups. There are, however, three reasonable comparisons that might offer insight into this potentially high-risk occupation: (1) longevity of presidential parents (Table 1.1); (2) longevity of cabinet officers (Table 1.2); and (3) longevity of Supreme Court Justices (Table 1.3).[3]

Longevity of Presidential Parents

The comparison of presidential longevity with the longevity average of his parents is distributed into two major groups. From George Washington (first president) to Abraham Lincoln (sixteenth president), data are available on fourteen sets of parents (group I). From Andrew Johnson (seventeenth president) to Richard Nixon (thirty-seventh president and the last president to die) data is available on all eighteen sets of parents (group II). Over the course of history, sixteen presidents lived longer than did their parents, while sixteen lived a briefer span. However, there is a striking difference between the earlier and later groups. Among the earlier presidents, nine of fourteen lived longer than their parents, but eleven of eighteen among the more recent group died at a younger age than their parents.

Longevity of Cabinet Officers

The second comparison group is also divided into two subgroups. The first begins with George Washington and ends with Abraham Lincoln, while the second starts with Andrew Johnson but ends with Dwight D. Eisenhower. The decision to choose a different endpoint in this sequence than with the first comparison group is based on the fact that cabinet officers from subse-

Table 1.1

Longevity of Presidents Compared with Longevity of Their Parents

	Presidents who lived longer intervals than parents	Presidents who lived shorter intervals than parents
Group I Washington to Lincoln		
Number of presidents	9	5
Range of duration (years)	2–31	1–12
Mean duration (years)	10	7
Group II Johnson to Nixon		
Number of presidents	7	11
Range of duration (years)	2–55	4–28
Mean duration (years)	17[a]	12

Source: Data from W.A. DeGregorio, *The Complete Book of U.S. Presidents from George Washington to George Bush* (New York: Wings Book, 1991).

[a]If Herbert Hoover, who lived fifty-five years longer than his parents were to be excluded, the mean duration would be eight years.

Table 1.2

Longevity of Presidents Compared with Longevity of Cabinet Officers

	Presidents who lived longer intervals than their cabinet members	Presidents who lived shorter intervals than their cabinet members
Group I Washington to Lincoln		
Number of presidents	11	5
Range of survival (years)	4–24	5–20
Mean survival (years)	11	10
Group II Johnson to Eisenhower		
Number of presidents	3	14
Range of survival (years)	5–19	1–17
Mean survival (years)	13	10

Source: Data from W.A. DeGregorio, *The Complete Book of U.S. Presidents from George Washington to George Bush* (New York: Wings Book, 1991).

quent administrations are still alive. The trends in this comparison are similar to those seen with their parents' longevity. In the earlier subgroup eleven presidents lived longer than their cabinet officers. This trend was decidedly reversed in the second group, with fourteen of the seventeen presidents living a shorter span than their cabinet members.

Longevity of Supreme Court Justices

The comparison of the longevity of presidents with justices they appointed (with senatorial confirmation) to the Supreme Court is limited to the sixteen

Table 1.3

Longevity of Presidents Compared with Longevity of Supreme Court Justice Appointments

	Presidents who lived longer intervals than appointed justices	Presidents who lived shorter intervals than appointed justices
Group I Washington to Lincoln		
Number of presidents	3	1
Range of duration (years)	15–25	18
Mean duration (years)	19	18
Group II Johnson to Eisenhower		
Number of presidents	3	9
Range of duration (years)	1–15	3–16
Mean duration (years)	9	10

Source: Data from W.A. DeGregorio, *The Complete Book of U.S. Presidents from George Washington to George Bush* (New York: Wings Book, 1991).

presidents who appointed three or more justices. Excluded are those presidents whose appointees are still alive. Hence, the latest president included is Dwight D. Eisenhower. The trend is the same as with the two previous comparisons. Three of four earlier presidents lived longer than their appointed justices, but nine of twelve among the more recent group died earlier.

In each presidential campaign, interest in the longevity of the persons who seek the office of president of the United States becomes a new issue. In every election, the question surfaces: does the stress and strain of the presidency tend to shorten the lives of those who hold the office? Periodically, Metropolitan Life Insurance Company has analyzed the issue of presidential longevity. Their most recent study (1980) indicated that:

> in general Presidents do not live as long as their contemporaries in the general population—nor even as long as Vice Presidents and unsuccessful candidates for the Presidency.[4]

The study compares the actual number of years lived by each president after his inauguration with his average expectation of life on that date, based on cohort (generation) life tables developed by the Statistical Bureau of the Metropolitan Life Insurance Company (Table 1.4).[5]

The findings of the Metropolitan Life study vividly illustrate that the presidency is a high-risk occupation that itself predisposes its occupants to serious illness, as well as assassination attempts.[6]

Of the forty-one presidents who have completed their terms, eight have died in office, half by assassination.

Table 1.4

Presidential Life Expectancy (years)

Inauguration between	Presidential expectancy	Excluding assassinated	Vice presidents	Unsuccessful candidates
1789–1844	+3.7	+3.7	−3.7	−5.4
1845–1884	−9.0	−6.9	−5.5	−5.4
1885–1932	−4.8	−3.6	−2.1	−3.8
1933–1979	−1.6	+0.3	+3.4	+0.2
Overall average 1789–1979	−3.1	−1.5	−1.9	−2.6

Source: Data from "Longevity of Presidents, Vice Presidents, and Unsuccessful Candidates for the Presidency." *Statistical Bulletin* 80. no. 4 (July-September 1980): 3-8.

The first sixteen presidents, from Washington to Lincoln, lived an average of 72.6 years. However, since the Civil War to 1980 the average has been only sixty-three years of age, in spite of dramatic advances in medical care including antibiotics, surgical procedures, X-ray and other imaging techniques.

The study shows that the fifteen deceased presidents from Abraham Lincoln through Franklin D. Roosevelt lived an average of approximately eight years less than expected, or 6.6 years less if the three assassinated presidents (Lincoln, Garfield, McKinley) are omitted. The presidents prior to the Civil War had the opposite experience. They lived longer than their life expectations at the time of inauguration, by approximately 1.3 years.

Other categories of government and industry leaders may well experience serious medical problems, which may be the result of professional pressures and frustration. However, the dismal litany of death and morbidity among twentieth-century presidents reflects something unique about the state of the modern presidency. There are several factors that contribute to the high risk of illness inherent in this position. The first is the tension created by the disparity between presidential responsibility and presidential authority. Presidential responsibility is virtually infinite. In a nuclear age, the president shoulders the final and sole responsibility for decisions of unprecedented gravity and consequence. In contrast, the authority of the office is sharply restricted. Not only the judicial and legislative branches of government restrict it, but also the pressures of public opinion and news media limit the president's options. With increasing frequency, probing by the media and minutely detailed reporting of personal matters have caused embarrassment, if not worse, for presidents and their families. This trend has clearly accelerated with the information explosion in recent years, instant journalism, tabloid sensationalism, and the public's insatiable demand for gossip. Infinite responsibility and limited authority to respond to the intrusion of private matters by public media may cause stress with medical consequences.

A second factor producing presidential stress is the restricted time frame available to the president. The four-year term and the two-term constitutional limitation since 1953 further undermine his leverage. The first year of any presidential term is generally required for presidential orientation and initial staffing development. The last year with its preparations for reelection may undermine the president's effectiveness. No other elected federal official has this combination of statutory term limitation with virtually limitless burdens.

All levels of the federal judiciary are appointed for life. Despite continuing efforts to limit congressional terms, senators are eligible for an unlimited number of six-year terms, while representatives have only two-year terms, but also have no constitutional barrier to reelection. Many return for multiple terms. Not only is the term of service indefinite for legislators and judges, but also rarely are they subjected to the intense, continuous, detailed personal, financial, and family analysis that became routine for a president in the twentieth century. Hence, the pressure to achieve formidable goals within a narrowly restricted time frame is intense and unique to the presidency as a political position.

In the twentieth century, only three of the ten presidents who served after Roosevelt (Dwight D. Eisenhower, Ronald Reagan, and Bill Clinton), and only one of the seven who preceded him (Woodrow Wilson), served two consecutive elected terms of office. This illustrates both the political and medical hazards of the presidency and demonstrates its restricted time frame.

A third factor that contributes to their vulnerability is the unrealistic expectations demanded by the symbolic dimension of the position. The president is not merely the chief executive, but he is also the cultural and societal leader of the nation. Virtually all frustrations and grievances perceived by the public are directed against the president personally, making him a natural target for verbal as well as physical attack. Unlike the royalty of many nations, ancient family lineage and indefinite tenure do not protect him.

Pre-presidential health related factors should also be mentioned in the context of the presidency as a high-risk occupation. It is expected that presidential candidates will have reached stature and political maturity. To achieve this level of personal development, the candidate will usually be at least middle-aged.[7] In later middle age, naturally health problems begin to develop with greater frequency than in younger years. Thus, some presidents are likely to have a history of preexisting illnesses which could be intensified by the stresses of office. A number of presidents have been vulnerable due to earlier illnesses.

Warren G. Harding, by his own admission, was unqualified for office af-

Table 1.5

Twentieth-Century Mortality and Morbidity in Presidents of the United States

McKinley	Assassinated
T. Roosevelt	No known serious illness; wounded as ex-president in assassination attempt
Taft	No known illness
Wilson	Disabled by stroke, October 1919 to March 1992
Harding	Died in office (age 57) from "apoplexy"
Coolidge	No known illness —possible depression
Hoover	No known illness—possible exhaustion
F.D. Roosevelt	Died in office (age 63); hypertensive congestive heart failure; paralysis; attempted assassination
Truman	Attempted assassination; no known illness
Eisenhower	Myocardial infarction; Crohn's disease; mild cerebrovascular accident
Kennedy	Assassinated; Addison's disease
Johnson	Gall bladder disease; renal stones; prior myocardial infarction
Nixon	Phlebitis; pneumonia; probably emotional disorder
Ford	Two assassination attempts; no known illness
Carter	No known serious illness
Reagan	Wounded in assassination attempt; colonic cancer
Bush	Atrial fibrillation, secondary to hyperthyroidism; later hypothyroidism
Clinton	No known serious illness

Source: Notes 8–15.

ter having suffered several "nervous breakdowns" as a younger man.[8] He suffered the first of these even prior to his election to the U.S. Senate in 1914.[9] The stress of scandal caused by widespread corruption, including two appointees who were later sentenced to prison, may have contributed to his unexpected collapse and death at the age of fifty-seven. His predecessor, Woodrow Wilson, was hypertensive and suffered apparent strokes in 1896, 1906, and 1907. He was also blind in the left eye, and displayed functional disability in the years prior to his presidency.[10]

The voting public became aware of Eisenhower's coronary thrombosis in 1955, his attack of ileitis in the third year of his first term (June 10, 1956), and a slight stroke in November of 1957. However, there was not an awareness of the fact that he had experienced episodic labile hypertension and intestinal disorders during his military service in World War II, and a possible heart attack in 1947, all preexisting conditions.[11] Lyndon Johnson had a severe heart attack when he was majority leader in the Senate. John F. Kennedy suffered from Addison's disease, a deficiency of the adrenal gland.[12] Richard Nixon's emotional state prior to and during the presidency has been the subject of much speculation, but the evidence of psychiatric disability is only inferential not absolute (Table 1.5).[13]

Disease, whether or not it affects the individual's fitness for office, tends to be viewed as a flaw in a president. Illness in this setting takes on an irrational quality. Subconsciously or consciously, in art and history, a leader's impairment has been associated with a message from Divine Providence, as exemplified by Richard III's withered arm or epilepsy in Julius Caesar and Alexander the Great.

Leadership, particularly on a national level, is often mythologized—making the leaders perceived as greater than the average persons—stronger, smarter, more knowledgeable, more physically fit, more moral and ethical, or more evil and devious. Some presidents have been demonized (Nixon and Hoover), others marginalized (Ford and Carter), and a few glorified if not deified while in office (Theordore Roosevelt, Wilson, Franklin Roosevelt) or posthumously (Kennedy). When these larger-than-life leaders become ill, the disease becomes magnified. Political considerations have required the denial of serious illness or its minimization. Presidential leadership—no matter how nominal, transient, and seriously compromised—requires the illusion of strength and therefore of excellent health. Increasingly, the public's concern with presidential vigor has been taken to the extreme. The exhaustion shown by Jimmy Carter while jogging amplified the popular impression of his awkwardness and lack of political acumen. Gerald Ford's slip on the steps of an airplane and George Bush's bout of nausea, emesis, and fainting at a state dinner in Japan in January 1992 were both instantly televised. The two minor incidents served to undermine their effectiveness and subjected them to ridicule for trivial but symbolic reasons.

At times, past illness or the potential reoccurrence of past illness are perceived as flaws in candidates for the office. This perception denied Senator Thomas Eagleton an opportunity to be the running mate of George McGovern in 1972. After his voluntary entry into a psychiatric clinic for depression was made public, the response of the voters was immediate. The fear of recurrence removed the illusion of strength required of a potential president.

Medical care that is politically determined can significantly compromise presidential health. The medical care of the president is at times modified, if not undermined by his political objective of presenting a strong, medically sound figure to the people. In 1893, during a depression, Grover Cleveland was involved in a major political struggle as opponents sought to replace the gold standard with a silver one. Medical examination discovered that a malignant growth had involved the bone of his upper jaw, requiring an imminent operation.[14] It was thought that public knowledge of his condition and a belief that he would not be able to continue as president could adversely affect the financial markets of the nation. His physician, Robert O'Reilly, organized a team of surgeons to secretly perform the surgery while President Cleveland was on a yacht journeying to his summer residence at Buzzards Bay.[15]

Sometimes the president himself makes a health decision based on political factors. Suffering chills and fever on the night of December 16, 1968, Lyndon B. Johnson was advised to enter the hospital. R.E. Gilbert notes that the president chose not to take that advice.

> . . . [T]he president thought it best to wait four or five hours because to go in the night would have negative effects on the stock market and would set off the "rumor machine."[16]

In the case of Roosevelt, military necessity called for the importance of perceiving the president as a vigorous commander-in-chief directing a global war against America's enemies.[17] All these examples indicate that successful presidential leadership requires the perception of strength.

The physical stamina and emotional stability required for survival in a modern presidential campaign provide an example of Darwinian selection, creating a medical screening process. Candidates aware of serious health problems are usually eliminated from the process of selection. If they choose to enter the lengthy, arduous, intensely and intimately probing primary process for the party's nomination, it is unlikely that they will be able to succeed and even more unlikely that they will successfully complete the presidential contest. The campaigns are too physically demanding and the scrutiny too harsh for candidates without the sufficient stamina and emotional stability needed for success.

For those candidates who succeed and are elected to the office of the president of the United States, the stresses and pressures of the position become apparent. This awareness has led many presidents to describe their office in the harshest of terms. Warren G. Harding remarked to a friend that "this is a hell of a place for a man like me to be."[18] Herbert Hoover called it a "compound hell."[19] Truman complained that "with the first months I discovered that being a president is like riding a tiger, a man has to keep riding or be swallowed. The fantastically crowded nine months of 1945 taught me that a president is either constantly on top of events, or, if he hesitates events will soon be on top of him. I never felt I could let up for a minute."[20] Wilson also felt the pressure: "I feel so weak and useless I would like to go to bed until I get well or die."[21] Some of these complaints may reflect political setbacks or momentary indulgences in self-pity, but they are consistent with the inherent frustrations of the presidential office.

The pattern of poor health and subsequent shortened life spans among twentieth-century presidents resulting from conditions inherent to the office

Table 1.6

Longevity of FDR's Vice Presidents and Cabinet Members

Name	Dates	Age at death
Vice presidents		
John N. Garner	1868–1967	99
Henry A. Wallace	1888–1965	77
Harry S. Truman	1884–1972	88
Average		88
Cabinet members		
Cordell Hull	1871–1955	84
Edward Stettinius, Jr.	1900–1949	49
William H. Woodin	1868–1934	66
Henry J. Morgenthau, Jr.	1891–1967	76
George H. Dern	1872–1936	64
Henry H. Woodring	1890–1967	77
Henry A. Stimson	1867–1950	83
Claude A. Swanson	1862–1939	77
Charles Edison	1890–1969	79
Frank Knox	1874–1944	70
James V. Forrestal	1892–1949	58
Harold L. Ickes	1874–1952	78
James F. Farley	1888–1976	88
Frank C. Walker	1886–1959	73
Homer C. Cummings	1870–1956	86
Frank Murphy	1893–1949	57
Robert H. Jackson	1892–1954	62
Frances Biddle	1886–1968	82
Daniel C. Roper	1867–1943	76
Harry L. Hopkins	1890–1946	56
Jesse Jones	1874–1956	82
Henry A. Wallace	1888–1965	77
Frances Perkins	1882–1965	83
Claude R. Wickard	1893–1967	75
Average n = 24		73.4

Source: Data from O.L. Graham, Jr. and M.R. Wander, *Franklin D. Roosevelt, His Life and Times: An Encyclopedic View* (New York: DaCapo Press, 1985).

Table 1.7

Longevity of World Leaders During Roosevelt's Presidency

Leader	Born	Died	Age	In office	Years
Chiang Kai-shek	1887	1975	87	1945–1975	30
Winston Churchill	1874	1965	91	1940–1945	
				1951–1955	9
Charles DeGaulle	1890	1970	80	1945–1946	
				1958–1969	12
Joseph Stalin	1879	1953	74	1928–1953	25+

Source: Data from O.L. Graham, Jr. and M.R. Wander, *Franklin D. Roosevelt, His Life and Times: An Encyclopedic View* (New York: DaCapo Press, 1985).

is disturbing. The illness of the nation's leader is a matter of general concern to all citizens. There may be need to restructure both the selection process and the time limitations in order to prevent potential disasters. The factors contributing to the pattern of medical problems among presidents form a structural basis that could be described in medical terms as a pathogenesis (cause of disease). In his study, *The Mortal Presidency*, Robert E. Gilbert discusses the relationship of the office to the illnesses of the incumbent:

> Those who reach the office of President find themselves subjected to a constant stream of stressful situations that may well compound their susceptibility to cardiovascular disease and also increase the likelihood of their contracting non-cardiovascular illness as well.[22]

The medical history of Roosevelt offers a striking example of the detrimental effect which the demands of the position have on the health of the incumbent. His death at sixty-three years contrasts with that of other vice presidents and cabinet members (Table 1.6) and contemporary world leaders (Table 1.7). This chapter has offered a framework in which to consider Roosevelt's clinical course while in office. An examination of Roosevelt's progressively deteriorating health and the methods chosen to conceal that information from the public suggest new approaches to the medical problems of presidents in the twenty-first century.

~ 2 ~

Pre-Presidential Years:
The Defining Experiences

Of the eighteen chief executives in the twentieth century, President Franklin D. Roosevelt was by nature and personal history probably the best prepared for the emotional strains and hazards of the presidency. Young Franklin was born into a life of wealth and privilege, the single focus of two devoted parents. (Although his father had a son, James Roosevelt Roosevelt, by his first marriage to Rebecca Howland, that son was the age of Franklin's mother, Sara.) He was born in what a neighbor in Hyde Park would later define as "socially favorable conditions."[1]

His later personal strengths were fortified by his early good fortune, and sharpened by his later personal struggles. The combination of good fortune and personal struggle produced an adult whose self-esteem and confidence were key ingredients of his later political success. There were perhaps a few others in the privileged group of wealthy persons who lived in country estates, maintained homes in New York City, summered in the mountains, at the shore, or in Europe, who were as well prepared educationally, as well supported financially, and as well connected politically as Roosevelt. There were probably few public leaders who approached his confidence level. According to a current biographer:

> There were always wiser men and women than Franklin Roosevelt in American public life, people who were better informed, more consistent, less devious. But there were none whose power to inspire both love and loathing was so great, none whose political success or apparent self-assurance exceeded his.[2]

This self-esteem and confidence were nurtured from infancy as an only child, the sole only child to ascend to the presidency in the twentieth century.

14

He grew into adulthood in an environment of rarefied social status, combined with independent wealth—a circumstance shared by only four other presidents of his century—his cousin Theodore Roosevelt, William Howard Taft, John F. Kennedy, and George Bush.

During the course of his political career he was able to dispel the stigmatization attached to his handicap. Jerrold Post makes the argument that "Roosevelt even managed somewhat to convert his handicap into a political virtue, a mark of courage and perseverance," noting that "his affliction softened his patrician edges."[3] He did not perceive himself as disabled, nor did the voting public. This perception was a major foundation of his political career. It seemed to be a well thought out strategy.

> This was not by accident. It was the result of careful strategy by the president. The strategy served to minimize the extent of his handicap, to make it unnoticed when possible and palatable when it was noticed. The strategy was eminently successful, it required substantial physical effort, ingenuity, and bravado. This was FDR's splendid deception.[4]

Perhaps the strongest influence in Roosevelt's life was his mother, Sara Delano Roosevelt. For eighteen years, his father, James, Sara, and Franklin lived a life in which FDR's development was the major objective. Even upon the death of his father, the maturation of FDR into manhood was a prime concern as shown in the wording of his will:

> I do hereby appoint my wife sole guardian of my son Franklin D. Roosevelt and I wish him to be under the influence of his mother.[5]

Sara Roosevelt was strong of will, held the family purse strings closely, and was often thought to micromanage her son's life, with profound psychological impact. That impact can be evaluated as positive or seen as detrimental. There is no doubt, however, that Sara Roosevelt was dedicated solely to the welfare of her son. Until her death in September of 1941, she shaped her life with the one purpose of providing a setting in which Franklin could accomplish his goals in life with as few extraneous concerns as possible.

> For sixty years her graciousness, charm and sense of social position graced the home at Springwood. Even though she did not always appreciate or understand the mystical love affair between F.D.R. and his neighbors, she did accept the inconvenience of that relationship because of her love for her son Franklin.[6]

She delayed changing this relationship and did not enroll her son in preparatory school until he was over age fourteen, later than was customary. She continued to give him advice: "Keep up your position and character and let no one make you feel small, go ahead your own way, and be kind to everyone if you have the chance."[7] His mother's view clearly took priority over almost everyone else's, even into adulthood and through the early stages of Roosevelt's marriage to Eleanor. The predominance of Sara's views was reflected in many areas of the relationship between the young couple. An outstanding example was her construction of two adjoining brownstones with adjoining interior doors, at 47 and 49 East 65th Street—Franklin and Eleanor to live in one and Sara in the other.

Even when Franklin's relationship to Lucy Mercer was revealed to Eleanor through Lucy's letters, Sara's opinions became predominant. Eleanor confronted Franklin and they discussed divorce. There were financial, political, and family reasons, as well as future positions to consider which Sara emphasized. One biographer believed that the major reason for Eleanor and Franklin remaining together was because he could not defy his mother. He concludes that "Sara was the unifying force that kept the marriage together."[8]

Sara's dominance continued into the presidency. Following the dedication of the Triborough Bridge in New York City in April 1936, Roosevelt was taken to his mother's townhouse on East 65th Street. She proceeded to rebuke her son, the president, for dressing inappropriately for the cool weather and did it in a style more appropriate for admonishing a schoolboy than the 53-year-old chief executive of the nation. The president meekly agreed.[9]

It was possible that the course of the mother-son relationship was set by the circumstances of his delivery. Roosevelt's birth on January 30, 1882 was difficult because at ten pounds he was an unusually large baby. The nurse, Carrie Lee, had feared for the infant's survival. The attending physician, Dr. Edward Parker, successfully concluded a prolonged and dangerous labor with a dose of chloroform. The infant did require resuscitation, but revived almost immediately. On medical grounds a second pregnancy for the mother was considered ill advised and thus Roosevelt was an only child.[10] Sara enjoyed excellent health and nearly outlived her son, dying in September 1941 at the age of eighty-seven.

As an only child at the Hudson River Springwood estate, Roosevelt was probably not exposed to many of the usual childhood infections. However, throughout his childhood and adolescence, he suffered repeated episodes of upper respiratory tract illnesses, sinusitis, and bronchitis. These would recur throughout his adult life. These illnesses were described in many of his letters to his family. A letter (apparently his first), at age five, addressed to "Dear Sally" (a nickname for Sara used only by the adults in the family) concerned a cold he had.[11] As he grew older, the list of pre-presidential illnesses increased.

In 1898, he and several other students at Groton developed the burning throats and chills associated with scarlet fever. This illness prevented him from joining his cousin Colonel Theodore Roosevelt and the Rough Riders in Cuba. Geoffrey Ward, in discussing Roosevelt's prep school days, notes that Roosevelt seemed "susceptible to every Groton germ. He suffered not only from frequent colds and chronic sinus trouble, but also from prolonged sieges of measles and mumps."[12]

As well as measles and scarlet fever, his illnesses included at least two episodes of typhoid fever—the first when he was eight years old and traveling in England, the second in 1912 following a trip to Mexico with his wife. An article in the *New York Times*, August 25, 1912, mentions that Roosevelt was designated for renomination to the state Senate on August 24, 1912. Roosevelt was afflicted with typhoid fever in September 1912 and was bedridden until after the election. This became the first time that an illness had direct effect on his campaign activities. His slow recovery, lasting several months, meant that he had to rely on proxies, including Eleanor and Louis Howe, his confidant, to conduct his successful campaign for reelection to the New York state Senate. When the legislature reconvened (January 1913), he appeared ill and haggard. His wife who contracted typhoid fever at the same time, had recovered promptly.

For the next eleven years he continued to experience a series of illnesses. By the time he arrived in Washington to assume his duties of assistant secretary of the Navy, he was still writing to reassure his mother that he was making progress on a stomach ailment. "It's nine o'clock and I'm really feeling better tho' Tummy isn't according to Hoyle yet."[13] On July 1, 1915, he was stricken with acute appendicitis and the appendix was removed at Washington Naval Hospital. In August of that same year, he writes Eleanor of "lumbago or rheumatism between the shoulders."[14]

By February 1916 the throat infections had returned to such an extent that he spent two weeks at the boardwalk in Atlantic City seeking to recover. He writes Eleanor: "This 'health resort' is purgatory. . . . Except for throat I feel better as to strength."[15] Throat infections would plague Roosevelt all his life. In the summer of 1916, Eleanor journeyed to Washington to be with him while he recovered in the hospital.[16] As the war drew to an end, Roosevelt had a desire to see the conflict in progress but a bout with pneumonia almost prevented the trip. Finally, Roosevelt was able to see the battlefield, but on the return trip he was bedridden, as were shipmates, some fatally, with "double" pneumonia. Upon arrival in New York he was carried home on a stretcher.[17] (It was during his unpacking that Eleanor discovered FDR's love letters exchanged with Lucy Mercer.) He later had several episodes of quinsy, an acute inflammation of the tonsils, known as peritonsillar abscess, which led to a tonsillectomy at New York Hospital in 1920.

Reacting to the severe 1916 poliomyelitis epidemic, as mortality in diagnosed cases reached 25 percent, Roosevelt expressed his continued concerns and obvious anxiety in letters to Eleanor. On August 5, 1916 he wrote from Hyde Park to Eleanor at Campobello: ". . . the infantile paralysis is gaining, 6 more cases in Poughkeepsie. . . ." A few days later he would write that "the infantile paralysis is gaining headway rather than abating."[18]

The increasing severity of the epidemic made it necessary to change travel plans for the family to leave their summer home in Campobello. The thought of his family returning by train was a great concern to Roosevelt, as he wrote to Eleanor on August 18, 1916.

> I am really upset at the thoughts of bringing you all down by rail. There is much I.P. [infantile paralysis] in Boston, Springfield, Worcester, etc., and even in Rockland and other Maine points. Also the various villages are keeping motorists with children out and it would be difficult to get to Hyde Park by motor.[19]

The solution was to bring the family by boat (in a yacht named *The Dolphin* belonging to Josephus Daniels, secretary of the Navy). In preparation for the trip, Roosevelt was still slightly anxious about the poliomyelitis cases in Dutchess County. In a letter to Eleanor on September 19, 1916, he expressed his hope that the Butler child (from a family connected to the Roosevelt estate) would "be out of quarantine and everything fumigated."[20] The trip on board *The Dolphin* was finally completed the first week in October 1916.

There are no signs that Roosevelt's emotional health was anything less than excellent. The only expressed fear seems to be related to fire. When he was only two his mother's sister Laura died in a fire at the family home in Newburgh while he was a guest there. Apparently he heard her screaming, but did not witness the event. The story probably remained a part of the family oral history as Roosevelt grew older. Much later, a chimney fire occurred in their apartment in New York City, but caused no damage. As a resident of Washington, he would write to Hyde Park suggesting that the fireplaces be pointed and the extinguishers checked. His paralysis after 1921 intensified this fear and he took particular precautions to avoid such threats. Geoffrey Ward describes in detail the various encounters Roosevelt had with fire at Springwood, Groton, and Harvard—experiences that led him to fireproof many of the walls when Springwood was remodeled.[21] There is no evidence that other fears were made manifest either to his physicians or family. There is, however, evidence that while on their honeymoon, Roosevelt suffered from sleepwalking, nightmares, and hives which he had never experienced before nor afterwards. His mother had adamantly opposed the marriage and perhaps his defiance of her will and his separation from her caused a temporary disturbance. For the rest of his life he was known for his calm, confident demeanor and was a sound sleeper.

Poliomyelitis—1921

The defining event in Roosevelt's life was his battle with poliomyelitis and its effects. He became ill on August 10, 1921 while vacationing with his family on Campobello Island. He was thirty-nine years old and until that day had led a physically active life, which included golf, tennis, horseback riding, dancing, bicycling, boating, and walks. After a swim in the very cold waters of the bay, Roosevelt returned to his cottage and experienced a chill, which eventually led to pain in his legs and anorexia (loss of appetite). His was a classic case of poliomyelitis. There was the onset of fever; anorexia and lassitude leading to paralysis, which progressed above the initially involved legs to include the trunk, part of the face, and the fatty and muscular part of the hand above the thumb. Bladder and bowel functions were only temporarily lost, as is also typical of this disease.

Diagnosis was not easily accomplished. A local physician, Edward Bennett, first diagnosed "a severe cold." A second physician, the 84-year-old retired surgeon W.W. Keen, decided the patient was suffering from thrombosis of a vertebral artery causing temporary reversible paralysis. On August 18, 1921, Eleanor told Roosevelt's half-brother "Rosy" that the clot theory had been discarded and Dr. Keen thought the problem was caused by a lesion in the spinal cord. This was a more serious diagnosis, but Keen still believed Roosevelt eventually would get well.[22] His fee was an astronomical $500 (well over ten times of what it would be in today's dollars for this house call, the erroneous diagnosis notwithstanding). Two weeks after the onset of illness, the family contacted Dr. Robert A. Lovett, a professor of orthopedic surgery at Harvard University, and an acknowledged leader in the field of poliomyelitis. He arrived in Campobello on August 25 and his examination, conducted with the two previous physicians present, revealed a classic case of poliomyelitis.

Finally on August 27, 1921, Eleanor wrote to inform Sara. Even after all the problems with diagnosis, Eleanor did not seek to explain in detail. She only wrote: "Franklin has been quite ill and so can't go down to meet you on Tuesday to his great regret. . . ."[23] In her autobiography, Eleanor would later refer to these days immediately following the onset of polio as a time of "trial by fire."

Initial paralysis of his trunk and hands gradually receded, but the atrophy of the major muscle groups of the legs worsened. Completely paralyzed from the waist down, Roosevelt was very weak and in constant pain in these early days. He was treated with deep massage, which probably intensified the degree of permanent paralysis and surely served to prolong the pain. Until Dr. Lovett stopped the massage, Eleanor faithfully followed the doctor's orders.

In this critical instance, Roosevelt did not receive the best medical care. Failure to establish a prompt diagnosis was inexplicable, since in all respects his was a typical case. Avoidance of manipulation in the acute states was a well-established principal of initial management and still is today. Major medical textbooks from the early twentieth century to the present emphasize the need to leave the painful paralyzed extremities alone for at least the first two to three weeks. At most, very gentle movement and warm compresses can be applied. Had the diagnosis been promptly established or, even without proper diagnosis, had his legs been left alone, the outcome would have been presumably more favorable and the paralysis milder. Roosevelt was transported with great difficulty and peril from Campobello to his home in New York City in September. He was admitted to Presbyterian Hospital for six weeks and later received outpatient treatment at Children's Hospital of Boston.

Why this illness occurred at the somewhat advanced age of thirty-nine is not clear. Several theories have been suggested to explain the fact that he was in the oldest 5 to 10 percent of polio cases. One theory suggests that he may have acquired the virus during a visit to the Boy Scout Camp at Bear Mountain, New York, on July 27 just two weeks before the onset of his paralysis.[24] A second suggests that he could be considered vulnerable because of his elevated social status. Poliomyelitis in that era was recognized as a disease of the middle class and affluent, being more prevalent among Caucasians than African Americans. A less fortunate child, living in crowded tenement situations was more likely to a have a relative degree of immunity due to natural subclinical infection which served as a form of immunization. To a person in this situation, the virus would invade the intestinal tract causing no symptoms or gastroenteritis at most, and the nervous system would be spared. The immune system would produce antibodies, thus providing life-long protection.

A third theory places Roosevelt in a position of vulnerability to the polio virus due to exhaustion and emotional strain. The emotional stress would be related to the inquiry by the Senate Naval Affairs Committee into Roosevelt's investigation of problems at the Portsmouth and Newport Naval Training Station. Responding to reports of homosexuality, drug use, gambling, and alcoholism, the Office of the Secretary of the Navy set up an investigative squad under Roosevelt's direction to correct the situation. Hence, he was the target of the committee which severely criticized the squad's procedures and effectiveness. The initial report of the committee posed a potential major political problem for Roosevelt. In all probability it contributed to his irritability and fatigue as he left for Campobello in the summer of 1921.

A fourth theory was suggested by Dr. Noah B. Fabricant, an otolaryngologist. Writing in a professional journal in 1957, he states that ". . . it is conceivable that his tonsillectomy (over a year earlier) could have been a contributing factor in Franklin D. Roosevelt's poliomyelitis attack."[25]

He indicated that studies in Minnesota, Detroit, and Boston all suggested that the incidence of nonparalytic and paralytic polio was higher in patients without tonsils than in patients with tonsils. However, the interval between the surgery and the attack of polio, and the clinical manifestations in Roosevelt's case cast doubt on this association.

On a personal level, the onset of polio brought Eleanor and Franklin together physically and emotionally during this crisis. With the first indication of Franklin's illness, Eleanor suggested that the other family members in the house at Campobello go on a camping trip. During these early days, she was the person to carry out the doctor's orders. With only minimal instructions she gave excellent nursing care, which prevented urinary tract infection and sustained Roosevelt during the darkest days of his illness. Specifically, she catheterized his bladder during the interval of atony (nonfunction) thereby relieving urinary obstruction. She also gave enemas since the bowel was also transiently paralyzed. Nurses, physical therapists, and other skilled professionals would enter the picture later, but she alone was there at this early critical time. Her support maintained his morale during the psychologically devastating interval following the definitive diagnosis. In a sense, she began to define the role that she would play so well during his years as president— becoming his eyes and ears in the public.

The onset of polio did change and emphasize certain personality characteristics. His daring became more extreme, his need for power and control perhaps more exaggerated. In his presidential years he was given to occasional irritability or sarcasm, and sometimes displayed a distracted attitude. These traits may have reflected some maladjustment to his disability rather than effects from later illnesses or fatigue. If he felt despair with his illness, it was a transient feeling. There is no indication in Roosevelt's medical history of anything less than fine emotional health even after the paralysis. In her early letters to Roosevelt's half brother, James "Rosey" Roosevelt, Eleanor did mention that Roosevelt was "getting back his grip and a better mental attitude. . . ."[26]

Although the polio had such a detrimental effect on his health, it had perhaps a positive effect on his political career. In July of 1921, the Senate Naval Affairs Committee released its report of the Navy Department's handling of the scandal at the Newport Naval Training Station. It was highly critical of former assistant secretary Franklin D. Roosevelt. At the time, he argued against the accusation that he had "committed all sorts of high crimes and misdemeanors [that] are nowhere supported by the evidence."[27] The committee denied Roosevelt access to the 6,000 pages of testimony until the majority report had been distributed to the newspapers. Within a short time, Roosevelt filed a complete answer to all the charges:

> Throughout their report I accuse them of deliberate falsification of evidence, of perversion of facts, of misstatements of the record, and a deliberate attempt to deceive.[28]

Roosevelt was fearful that the case and the charges would be revived. However, with the advent of his disability it would seem that he was not eligible for future elective or appointive office, and hence the investigation was not pursued when Congress reconvened after their summer recess. The charges were eventually dropped.

Polio forced a seven-year hiatus in Roosevelt's political career. When he did finally return, it was with new stature. From that dreadful summer of 1921 in Campobello until the campaign for governor of New York state, most of Roosevelt's energy and much of his personal fortune were spent at Warm Springs, Georgia, although he pursued a variety of business ventures and leisure activities, especially boating. Within a year of his first visit in the fall of 1924, approximately twenty-five persons who had been afflicted with polio had come to Warm Springs for rehabilitation. The springs which flowed at a rate of 1,800 gallons a minute at a constant eighty-eight degrees, and its highly mineralized content provided an invigorating swim for persons whose illness prevented them from being totally mobile when out of the water. With the formation of the Warm Springs Foundation for treatment of patients with poliomyelitis, Roosevelt became identified with the handicapped, the disabled, and the disadvantaged.

His excitement about Warm Springs and its facilities was continually reflected in his letters. To Sara he wrote: ". . . I spent over an hour in the pool this A.M. and will I think do great good."[29] During that same first visit he wrote to Eleanor: "Dearest Babs. . . . The legs are improving a great deal."[30] And also to his half-brother Rosy: "This exercising in warm water seems to be far and away the best thing."[31] Even in these early months he was busy envisioning the future, which he confided to his mother: "I feel that a great cure for infantile paralysis and kindred diseases could well be established here."[32]

During the seven years when Roosevelt was so totally consumed with Warm Springs and polio rehabilitation, Eleanor saw her life in a different light. In her autobiography she refers to the period from 1921 to 1927 as "The Private Interlude."[33] Roosevelt remained active in Democratic Party politics, and Eleanor became increasingly involved in public affairs—the League of Women Voters, the Trade Union League, and as finance chairperson of the Democratic State Committee. Additional involvement as a newspaper columnist and radio commentator not only educated Eleanor in party politics, but also served to keep Roosevelt and his name in the political limelight. Public appearances by Roosevelt at the Democratic National Conventions at Madison Square Garden, New York City, in 1924 and in Houston, Texas, in 1928, reflected an aura of nobility born from his courage and determination in overcoming his severe physical handicap. Much effort and advance planning was required for him to mount the podium to nominate Governor Alfred E. Smith for president.

The 1920s were Republican years on the national scene. Republican victories in the presidential races of 1920, 1924, and 1928 were achieved with substantial margins of victory:

	1920	1924	1928
Republican Electoral Vote	404	382	444
Democrat Electoral Vote	127	136	87

In New York state, Republican Herbert Hoover swamped Alfred E. Smith, his Democratic opponent, by 100,000 votes. This was a stunning defeat since Smith was a four-term governor of the state. Roosevelt had been identified closely with Smith, after having nominated Smith at two national conventions. However, in 1928 Roosevelt was able to swim against the tide and achieve victory. Of the total 4,500,00 votes cast in the election, Roosevelt won by a margin of only 25,000.

His paralysis played a key role in the outcome of the 1928 election. Prominently reported from the beginning, featured in Sunday magazines, the disability was not something that could be ignored. Instead, it became an integral part of the campaign and he made shrewd use of it. He may have felt that an open approach was necessary because of previous widespread publicity. His humor, which came with a slightly sarcastic edge, put his disability in a positive perspective. His courage and formidable stamina in the face of long days of campaigning charmed the voters. In effect, the paralysis enhanced his standing, distinguished him from all other political leaders, and may have contributed significantly to his victory in the New York gubernatorial race.

Had the arc of his career continued unchanged by paralysis, Roosevelt's opportunities to succeed on the national level would have been dim. By the time of his polio attack in 1921, he had lost a national election and been the focus of an investigative inquiry by the Senate Naval Affairs Committee: How Roosevelt would have fared at a legislative level, as a congressman or senator, is speculative. His career, character, and style seemed more suitable to administrative and executive responsibilities. The paralysis that resulted from polio altered his ambition and his timetable, changes which turned out to be especially fortuitous. It may well be argued that without this delay he would never have achieved the presidency.

Franklin D. Roosevelt, as a patient, exhibited a repertoire of coping skills. At first he became what might be referred to as an "identifier." He gained widespread public recognition and respect based on the illness, which had positive short-term consequences for his career. In the next phase of his life, as president, he was a "minimizer." He masked his disability, rationalized it, and rarely referred to it. He maintained his belief that given sufficient time he could relearn to walk, even though medical evidence was clearly to the contrary. Along with this denial and minimization, he developed a style of highly imaginative distraction. The endless stream of jokes, puns, the use of theatrical props, an old hat, a cape, the pince-nez glasses, the cigarette holder, the ever-present exuberance, and disarming charm were all exaggerations of his pre-paralysis style. Especially when moving from one position to another he would divert attention from his slow movements, his canes and crutches, his aides, by engaging in highly animated, good-natured banter, joking and smiling constantly. While he minimized his physical disability, his personality did not greatly change. His son Elliott, in explanatory notes accompanying the edited Roosevelt letters noted that:

> Life as a cripple intensified all the characteristics shown in his letters prior to 1922. His stability became more stable, his optimism more optimistic, and notwithstanding his inability to walk, even his independent nature was intensified.[34]

The trips to Warm Springs prior to 1928 provided endless opportunities for Roosevelt to communicate directly with individual polio patients who were there seeking rehabilitation through hydrotherapy. The photographic record of these visits to Warm Springs show in great and joyful detail his interaction with the patients. After 1928, during the governorship and presidency, those opportunities became more and more limited. However, he continued as advocate for polio victims with the nationally publicized annual Birthday Balls each January 30. Generally, his status as a patient was downplayed. Only the rare photograph clearly showed the true extent of his disability. The photographs from Warm Springs and elsewhere in some instances showed the leg braces seen below his trouser cuff. Others revealed the wasted leg muscles as he sat by the pool. As governor, and later as president, he rarely used crutches and was rarely seen with a wheelchair, preferring to use a cane, a milder and less medical symbol of disability.

Once Roosevelt was elected governor in 1928, there seemed to exist an agreement between the administration and the media that he would not be portrayed as a person with a major disability. There is some indication that

Roosevelt had made this prohibition so that he would not look helpless or not in command.[35]

Roosevelt experienced the economic catastrophe following the Wall Street crash of 1929 as governor of what was at the time the most populous state in the union. New York was a microcosm of the entire nation. As governor he was familiar with the profound effects of a severe and unremitting unemployment that left a quarter of the work force idle; the collapse of agriculture with crop prices inadequate to permit shipment to markets; the bank failure and loss of life savings for many people; a plummeting stock market, with nearly a tenfold decline in the Dow-Jones average; mortgage foreclosures on homes and farms; bankruptcies; and a resulting sense of hopelessness, despair, and gloom.

At Warm Springs Roosevelt began to develop a doctor-patient metaphor, which would carry through the remainder of his political life. In the early days of his presidency, the "Doctor Roosevelt" of Warm Springs changed into "Dr. New Deal" and later "Dr. Win the War." Fresh from his Warm Spring experiences and the governorship, Roosevelt chose to use a metaphor that probably had grown out of his effort to cope with paralysis. He was the doctor; the country was the patient. His findings of systemic failure comprised the "physical examination." No laboratory studies were needed to confirm the profound, worsening condition of the patient in the middle of the Great Depression. The disease was unusually severe, seemingly unique, since recovery from other more limited depressions had occurred spontaneously, with little therapy required as part of the "normal" economic cycles. In the new case of the 1930s, however, conventional treatment was ineffective and the patient was physically *in extremis* with severe psychological damage being inflicted as well.

The guiding principle for physicians is *primum non nocere*, "above all do no harm." But in this extraordinary crisis, Roosevelt argued, only novel, untried measures, those which would be considered experimental, would avail. They were urgently needed in view of the gravity of the situation. "Dr. Roosevelt" could not only recognize the need for improvisation, for unusual measures, but unique among political leaders, he could provide an example. His belief in his own recovery never wavered, even though it lacked any medical or scientific foundation. By the time of the 1928 campaign he was describing himself as a recovered polio patient. For a nation in the moment of calamity, the example and the approach of "Dr. Roosevelt" were what was needed. Beyond the specific measures taken to redress the economic crisis was Roosevelt's remarkably buoyant spirit instilling a sense of optimism, enhancing the psychological recovery of the public, and thereby helping to sustain the physical recovery of the economy.

25

~ 3 ~

Presidential Years 1933–1943: The Picture of Health

When inaugurated on March 4, 1933, Franklin D. Roosevelt was healthy, except for the paralysis resulting from his attack of poliomyelitis. He had just turned fifty-one at the end of January and was in excellent physical and emotional condition. He had withstood the rigors of a vigorous election campaign and suffered no ill effects from the assassination attempt in Miami on February 15, in which Mayor Anton J. Cermak of Chicago died.

In 1930 a decisive win in his second campaign for the governorship of New York state made Roosevelt a viable candidate for the presidency in 1932. A few short months later, on April 29, 1931, Governor Roosevelt had a complete physical examination by doctors Samuel W. Lambert, Russell A. Hibbs, and Foster Kennedy. Their findings pictured a man in the best of health.

In October 1930, Roosevelt had applied to the Mutual Life Insurance Company of New York for a policy with the face value of $560,000. The Warm Springs Foundation was named as beneficiary. On October 3, 1930, the medical examiner for the insurance company examined Roosevelt. Weighing 182 pounds, at 6'1½" in height, with a 43½" chest, and a blood pressure of 128/82, the patient reflected exceptional health.[1] The examiner even answered "no" to such questions as; does the applicant look older than the stated age?; is there anything unfavorable . . . such as delicate or sickly appearance?; is there any undue hazard to life or health from occupation? The medical examiner's notes provided support for the life insurance policies. The doctors' report a few months later served a more political cause.

As the continuing events of 1931 reflected Roosevelt's increasingly probable candidacy for the presidency, the questions relating to his ability to assume the burdens of that office inevitably arose. There was a public challenge from a supposed Republican, Earle Looker, for Roosevelt to have a complete physical. The report of the three doctors was the result, which read[2]:

> We have, today, examined Franklin D. Roosevelt. We find that his organs and functions are sound in all respects. There is no anemia. The chest is exceptionally well developed, and the spinal column is absolutely normal; all its segments are in perfect alignment and free from disease. He has neither pain nor ache at any time. Ten years ago, Governor Roosevelt suffered an attack of acute infantile paralysis, the entire effect of which was expended on muscles of his lower extremities. There has been progressive recovery of power in the legs since that date; this restoration continues and will continue.
>
> Governor Roosevelt can walk all necessary distances and can maintain a standing position without fatigue.
>
> We believe his power of endurance are such as to allow him to meet all the demands of private or public life.
>
> Signed: Samuel W. Lambert, M.D.
>   Russell A. Hibbs, M.D.
>   Foster Kennedy, M.D.

Earle Looker was later to ghost-write articles that appeared over Roosevelt's signature in *Liberty Magazine*. Roosevelt requested that the doctors send a copy of their report to Looker, and they replied to the request on April 29, 1931. Writing in the July 15 issue of *Liberty Magazine* Looker made use of that information:

> In so far as I had observed him, I had come to the conclusion that he seemed able to take more punishment than many men ten years younger. Merely his legs were not much good to him.[3]

This information was used by Roosevelt and his staff to allay the fears and concerns related to his health and the presidency.

The first ten years of Roosevelt's presidency appeared medically uneventful, despite the onset of hypertension after his first four years and reports of several respiratory tract infections. As late as November and December of 1943, his photographs and newsreels reflect vigor and a reasonable state of health. He resonant voice, heard frequently on the radio, likewise reflected positively on his well-being.

On assuming the presidency Roosevelt developed a role as a wise if somewhat controversial, optimistic, and benign therapist. His personal concern for health and treatment of illness became reflected in his approach to his role as president. The clearest explanation by Roosevelt of his "doctor" terminology was given at a press conference on December 28, 1943, when he was asked about the use of the term "New Deal."

> . . . [H]ow did the New Deal come into existence? It was because there was an awfully sick patient called the United States of America, and it was suffering from a grave internal disorder—awfully sick—all kinds of things had happened to this patient, all internal things. And they sent for the doctor. And it was a long, long process—took several years before those ills, in that particular illness of ten years ago, were remedied. But after a while they were remedied. And on those ills of 1933, things had to be done to cure the patient internally. . . . The remedies that the old Dr. New Deal used were for internal troubles.[4]

In his Fireside Chat of March 12, 1933, he spoke of a major "internal" disorder—the banking system. He noted that the banks were "on holiday" rather than closed, and would reopen in sound condition, or were to be reorganized so that sound banks would be created. He offered hope, indeed certainty, that the patient, the country, would recover, for "we have provided the machinery to restore our financial system."[5] Credibility was enhanced, as in the conventional doctor-patient relationship, by clearly defining the magnitude of the "illness." In the Fireside Chat of May 7, 1933, he proceeded to define the illness by saying the economy was dying and proceeded to speak of methods of treatment.[6] In evaluating the practice of Dr. New Deal, at his press conference in December 28, 1943, he noted:

> The remedies that the old Dr. New Deal used were for internal troubles. He saved the banks of the United States and set up a sound banking system.[7]

Specific treatments were designed to provide relief. Old Dr. New Deal ". . . he put in old age insurance, he put in unemployment insurance."[8] Continuing treatments sought to provide food and shelter and income for such. The Federal Aid system cared for the infirm, the crippled, and the blind. The Civilian Conservation Corps, the P.W.A. (Public Works Administration), and the W.P.A. (Works Progress Administration) provided jobs by the thousands. The National Youth Administration worked with thousands of underprivileged young people. More substantial therapy came in the form of banking and stock market reform, increased regulation of utilities, and the establishment of social security. Also important on the list, Dr. New Deal would later mention the various ways of conserving natural resources:

> The resettlement of farmers from marginal lands that ought not to be cultivated; regional physical developments, such as T.V.A. (Tennessee Valley Administration); getting electricity out to the farmers through the R.E.A.(Rural Electrification Administration); flood control; and water conservation; drought control and drought relief; crop insurance, and the every normal granary; and assistance to farm cooperatives.[9]

The "doctor knows best" and "doctor's orders" style of physicians of that era closely blended with Roosevelt's approach to the nation's problems. The desperately afflicted patient of March 1933—the nation—preferred the control, the dictation of the responsible "physician" to the endless debates of the Congress. Indeed bills were passed during Roosevelt's First One Hundred Days in the fashion of a rapid infusion of medication to a critically ill patient in intensive care. The crisis, as with a patient in shock, was so severe that the rapid, drastic therapy "Dr." Roosevelt prescribed was taken gratefully and surely without question.

Indeed, it was only when the acute phase of the crisis ended that Roosevelt's prescriptions were subjected to second opinions and the initial reflexive acceptance replaced by discussion, debate, and doubt. In the second term, the good will so evident in the legislation of the first hundred days of the first term disappeared in the turmoil of the Court Reform crisis. Pages of criticism began to fill the newspapers such as the *New York Times*, the *Washington Post*, and the *New York Herald-Tribune*. Even the Scripps-Howard chain joined in the negative positions against Roosevelt, whom they had supported during the previous election. The physician's reservoir of good will sustained him in other, less severe crises, but it was inevitably drained away when the situation seemed more about Roosevelt's power than about the crisis involving the nation. At the time of his first election in 1932, 41 percent of American daily newspapers and 45 percent of the weeklies supported Roosevelt. By the end of the 1940 election, those percentages had dropped to 25 percent and 33 percent respectively.[10]

With the Japanese attack on Pearl Harbor, the patient needed treatment. Roosevelt's "Dr. New Deal" called on his partner "Dr. Win-the-War," as he explained in the December 28, 1943, press conference:

> But since then, two years ago, the patient had a very bad accident—not an internal trouble. Two years ago, on the seventh of December, he was in a pretty bad smashup—broke his hip, broke his leg in two or three places, broke a wrist and an arm, and some ribs; and they didn't think he would live, for a while. And then he began to "come to"; and he has been in charge of a partner of the old doctor. Old Dr. New Deal didn't know "nothing" about legs and arms. He knew a great deal about internal medicine, but nothing about surgery. So he got his partner, who was an orthopedic surgeon, Dr. Win-the-War, to take care of this fellow who had been in this bad accident. And the result is that the patient is back on his feet. He has given up his crutches. He isn't wholly well yet, and he won't be until he wins the war.[11]

The Dr. Win-the-War role was far more complex, with stakes escalating even beyond those of the Depression. The patient in 1933 knew all too well how serious the illness was—there was a lack of adequate food, clothing, and shelter. They understood Dr. Roosevelt's diagnosis, stated in his second inaugural speech: "I see one-third of a nation ill housed, ill-clad, ill-nourished."[12] The country could continue to accept Roosevelt's treatments for its internal illnesses.

Even as Dr. New Deal was seeking to remedy the country's illnesses, conflict was spreading in other lands. At a conference in Munich, Great Britain and France agreed to allow Germany to take over the Sudetenland. A few short months later, in March 1939, Germany invaded Czechoslovakia; and finally on September 1, 1939, Germany began a major invasion of Poland.[13] There was no doubt that a virulent epidemic of war had began. Most newspapers reflected the view that the majority of American people wanted to stay out of the European war, even in light of the aggressive actions of the Nazi war machine.[14] The American people had traditionally been reassured that the oceans separating the New World from the Old formed barriers that could not be breached.

The oceans could clearly permit a quarantine of the aggressors in Europe. Most Americans responded at first to the European conflicts with a belief that isolationism would effectively protect America from the infection of war. As long as the United States was asymptomatic and the infection of war was remote, Americans wished to remain separated from the battle. In May 1937, Roosevelt signed the Third Neutrality Act that prohibited exporting arms to belligerents.

Even prevention in the form of buttressing our prospective allies was received ambivalently. As the United States sold munitions to France and Great Britain, Roosevelt insisted that secrecy be maintained.[15] In his conversations with the American public, Roosevelt continued to tell the voters why it was important to assist the allies while not entering the conflict. In a Fireside Chat in December 1940, he reminded the listeners that, "We must be the great arsenal of democracy. . . . For us this is an emergency as serious as war itself."[16] Only after the invasion of Poland by Nazi Germany was the administration able to achieve repeal of the embargo of arms to England and France. His promise not to send American boys to fight on foreign soil was not to be fulfilled. The desire to quarantine war's infection would collapse with the attack on Pearl Harbor, an event that would also dispel the illusion held by many Americans that they could be immune to the infection that was afflicting other countries.

America had been healing under the direction of Dr. Roosevelt. However, following the physical and psychological trauma of Pearl Harbor, new treatments and healing skills were needed. In Roosevelt's words, Dr. New Deal knew only about internal trouble, and nothing about surgery. Therefore, it was necessary after December 7, 1941, that the United States needed another approach. So Dr. New Deal gave way to Dr. Win-the-War. Roosevelt's skills took a new approach. He did not soft pedal the magnitude of the difficulties faced by the nation, which were severe and global. The prognosis was as dire as had been the events of 1933.[17]

The treatment of the crisis would be drastic. Massive amounts of money, goods, and people were to be involved in meeting the infection of war. By the spring of 1942, Roosevelt had increased the goal of the draft to more than 5 million persons. The industrial production considered feasible for 1942 was $62 billion. Within months the shipyards had begun to complete large numbers of ships, from twenty-six in March to sixty-seven in June.[18]

As a nation, Americans became involved in seeking to combat the epidemic of violence and war that had engulfed the world. As individuals, they were no longer just spectators in the process of winning the war and healing the pain it created. Their involvement in the process of getting better included conservation measures, victory gardens, scrap metal and rubber drives, war bond purchases, and a seemingly endless array of morale-boosting songs, movies, radio broadcasts, and parades. In his formal role as commander-in-chief and in his informal role as Dr. Win-the-War, Roosevelt evaluated the status of his patient in realistic but reassuring terms. In 1943 as the tide of war began to turn, Roosevelt's authority was more freely questioned. Only at the depth of the crisis was his authority absolute.

During the war, Roosevelt continued to employ medical imagery explicitly. Admiral Ross McIntire related a conversation between Roosevelt and a young Marine who had removed his own leg on the battlefield of Saipan. After the president had been told this, he greeted the Marine by saying: "Good morning, Doctor. I understand that you are quite a surgeon. . . . Well, I happen to be a pretty good orthopedist myself, so what about a consultation?"[19]

To compensate for his total dependence on others for mobility, Roosevelt felt the need to be daring, a need to push the political process as far as possible. His paralysis was the foundation on which his authority was built. According to Hugh Gallagher: "His visible handicap was a badge of courage that men respected and responded to. . . . It was no small part of Roosevelt's magnetism and authority."[20] That magnetism attracted the talents of those New Deal administrators from the fields of law, finance, and education to help Dr. Win-the-War fight the infection of totalitarianism. That authority created an atmosphere in which the doctor's orders for war production were readily accepted and obeyed. His assurance that others could do the impossible was a reflection of the optimism stemming from his own struggle over the handicap of paralysis.

His self assured, and daring approach to his role as president resulted in new and innovative activities. In 1932 he had become the first presidential candidate to expand the scope of his campaigning by use of airplanes, still a new and hazardous mode of transportation. During the war, the "physician" continued to travel to see the progress of his efforts—cross-country tours in 1942 and 1943, international conferences at Casablanca, Cairo, and Teheran, flights to Hawaii and Alaska in 1944, and finally Yalta in 1945. He was the first incumbent president to visit Africa, the first to fly overseas, and the first to visit a battlefield since Lincoln.

Because of his exaggerated need to centralize all authority, he failed to develop a politically suitable successor. The few men suggested as potential nominees were clearly doomed to failure for reasons of their religious background (Roman Catholics such as James A. Farley and Joseph P. Kennedy), or age (Cordell Hull). Selective rejection of help from former adversaries, even during World War II, also reflected this need for centralized authority. Hence the talents of a wide range of public figures who offered their services to Roosevelt in the emergency following Pearl Harbor were denied to the nation. Colonel Charles A. Lindberg and former president Herbert Hoover were in this category.

Physically confined to a wheelchair, Roosevelt found liberation in defying conventional restraints. No other president, no matter how popular (except perhaps his cousin Theodore and, unrealistically, because of his stroke, Woodrow Wilson), ever envisioned defying George Washington's proscription against a third or fourth term in office, regardless of military or political exigencies. His hubris made him larger than life to the nation and the people around him. He created an aura of invincibility and may have convinced himself he was invincible. His choice to ignore his physical limits almost certainly hastened the decline of his health and his early death.

Coverage and Coverup

The relationships of Roosevelt and the media were complex. In their study of *The Press and the Presidency*, John Tebbel and Sarah Watts state their belief that Roosevelt controlled the flow of news from the White House beginning with his first press conference. After the excitement of a new president and a new type press conference passed,

> . . . it did not occur to them [the press] that what had happened was a laying down of rules which would guarantee, if followed, that the president would control the dissemination of news at his pleasure. And they learned, as time went on, that his control was sophisticated.[21]

Roosevelt and his closest associates—people like Louis Howe and Steve Early—worked diligently to make the tasks of the journalists easier and more efficient. The number of administration sources, such as public information officers, seemed to multiply. This approach also served the self interest of the administration. One analyst notes: "By aiding the press in their work and particularly by aiding the journalists personally, they maximized positive results for the administration."[22]

Just how sophisticated Roosevelt's control happened to be is illustrated in the interplay of Roosevelt and the press during the discussion surrounding the nomination of Alabama Senator Hugo Black to the Supreme Court. At the press conference on September 21, 1937, no minutes were taken for approximately five minutes of discussion during the questioning of Senator Black's Klan affiliations.

The force of Roosevelt's personality and his superb voice heard when he delivered his speeches were great contributions to his control of radio.[23] More closely related to this discussion were the continuing efforts by Roosevelt and his staff to control his image as presented through photographs in the media. Memoranda from Steve Early to the photographers covering the president outlined the rules for photographing Roosevelt, including candid shots.[24] Even prior to his election to the presidency, Roosevelt had established the ground rules for his image control. According to one biographer, "News photographers in the 1920's voluntarily destroyed their own plates when they showed Roosevelt in poses that revealed his handicap."[25] The management of his public image was so effective that few people were conscious of his crippled legs. The reaction of the head usher at the White House was typical of public reactions:

> Everybody knew that the president had been stricken with infantile paralysis, and his recovery was legend but few people were aware how completely the disease had handicapped him.[26]

Throughout his presidency there was intense interest by the public and the press in Roosevelt's health. Ignorance regarding poliomyelitis was partly the reason. Some people did not understand that his condition, however severe, was static—that the paralysis would not spread to other parts of the nervous system or elsewhere.[27] Because he often traveled, large numbers of people were able to see the president in person, helping quell the whispering campaigns about his ill health. However, the media coverage reflected public concern and managing public perception of the president's health became a preoccupation of the White House.

Hugh Gallagher noted that many rumors surfaced that had to be denied by the White House staff:

> It was said that the polio had affected FDR's brain; that he was permanently institutionalized in a lunatic asylum somewhere on the Georgia Warm Spring Foundation grounds. It was said that certain reporters had certain friends who had seen the President being smuggled into the Mayo Clinic for a major cancer

operation. It was said that the President had suffered a heart arrest during a Cabinet meeting, but that the Cabinet had decided to keep it a secret.[28]

Most of these rumors were repeated after Roosevelt's death in an article by Dr. Karl C. Wold in *Look* magazine. Wold claimed that during a visit to the Mayo Clinic in 1938 where his son James Roosevelt was a patient, the president had the first in a series of strokes. He also mentions a cerebral hemorrhage in March 1945 at Hyde Park, and a secret trip to the Mayo Clinic where examination revealed an inoperable tumor, possibly malignant, of the prostate gland. In 1949, Roosevelt's son Elliott published a rebuttal of Wold's article because "every member of his (FDR's) family has been indicted for negligence by his article."[29]

The coverage of Roosevelt's health in the *New York Times* over the course of his administration is particularly revealing. In April 1934, the *New York Times* reported that Roosevelt's son Elliot responded to rumors of serious illness or injury, assuring reporters that his father's health was "swell" and that he was enjoying a fishing trip to Florida.

Extensive detailed observations of White House physician McIntire reached the front page of the *New York Times* twice in 1934, on March 3 and December 20. The reports that "FDR was in better physical shape than at any time since entering the White House" were to become a standard. They would be repeated over the years with little variation. At the beginning of Roosevelt's second term, McIntire told Frederick A. Storm of *Liberty Magazine*:

> The President is in better shape now [1932] than [when] he initially entered the White House on March 4, 1933. His muscle tone is excellent . . . he has the ability to relax and therein lies the secret of his ability to "take it."[30]

These White House claims, however, were not effective in stopping rumors or preventing opponents from raising questions about Roosevelt's health. The *New York Times* in its "News of the Week in Review" of July 14, 1935, ran a story in response to an especially vicious, politically motivated rumor campaign in the summer of 1935.

> Whispering campaigns against men in public life in this country ordinarily involve either morals or health. In this instance it was health; residents of Washington, returning to their homes after trips to places far distant from the capital, carried with them all sorts of stories heard in those distant places. They had been assured, on the straightest of straight information that the president's health had broken, that his nerves were shot to pieces, that the main concern of those close to him was to keep the awful facts from the public.[31]

When a reporter at a press conference cautiously probed, "Are you in a little bad health?" Roosevelt laughed it off and displayed his vigorous grin and radiant appearance in response. The response of the editors to the gossip was essentially to note that before the summer was over millions of Americans would have the opportunity to see for themselves just how healthy the president really was. The coverage of the medical allegation was extensive and several major political leaders denounced this strategy.[33] In the wake of this rumor-mongering, an employee of the Thomas A. Edison Industries of West Orange, New Jersey, wrote a letter of abject apology to Roosevelt expressing his shame at having started the campaign: "Having publicly acknowledged that I am ashamed. . . . Permit me to make the same acknowledgment to you."[33]

Still, stories concerning Roosevelt's health continued to appear. During 1937 there were a total of twenty-six articles in the *New York Times* related to Roosevelt health. In December 1937, the *Times* ran eight stories about the president's dental infection, six of them on the front page. The first of the front-page articles on December 1, 1937, noted that "Roosevelt Off Dry Tortugas for Gulf Fish; Still Feels Tooth Infection, but is Gaining." A radio bulletin from his son mentioned that the tooth infection was showing "satisfactory improvement." The reassuring headline in the last of these, "Jaw Healed," confirmed previous reports of his good general health.[34]

In 1939 solicitous concern for the president's well-being was expressed by columnist Arthur Krock, the *New York Times* Washington bureau chief for many years. A section of his column for February 17 was entitled "A Crop of False Rumors." Krock argued that when a president is reported ill and cancels appointments, "groundless rumors concerning his condition fill the air" and "since Mr. Roosevelt went to bed with the grippe, the usual nonsense has been circulated."[35] The next day's front-page story reported a press conference in Roosevelt's private railroad car on the way to Key West. The article described the president as "a bit pale and professedly tired."[36] In truth, a previous blood pressure level showed an increase, but the White House did not acknowledge that[37]; nor could such an elevation necessarily be the cause of the symptoms described.

With very little information, the press continued to speculate, often merely repeating inaccurate official statements. In May 7, 1941, when the president was experiencing bleeding hemorrhoids, the front page of the *Times* reported that Roosevelt was confined to his living quarters "with a slight temperature caused by a gastro-intestinal disorder." It further quoted the White House physician as stating that it was "nothing serious at all, something he ate, and the condition should clear up promptly."[38] The White House physician made no comment, nor did any spokesperson, even though hemorrhoids are a common, benign, treatable abnormality.

On May 8, 1941, the *New York Times* in reporting Italian reaction to a speech by Secretary of War Henry Stimson, noted that his mention of "the spirit of Woodrow Wilson is enough to arouse the irresistible disgust of the Italian people." The report linked the Italian reaction to a rumored health problem of Roosevelt's— "Roosevelt has entered a hospital"—and continued to describe a sort of breakdown that required an indefinite rest, but then issued a disclaimer of this politically motivated report one day after its release.[39]

In the immediate aftermath of Pearl Harbor, the *New York Times* reported that the president was medically unaffected by the strain of war.[40] As 1942 progressed it noted that the president suffered from colds in February, April, and December.[41] The effect of the continued preoccupation by major newspapers with rumors of ill health may have further dampened the public's response to signs of the president's later decline. Roosevelt's health was an old story by the time of America's entry into World War II, a media perennial which in earlier instances had revealed no serious problems. However, the cover-up related to health issues was beginning.

Franklin D. Roosevelt was vigorous and in a reasonable state of health for the first ten years of his presidency. His schedule for most of those years, as recorded in the diaries of the White House Usher (which lists all presidential appointments in the Executive Office) reflected an energetic, even indefatigable executive with a wide range of interests and a six- or seven-day work week. The diaries list Roosevelt's press conferences. Held twice weekly, they were unprecedented in number and open in style. The diaries show that cabinet meetings were frequent, as were meetings with the vice president and congressional leaders. Other meetings were scheduled for most weekends, further reflecting his usually high energy level.

However, the full range of Roosevelt's work hours is not completely shown. His morning paperwork before scheduled appointments is not included, nor are meetings held outside of Washington. Clearly, he worked a long day, typically in excess of twelve hours. There were also secret meetings that were omitted from the Usher's Diaries.[42]

While there were brief periods of illness during the first ten years of his administration, none were serious and he always recovered, similarly to what the papers reported. The subtle nature of his hypertension and its progress made it possible for Roosevelt to fool the nation and himself. There was always a degree of concern about the president's health in the press and among the public, which was relieved by the ready acceptance from both quarters of the optimistic assessments coming from the White

House. The continuous shadow of rumors eventually dulled the instincts of the press.

Curiously some of the rumors of the president's ill health came from Roosevelt himself. By the late 1930s, he sometimes referred to fatigue, "slowing down," but always in a highly political content. It is likely that such complaints to persons like Postmaster General James Farley were designed by the president to deter their rivalrous ambitions.[43] Some of the other reports of ill health came from disaffected associates, making them questionable. For example, William C. Bullitt, U.S. Ambassador to the USSR from 1933 to 1936, and to France from 1936 to 1941, recounted a supposed collapse at dinner in February 1940, at which Roosevelt's "friend" Marguerite "Missy" LeHand was also present. According to Bullitt, White House physician McIntire examined Roosevelt and reported to the others present that the president had a "very slight heart attack."[44] However, there was no public mention of this incident, no independent verification, nor even a source in the notes of a book later written by Bullitt in which the alleged heart attack was mentioned. To the contrary, the Usher's Diaries show a normal schedule of Roosevelt's appointments on the next day. When Roosevelt was ill, even with a cold, it was recorded in the Usher's Diary as an explanation for a light schedule, or indeed no appointment at all.[45] Clouding Bullitt's objectivity is the especially bitter, highly personal estrangement in 1943, which ended a long and previously friendly association with Roosevelt.

As Roosevelt began his third term, he did experience some real medical problems. In 1941 an EKG showed possible changes—low amplitude of T waves in leads I and V-4 were of a degree that could be considered abnormal.[46] On a May 2 trip to Staunton, Virginia, to dedicate Woodrow Wilson's home, Roosevelt was observed by a reporter from *Time* magazine, who noted that "FDR looked as bad as a man can look and still be about."[47]

On May 5, 1941, the president's hemoglobin level dropped precipitously—declining to 4.5 gm/dl (normal is 13–15 gm/dl)—due to bleeding hemorrhoids, which spontaneously improved. Ferrous sulfate (an iron supplement) was given, as was a blood transfusion, and the hemoglobin increased to almost normal—12 gm/ml on June 4.[48] A gastrointestinal series and barium enema examination were within normal limits suggesting that other causes of this anemia and rectal bleeding, such as polyps or carcinomas in the intestinal tract, were not evident.[49] There is no evidence that these tests were repeated during Dr. Howard Bruenn's physical examination of Roosevelt on March 28, 1944 nor thereafter.

Elevated blood pressure levels, indicating hypertension, were recorded as early as 1937—162/98 on April 22, 1937. The next known readings were on November 13, 1940—178/88. During his bout of illness in May 1941, the blood pressure declined transiently—148/80, 152/86, 162/84—associated with anemia (drop in hemoglobin attributed to bleeding from the hemorrhoids).[50] An upper gastrointestinal series given later in the summer of 1941 was within normal limits. An "irritable colon" was found, but there were no diverticula or polyps. Blood chemistry levels (blood urea nitrogen, uric acid, creatinine, glucose, sodium, chloride, carbon dioxide) were all normal in 1939 and 1941. Cholesterol levels were 190 and 155 in 1939 and 1941, respectively.[51]

The progressive effects of hypertension were silent until early 1944. The public would not be aware of any deterioration in Roosevelt's health. At no time were the repeatedly abnormal blood pressure levels disclosed, nor was the "perhaps abnormal" EKG mentioned above disclosed. There is no documentation that the potentially ominous significance of hypertension was discussed with the family or Roosevelt himself.[52]

Although doubtlessly exacerbated by relentless wartime pressures both physical and emotional, the president's hypertension progressed without even minimal treatment as noted in available records. The White House was, understandably, a very tense place during Roosevelt's third term, as emphasized by Roosevelt's daughter, Anna Roosevelt Boettiger: ". . . all of us were tense . . . everybody was tense."[53] There can be speculation about other possible contributing factors to his hypertensive condition.

Sympathomimetics (agents that tighten blood vessels) were probably given in the almost daily sprays administered to Roosevelt's sinuses. In addition, adrenaline or ephedrine were routinely applied to the surface of nasal mucosa. Sometimes an anesthetic such as novocaine was applied prior to irrigation of the maxillary sinuses. However, the effect of adrenaline or ephedrine given this way on blood pressure is thought by ear, nose, and throat specialists to be negligible. These agents were probably not factors in increasing hypertension.[54]

Smoking, however, could have been a factor in the president's increasing blood pressure. Since he was a heavy cigarette smoker, Roosevelt's physician said that despite the nasal irritations the best he could do was to get the president to cut back on cigarettes during sinus attacks.[55] One White House correspondent, Merriman Smith, notes that at his last press conference on April 5, 1945, Roosevelt was still smoking but having trouble fitting a cigarette into his famous ivory holder.[56] If Roosevelt had been cautioned to reduce his use of tobacco, he apparently disregarded that advice. At that time, the effects of tobacco use were poorly understood. A principal textbook of the period was dubious about hypertensive or other harmful effects, disdainfully commenting on "bogies flaunted by the anti-smoking propagandists."[57] Likewise, the role of alcohol in raising blood pressure levels was unrecognized at that time, but even so it would seem that Roosevelt's alcohol consumption was limited. There have been suggestions that poliomyelitis itself has been linked to chronic hypertension, but the results of studies are too varied to draw conclusions for any single patient.

The acute attack of poliomyelitis has a clear association with only transient hypertension of three to six months and is seen in only a few cases.[58] Furthermore, the association, when it does occur is especially pronounced in a very severe type, called bulbar polio, which requires artificial ventilation.[59] In Roosevelt's case his blood pressure was normal a decade after the onset of paralysis only to increase five to six years later. Hence, for Roosevelt there would not appear to be an association between poliomyelitis and hypertension.

The most serious health problem that Roosevelt had during his presidency was not his paralysis. It was hypertension which led to congestive heart failure, hypertension that went untreated even though periodic examinations indicated increases in blood pressure. As noted earlier, the dramatic elevations in blood pressure began in his third term (Table 3.1). Had his presidency concluded after his second term, Roosevelt would most likely have lived longer. Had he not run for the unprecedented third and fourth terms, and been spared the continued official wartime burdens, he would have experienced less stress and his hypertension would have been recognized and treated in a timely fashion. Congestive heart failure, anginal episodes, and ultimately fatal cerebral hemorrhage could have been delayed or avoided. Based on the life span of his parents, his children, and other family members (Table 3.2), it is reasonable to assume that had Roosevelt retired and become a country squire and leading private citizen, he would have survived well beyond the age of sixty-three years.

If Roosevelt had not run for a fourth term in 1944, after his health had declined dramatically, his hypertension could have been managed as a former president with lifestyle changes more feasible and effective. There is no indication that sedation was used more than minimally during his presidency and diuretics not at all. They could have been used more aggressively with a former president. Hospitalization could have been undertaken without political fallout by a former president relieved of his responsibilities as commander-in-chief.

The reality of wartime issues in 1939 and 1940 impelled Roosevelt to run for a third term. This decision had disastrous, indeed fatal medical consequences for him as his health deteriorated in the latter part of the third term. A similar situation existed in July of 1944. After the successful invasion of Normandy, allied troops were pushing into France but the outcome of the war was not absolutely certain and major challenges and decisions remained. Roosevelt's role in history was secure and a willingness to turn over his responsibilities in a planned, orderly fashion, might have been

Table 3.1

FDR's Blood Pressure

First, second, and early third term		Later third and fourth terms	
Date	Systolic/diastolic	Date	Systolic/diastolic
07/30/35	136/78		
04/22/37	162/98		
11/13/40	178/88	03/28/44	186/105
02/27/41	188/105		178/102
02/27/41	178/102	04/05/44	226/118
05/41	136/78	04/09/44	196/112 am
	162/84	06/14/44	194/96 pm
		9/44	180/100 low
			240/130 high
		11/18/44	210/112
		12/44	260/150
		2/45	170/88 low
			240/130 high

Source: Bruenn, H. "Clinical Notes on the Illness and Death of President Franklin D. Roosevelt." *Annals of Internal Medicine* 72:579–91, 1970.

Table 3.2

Longevity in FDR's Family

FDR's paternal ancestors				FDR and his children			
Name	Life span	Years	Relation	Name	Life span	Years	Relation
Nicholas	1658–1742	84	g-g-g-gf	FDR	1882–1945	63	
Jacobus	1692–1776	84	g-g-gf	Anna	1906–1975	69	daughter
Isaac	1790–1863	73	g-father	James	1907–1991	84	son
James	1828–1900	72	father	Elliot	1910–1990	80	son
				FDR, Jr.	1914–1988	74	son
				John	1916–1981	65	son
Average		76.8		Average		74.4	

Source: Collier, P. *The Roosevelts* (New York: Simon and Schuster, 1994.)

respected if there were a suitable replacement. However, he was still viewed by many Americans as the most experienced, even, indispensable leader. It is not clear that he or anyone else, except some of the physicians attending him, understood that he was a gravely ill man.

It is possible to understand the course of events and the president's medical history if one appreciates the forces at work throughout his presidency. Transient, trivial illnesses were manipulated for political purposes. The most prestigious newspapers in the country (i.e., the *New York Times*) carried front-

page stories about slight cases of "the grippe," toothaches, colds, sinusitis—
a seeming exploitation of the public's near obsessional preoccupation with
any variation in Roosevelt's health. This situation was enhanced by the secrecy of the White House staff and the failure of White House physician
McIntire to recognize and/or communicate to the American public a significant abnormality—hypertension—which would cause heart failure and ultimately a fatal stroke.

The role of the White House physician was naturally a pivotal one in the
medical history of the president. During Roosevelt's tenure, only two physicians occupied that position. Dr. Joel Boone, for approximately one month,
and McIntire for the remainder of the time Roosevelt was in office. Boone
had served as personal physician to President Herbert Hoover (having been
deputy physician to two previous presidents, Harding and Coolidge) and
expected to remain as the White House physician under Roosevelt. He was a
highly decorated naval officer, having been awarded the Congressional Medal
of Honor. After leaving the White House, Boone resumed his naval career,
retiring in 1951. Boone kept in close touch with the White House even though
no longer formally associated. A letter in his file shows that Roosevelt's
passing left him shocked and upset, yet not surprised (April 13, 1945).
McIntire responds to him, somewhat belatedly (May 10, 1945) addressing
him as "Dear Joel." The rationalizations continued, "I had not expected any
such disaster to come up on us and consequently I was in Washington at the
time." However, McIntire was still in a state of shock acknowledging, "I do
not believe that any of us fully realized what has happened . . . it will take
months before the world realizes it." [60]

One of McIntire's obituaries (December 8, 1959) in passing records his
opinion that he could learn more about the president's condition by his mood
than through a physical examination. Hence, he provides, perhaps inad-
vertently, the basis for a delay in diagnosis of Roosevelt's congestive
heart failure.[61]

McIntire attributed his obtaining the position to his relationship to Admiral Cary Grayson, the White House physician for Woodrow Wilson. In his
memoirs he wrote that "my appointment as White House physician came
through Admiral Cary Grayson." An otolaryngologist, McIntire wondered,
"What could an eye, ear, nose, and throat name possibly have to offer to a
victim of infantile paralysis?"[62]

It would be more likely that Boone, as a generalist, would have recognized and treated Roosevelt's hypertension early and appropriately. Given
his career history, Boone would have been more forthcoming with the American public, the "patient," and Roosevelt's family, than his successor turned
out to be regarding the president's medical condition. Boone had been one of

the physicians attending at President Harding's last illness. He also had attested to the medical fitness of President Hoover for his reelection in 1932. In 1923 he had candidly advised Secretary of Commerce Hoover that President Harding was significantly more ill than his official physician realized.[63]

In a chapter entitled "The Royal Physician" in their book *When Illness Strikes the Leader: The Dilemma of the Captive King*, Jerrold M. Post and Robert S. Robins claim that McIntire wrote his book *White House Physician*

> to dispel the rumors that President Franklin D. Roosevelt was more seriously ill than McIntire had said and also to counter the suggestion that Roosevelt's senior physician had withheld this information from the American public.[64]

One of the bases for making such positive claims about the health of the president was the fact that Roosevelt had annual checkups similar to those used by the military for their officer personnel. However, his was the only documentation for those records. They do not exist today. Dr. Bruenn stated that the clinical progress notes and results of various laboratory tests were kept in a safe at the U.S. Naval Hospital, Bethesda, Maryland, and that after the president's death they could not be found.[65]

There is some indication that Roosevelt's family, including his granddaughter Eleanor Seagraves, also had some concerns about the role of McIntire.[66] Seagraves commented on Roosevelt's tremor observed when he met vice-presidential candidate and senator Harry S. Truman in August 1944. She is aware of several members of the family known to have the same finding and it appears to be a benign familial tremor. Bruenn denied that Roosevelt had symptoms of Parkinson's disease.[67]

Assistant Secretary of the Navy Roosevelt on inspection tour of a United States Naval Air Station, August 18, 1918.

Roosevelt, president of the Boy Scout Foundation of Greater New York, on a visit to a Boy Scout camp at Bear Mountain on July 27, 1921, two weeks before he was stricken with poliomyelitis. Thought to be last photograph of Roosevelt before the paralysis.

Roosevelt at Warm Springs, Georgia, about 1923 or 1924. Note the well-developed upper arms compared with the thin, atrophic legs.

Roosevelt preparing to address the 1924 Democratic National Convention, Madison Square Garden, New York. He is using crutches as he approaches the rostrum.

Roosevelt at a 1927 picnic in Warm Springs, Georgia, on the Dowdell Knob. With him is "Missy" Marguerite A. LeHand (left).

Roosevelt driving the specially designed Model A Ford, equipped with hand-operated controls, at Hyde Park, New York.

Governor Roosevelt enroute to Warm Springs, Georgia, on the Pennsylvania Railroad, from New York City, November 18, 1931. Note jaunty smile, use of cane, and his leaning against the wall and holding a bar for further support.

President Roosevelt at Hyde Part, New York, February 1941 with 5-year-old Ruthie Bie (granddaughter of Christian Bie, caretaker of Hill Top Cottage) and Fala, his Scottie. One of the rare photographs taken with Roosevelt in a wheelchair.

President Roosevelt giving a radio address to the nation, January 11, 1944. This was the first year in which he did not personally appear before Congress to give the State of the Union address. His explanation was "the flu."

President Roosevelt with Prime Minister Winston Churchill at the Quebec Conference, September 11, 1944.

President Roosevelt flanked by Prime Minister Winston Churchill and Premier Joseph Stalin at the Livadia Palace, Yalta, during their conference, February 9, 1945.

President Roosevelt addressing a Joint Session of Congress on March 1, 1945, for the last time, to report on the results of the Yalta Conference.

President Roosevelt with the delegation to the United Nations, March 15, 1945. From left are Representative Sol Bloom, Dean Virginia Gildersleeve (Barnard College), Senator Tom Connally, Secretary of State Edward R. Stettinius, Jr., former Governor Harold Stassen, Senator Arthur Vanderberg, and Representative Charles Eaton.

Last known photograph of President Roosevelt taken April 11, 1945, or about twenty-four hours before his death.

~ 4 ~

Presidential Years
1943–1944:
Decline and Deception

In late fall of 1943, November 22–26, President Roosevelt and Prime Minister Churchill conferred with Generalissimo and Madam Chiang Kai-shek in Cairo, Egypt. The Declaration of Cairo confirmed that the three powers would continue the war against Japan until there was unconditional surrender; that Japan should be deprived of all Pacific lands acquired since 1914; Manchuria, Formosa, and the Pescadores would be returned to China; and "in due course Korea shall become free and independent."[1]

The first day of the Teheran Conference (November 28, 1943), Roosevelt experienced a brief, but alarming and unexplained bout of indigestion. By the next day, he seemed fully recovered.[2] Later, fears were expressed that he might have been poisoned.[3] Perhaps the basis for these fears was the fact that Stalin had urged the president and his party to move to the part of the city where he was residing (Churchill was next door) for security reasons. This rumor died quickly. Later, this incident would lend support to the theory that Roosevelt had, or did, die from cancer.

When Roosevelt returned home on December 17, 1943, Eleanor saw a man "exhilarated by the trips, full of new interests and seemingly in better health."[4] However, many of those closest to him saw a different person. The trips from Washington to Hyde Park increased as he sought rest and relaxation. From this time forward, expressions of concern for his health seemed to escalate. Many of Roosevelt's inner circle, including family, noted that during the winter of 1943–1944 he failed to rebound to his earlier vigorous self. They described a leader "who seemed to feel miserable,"[5] a boss who often dozed off during dictation,[6] a patient who was a concern to his doctor because of "continual coughing,"[7] "a President not looking so well,"[8] who was "getting tired more quickly and losing weight."[9] Even persons who dealt with the president only in a professional situation made comments about his appearances during this period. Newsman Merriman Smith used words like "listless," "poor of voice," and "increasingly quarrelsome" to describe Roosevelt in the context of his press conferences.[10] Even while still in Teheran, Churchill mentioned that Harry Hopkins said of the president: "He was asked a lot of questions and gave the wrong answers."[11] Roosevelt himself related changes to his new physician, Howard Bruenn. Bruenn later recalled that Roosevelt was aware that he was "tiring easily" and "not himself"—these being among his complaints in March 1944.[12]

There were also other staff members who noticed the physical condition of the president, but made no public mention of their observations. Harold G. Smith, director of the Budget, met with Roosevelt once or twice a month to discuss a wide range of domestic and foreign subjects. Many of his notes mention the health of the president. Meeting with Roosevelt on January 7, 1944, Smith expressed real concern that the president had never been "so listless . . . not his usual acute self, very tired . . . worried . . . worn out . . . his head nodded while reading." On January 21, 1944, Smith noted that on January 7, Roosevelt appeared "as though he had been drawn through a knot-hole."[13]

Many of his alarming symptoms could be explained as representing transient lapses, or taken separately could have had other plausible explanations. Napping or dozing is not uncommon in much younger and healthier individuals as part of their daily cycle. The weight loss could be explained as volitional, the result of the president over-responding to his physician's advice. Although some symptons could perhaps be explained away, there were still hints of serious deterioration. On December 24, 1943, Roosevelt addressed the American public utilizing his most effective media approach, a Fireside Chat. In this twenty-seven of thirty-one chats with the American public, he reported on the Cairo-Teheran conferences. For the first time since the fireside chats began over ten years before, in 1933, at two points he stumbled and his voice sounded weak. Two and a half weeks later, on January 11, 1944, he sent his State of the Union Address to Congress, rather than address it in person as in previous years. His explanation for not appearing was a case of a malady afflicting many at the time, the flu. Although he claimed to have recovered, his doctor, he explained, had not permitted him to go to the Capitol.

Roosevelt's physical decline may be explained by simple denial, wishful thinking, or political considerations, even necessities. Although many of the family and staff described Roosevelt's deteriorating physical changes in late 1943 and early 1944, political expediency rationalized the changes merely as a result of strain. Even Eleanor reflected the wishful thinking—mentioning in her *Autobiography* that, "We thought he had picked up a bug on the trip, or perhaps had acquired undulant fever from our cows."[14] The president's physical condition had finally declined to the point that a general medical examination was required.

World War II was moving toward a dramatic climax. By March 1944 the Allies had seized the offensive in both the Pacific and European theaters of war. American bombers massed to begin the daytime bombing of Berlin. The Russians, with American supplies, were crushing German military forces. And in the United States, the health of the president was visibly deteriorating. The increasing concern of staff and family led McIntire, White House physician and surgeon general of the Navy, to belatedly schedule a through examination of the president. Bruenn, an internist and cardiologist, finally examined the president on March 28, 1944.[15] According to all available records, this was the first time that a cardiologist had examined Roosevelt.[16]

Bruenn, a lieutenant commander in the Medical Corps., United States Naval Reserves, served as a cardiology consultant to the Naval Hospital in Bethesda, Maryland, and to the Third Naval District. After examining the president, Bruenn reported the results to McIntire. From that day on, for the last twelve and a half months of Roosevelt's life, Bruenn was responsible for the day-to-day medical care of the president.[17] Nevertheless, he reported to McIntire, who was nominally the president's physician, and who gave strict orders that as a naval officer Bruenn was not to discuss Roosevelt's health with anyone.[18]

Bruenn's checkup began with recording Roosevelt's medical history. It soon became clear that the increasing concerns of family, friends, and staff about the deteriorating health of the president were based in fact.

> During the latter part of December 1943 he had an attack of influenza with the usual signs and symptoms—fever, cough, and malaise. After this he had failed to regain his usual vigor and subsequently had had several episodes of what appeared to be upper respiratory infections. There had been occasional bouts of abdominal distress and distention, accompanied by profuse perspiration. Since the attack of influenza he had complained of unusual and undue fatigue. One week before this examination he had developed an acute coryza, which was followed two days later by an annoying cough with the production of small amounts of thick, tenacious, yellowish sputum.[19]

As the examination began, Roosevelt had a temperature of 99F, a pulse of 72/min, and a respiration of 24/min. To Bruenn he appeared very tired. His face was very gray and lips showed a trace of cyanosis. He moved with difficulty and coughed frequently. His blood pressure was 188/105 mm. Hg. Electrocardiograms showed some abnormality. Fluoroscopy and X-rays showed increase in the size of the cardiac shadow. Enlargement of the heart was confirmed on physical examination, specifically the left ventricle and aorta. Contractions of the heart, at least in some views were limited. This was conveyed to McIntire: "Accordingly, a diagnosis was made of hypertension, hypertensive heart disease, cardiac failure (left ventricular), and acute bronchitis."[20] In that era, Bruenn's diagnosis of severe cardiac failure implied a fatal outcome, because there was little that medicine could offer to slow, much less reverse the process. The handwritten notes of Bruenn's first examination of Roosevelt show profound congestive heart failure, which is even more ominous than what is implied in his published paper. However, in later interviews, Bruenn confirmed the congestive heart failure as very severe, four plus (on a scale of 1–4+).

The significant level of hypertension that had apparently gone untreated for seven years and the congestive heart failure placed Roosevelt at least in a moderately severe category of heart disease. Bruenn noted that the situation in March 1944 was "very serious," and the likelihood that "something would happen" before the four-year term ended is hard to quantify, but clearly is in the 70–80 percent range.[21] This estimate is very close to the actuarial analysis based on later studies by the Metropolitan Life Insurance Company on "Blood Pressure Levels and Mortality among Men."[22] As early as the 1920s, increased blood pressure increased mortality two- to eightfold. Treatment with sodium isothiocyanate was in vogue but not recommended by Bruenn, nor did he advocate Vitamin A therapy.

In view of the diagnosis, the doctor urged that the president be confined to bed for one to two weeks with nursing care; digitalization (treatment with digitalis to improve cardiac function) should be carried out; diet changed to restrict salt intake; codeine for control of coughing; sedation for rest; and a program of weight reduction. This regimen was not acceptable due to the demands of the presidency, and was modified with limitation of activity, curtailment of cigarettes, rest after meals, minimum of ten hours sleep, no swimming, low-fat diet, and use of mild laxatives. When these recommendations for bed rest, diet, and so on were read by McIntire, he replied: "You can't do that. This is the President of the United States!"[23]

There was disagreement regarding the digitalization. Two days after Bruenn's recommendations to McIntire, various staff doctors at Bethesda Naval Hospital met to discuss the situation—McIntire, Captain John Harper (officer in command, Naval Hospital), Captain Robert Duncan (executive officer of the Naval hospital),[24] Captain Charles Behrens (officer in command, radiology department of the hospital), Dr. Paul Dickens, and Bruenn. This group was referred to as the Board of Medical Consultants. They presented McIntire with a revised set of recommendations.[25] The board met for the second time on March 31, with two additional members—consultants Dr. James A. Paullin, internist-cardiologist and president of the American Medical Association, and Dr. Frank Lahey, surgeon, Lahey Clinic. On the afternoon of March 31, Paullin and Lahey examined the president once again.[26] The next day, the group met and Bruenn made his case for digitalization. Digitalization was approved and begun. Robert Ferrell, in his study *The Dying President*, notes that Bruenn said in the final discussion that unless the group would assent to his diagnosis and recommendations he would withdraw from the case.[27]

Bruenn continued to check Roosevelt every day. His color appeared to be good, lungs were clear, and heart unchanged. However, on April 3, his blood pressure rose to 208–210/108. On April 4, his blood pressure was 222–226/118. By April 5, Roosevelt was sleeping well and in good spirits, but his blood pressure was 218/120. Although digitalization brought positive results, the underlying hypertension could be treated on a routine basis only with changes in lifestyle and mild sedation, none of which had been previously recommended until this examination in March of 1944. The outlook was not positive. Ferrell notes that a medical textbook of the time (Cecil's *Textbook of Medicine* 1944 edition, pp. 248 & 249) states: "In malignant hypertension . . . retinal hemorrhage . . . and congestive heart failure commonly complicate the clinical picture. . . . The condition is invariably fatal."[28]

In a more recent interview Bruenn indicated he did not do a rectal examination because "it was not indicated" since there were no urinary or lower gastrointestinal symptoms. He was vague on the role of a rectal examination as part of a routine "head-to-toe" physical examination in a 62–year-old male.[29] The major reason for the omission was that the patient was the president.

Bruenn felt that Roosevelt's hypertension was "essential" with no evaluation done for pheochromocytoma, renal disease, or other possible cause. There was no evaluation of blood urea nitrogen or creatinine.

In Roosevelt's case, there was no major emotional cause for hypertension. He was generally even-tempered and rarely worried, calm even in crises. Episodes of anger or upset were transient. His longevity could have been improved by reducing his work hours and levels of stress. However, the president's hypertension was labile, but unremitting. The demands of his office precluded implementing an ideal regimen, including a schedule avoiding irritation and limiting his work hours to four each day. Even efforts by Bruenn to discourage family and staff from making unrealistic demands were not uniformly successful.

In one interview, Bruenn noted that Roosevelt would have been admitted to the hospital if he were anyone else but the president. In Bruenn's long career practicing cardiology, Roosevelt was the only patient with congestive heart failure *not* hospitalized by him but rather treated "at home."[30] At this critical time, health care management at the White House represented a compromise due to military and political conditions. On April 7, 1944, the Board of Medical Consultants met again to reevaluate the original recommendations. Although they called for a restricted daily schedule and exercise, they did not seek to hospitalize the president.

Such decisions were probably based on two fundamental considerations: 1) Roosevelt was vitally needed to continue strategic direction of the war, because no one else had the experience and capability to provide leadership even with a reduced workload; 2) Roosevelt had endured periods of severe illness before and always bounced back, hence his declining health in early 1944 was thought to represent the same pattern. The conclusion was simply that with an interval of rest, he would recover again from a presumably temporary setback. Bruenn's view of his patient's health was midway between the unjustified optimism of McIntire and the posthumous descriptions by other observers, including Lord Moran, Churchill's physician, who echoed the opinion of many who met the president that he was a very sick man.[31]

The health crisis during March 1944 was not only in the perception of those people close to Roosevelt. The White House Usher's Diaries for this period reflect and confirm the serious deterioration in the president's health. They reveal a decline in activity, measured by the number of daily appointments scheduled for Roosevelt, especially in March of 1944. Interpretation must include awareness that wartime responsibilities preempted much of his time and that some additional appointments were off the record. However, the range of visitors in the war years was similar to those in peacetime— political leaders, theatrical luminaries, distinguished clergy, family members, friends, staff, and foreign dignitaries.

Using March of each year as an index month, the number of appointments of 15–30 minutes each per working day at the White House is shown in Table 4.1.[32] The decline in number of daily appointments in March 1944 became especially significant starting on Sunday, March 19. From Monday to Thursday, March 20–23, there were no appointments, an unprecedented situation while Roosevelt was in residence at the White House. The only entries are lunch and dinner on a bed tray. He had three appointments on Friday, March 24, including a press conference, after which he went to Hyde Park. Roosevelt returned to Washington the evening of Monday, March 27. No appointments were scheduled for Tuesday and Wednesday. March 28 was the date of his examination by Bruenn. There was only one appointment

Table 4.1

Presidential White House Appointments Daily Average for March

Appointments/day		Appointments/day	
1934	7.9	1942	9.8
1937	7.4	1943	5.9
1939	8.7	1944	2.9
1941	5.0	1945	5.1

Source: White House Usher's Diary, Franklin D. Roosevelt Library.

on March 30, and two on March 31 (which were kept by his aide Major General Edwin "Pa" Watson). On April 3 he had two appointments. He had one appointment each on April 5 and 6. The week ended with a Friday morning press conference and an afternoon cabinet meeting. On April 8, he left for Hobcaw, the Baruch's estate in South Carolina and stayed there until May 6. This modest increase in his appointment schedule coincides with Bruenn's treatment, including digitalization, which brought relief to Roosevelt's congestive heart failure.

The *New York Times:* Escalating Concern About Roosevelt's Health

As president during the major times of crises related to the Depression and World War II, Roosevelt was the central figure in much of the news of the day. In turn, the state of his health was one of the central topics reported. From 1933 through 1943, most of the health coverage appearing in the *New York Times* concerned colds, flu, canceled appointments, and McIntire's continuing reassurances that the president was in perfect health. The first of the reassuring reports was on the first page in the spring of his first term:

> "Roosevelt 100 Per Cent Fit, Copeland Says After Visit"
> Senator Copeland, one of two physicians in the Senate, after paying one of his periodic calls at the White House today to see how the President is getting along said: "President Roosevelt looks 100 per cent this morning. He is in splendid health. . . .[33]

In March 1934, the *New York Times* carried the first of what would be many reassurances from McIntire, following a headline that proclaimed: "Roosevelt's Health Better Than Year Ago; Due to Optimism and Exercise, Says Doctor."[34]

> Because Franklin D. Roosevelt can keep smiling he has come through his first year healthier than when he became President, the White House physician says. Dr. R.T. McIntire . . . said today. . . . "There is no question in my mind that President Roosevelt is better today, in a general physical way, than when I first saw him in March of last year."[35]

The pattern was being established. In that same article he noted that "the few little colds the President has suffered have amounted to nothing at all" and "if they had happened to anybody else, that person probably would have gone to work as usual."

The number and type of articles appearing in the *New York Times* are revealing (Table 4.2). Most frequently the *New York Times* quoted McIntire's reassurances to the American people that the president was in good health. The following year, 1935, he once again reassured the public under the headline: "Dr. McIntire Asserts that the President Is in the Best of Condition."

> In my opinion, said Captain McIntire, Mr. Roosevelt was never in better condition at any time since he has been in office. . . . Captain McIntire said the diet of Mr. Roosevelt is unlimited and he eats what he pleases.[36]

McIntire's reassurances also appeared in articles that were more political in nature. A special report to the *New York Times* in September 1936, when Roosevelt was enroute to Washington state to review the drought there, included a medical report: "Dr. Ross T. McIntire, White House physician, said today that Mr. Roosevelt was in perfect health."[37] As the second term began, the Associated Press reported on the president's health: "Roosevelt in Fine Health. President Roosevelt rounded out one of the most active years of his long political career tonight in what his physician described as the best of health."[38]

The political uses of McIntire's reassurance is seen in the summer of 1938 as Roosevelt endorsed Lawrence Camp in his race for the Georgia U.S. Senate seat occupied by Walter F. George. After a long political analysis, the reporter noted:

> It was a rugged and invigorated Franklin D. Roosevelt who drove his own car away from the railroad siding this morning and back again tonight. Dr. Ross McIntire, his physician, said the President was in better physical condition "in many respects" than when he assumed office in 1933. This professional opinion was borne out in Mr. Roosevelt's appearance.[39]

Although the reassurances by McIntire and the patterns of reporting presidential health were present in the press from 1933 to 1943, the president's health in the first two terms was good, with the significant exception of hy-

Table 4.2

New York Times: Number of References to FDR's Health

Year	Total	Appearing on page 1	Vice Admiral McIntire	Colds, flu	General
1933	17	5	0	8	9
1934	06	2	1	1	4
1935	19	2	1	1	17
1936	05	0	1	0	4
1937	25	9	0	2	23
1938	07	0	0	6	1
1939	14	2	0	7	7
1940	20	4	0	5	15
1941	30	5	1	14	15
1942	05	0	0	3	2
1943	15	0	0	9	6
1944	50	10	8	4	46
Jan	12	1			
Feb	3	0			
Mar	6	1			
Apr	10	3	1		
May	5	2	1		
June–Dec.	15	2	4		

1945	8	1 (before death)
	3	0 (after death)

Source: *New York Times* volumes in Franklin D. Roosevelt Library.

pertension. These reports were not helpful to the American public in knowing more completely about Roosevelt's health, but did not seem to be deliberately misleading as yet.

However, after the conferences at Cairo and Teheran (November–December 1943), the relationship of presidential health reporting and the actual state of the president's health were far more divergent than earlier. An examination of the *New York Times* coverage, when compared to the actual events, indicates a deliberate misleading of the American public in a time of global war.

The reassurances of McIntire continued into the critical medical period of the spring of 1944, when Roosevelt would be diagnosed with hypertension and congestive heart failure.

In 1944, the number of articles on Roosevelt's health in the *New York Times* increased dramatically—by June 1944 thirty-six articles had appeared. This increased number is even more significant when seen in the context of massive wartime coverage. The *New York Times* devoted its front pages and much of the remainder of the paper, including the Sunday magazine section and "News in Review," mostly to military campaigns. A daily index was solely devoted to war news. Domestic issues relating to labor unrest and strikes, taxation, reconversion to a peace-time economy, voting rights for GI's, city and state budgets, and crime were not ignored, but received less than customary notice. Daily casualty lists from the tri-state area filled pages two and three, eight columns each, supplemented by stories of heroism and other battlefield vignettes. In responding to an assumption that reading these daily casualty lists sharply increased tension in the White House severely straining Roosevelt, Bruenn readily agreed. His response was couched in a sharp retort, "Well, what could we do about it?" His tone was a unique exception to his calm answers in all other interviews.[40] So it is significant that during the first five months of 1944 front-page notice was given to Roosevelt's health on seven occasions: once in January, once in March, three times in April, and twice in May. In the first month of 1944, Roosevelt's health was mentioned in twelve stories in the *New York Times*.

Most statements from the White House continued to follow the pattern of reporting the president's health that had been set in the first two and a half terms—minimization of the severity and/or duration of the illness, followed by optimistic descriptions of recovery. This pattern is clearly seen in several of McIntire's stories to the press. On January 1, 1944, William D. Hassett, a White House secretary, reported that the president "has a case of the grippe."[41] On January 2, the headline reported the "President on the Mend," while his condition was reported as making "satisfactory progress."[42] January 4 brought the news that this mild case of grippe might prevent the president from delivering his annual message to Congress, but that would depend on the advice of his physician.[43] Finally, on January 29, the *New York Times* article headlined:

> "President's Health Called Better than Ever; McIntire Hails His Ability to Bounce Back"
>
> "President Roosevelt, who will celebrate his 62nd birthday anniversary Sunday, is in better health than at any time since he came into office in 1933," Dr. Ross T. McIntire, his personal physician, said today. Dr. McIntire maintained his basic line, telling the press that the "president was in his best health ever . . . snaps back from extra-heavy strain or some little illness—the only kind he has had since becoming president. . . ." For Dr. McIntire, his client is "just an average patient with no operations and no interesting complaints".[44]

At the end of February, Roosevelt took a week's rest at an undisclosed location. Noting that "Roosevelt Keeps in Touch With Capital," the *New York Times* quoted White House Press Secretary Stephen T. Early that "the President's health was good, that he was entirely alright, but just needed a rest."[45] This was in response to speculation by some members of the press that the president was out of town because of health-related matters. On March 1, 1944, Roosevelt returned to Washington to meet with military leaders. There were others visitors to the White House that day, including Arthur G. Klein, Representative from New York. Klein observed that the president was "in excellent health and fine spirits."[46]

On March 22, 1944, Early was quoted on page one of the *New York Times* that the president was confined to his quarters with a head cold, but no fever. In the same short article, McIntire "later described Mr. Roosevelt's condition as definitely improved."[47] The next day the *Times* reported the "President 'Decidedly Better.'"[48] On March 24, the president returned to the Executive Office. Most articles were "Special to the *New York Times,*" without specific authorship. On March 24, neither McIntire or Early had any comments.

> Correspondents attending the [press] conference noted the apparent effects of his illness in his voice and appearance. He had no color, and his voice was out of usual pitch, probably owing to the cold. The illness from which he was then recovering was his second that year. Earlier, he was confined for two weeks with the grippe, from which he recovered slowly. He was reported to have lost ten pounds at that time.[49]

Not only were the correspondents concerned about his appearance, but so was his one known visitor. Aubrey Williams, an early New Dealer, Roosevelt protégé, and former director of the National Youth Administration, was a dinner guest at the White House on March 23 or 24. Again, he was probably the only non-staff member to visit Roosevelt at that time. The *New York Times* on March 26, quoted a story from the *Atlanta Journal* in which Williams stated that he did not believe the president would run for a fourth term and also that, "He [Roosevelt] looked so tired and worn that I was shocked."[50]

As the day approached when Bruenn performed the physical examination of the president, it is important to recall the context in which these health events were taking place. Since the beginning of 1944, Roosevelt and Churchill had exchanged messages almost daily, continuing a pattern which started in 1939. Several major topics were regularly discussed—the establishment of United Nations machinery for postwar economic collaboration, plans for the division of postwar Germany, Russian convoys, Operation Overload, redrawing of boundaries in Poland, and diplomatic relations of Poland and Russia.[51]

The fighting intensified in 1944. The Allies landed at Anzio on January 22. Rome fell to the Allies on June 4. Merrill's Marauders, under the command of General Joseph Stillwell, moved into northern Burma to deprive the Japanese of fighter support. Some of the captured Italian fleet were turned over to the Russians. The siege of Leningrad ended in January, and in March Russians opened a major offensive in the Ukraine. Tito joined the Allies while civil war broke out in Greece. The editors of the wartime correspondence of Roosevelt and Churchill suggested that the first five months of 1944 were a preview of the many problems that lay ahead.[52]

It was also interesting that on March 24, just four days prior to this physical examination, Roosevelt made one of his few explicit communications regarding Jews and the Holocaust during his press conference. He warned the Germans about their persecution of the Jews and implored them to assist this oppressed group. He was now more willing to speak out partly because documentation of the Holocaust through undeniable eyewitness accounts increased confirming numerous earlier reports. The establishment of the War Refugee Board (January 1944) and the forced expulsion of Hungarian Jews, who had been previously protected because of Germany's alliance with Hungary, made his forthright statement especially timely. The appointment calendar was nearly empty for an unprecedented interval, reflecting his ebbing strength. This may have been one instance when he was casting an eye to history and trying to confirm his concern for victims of the Holocaust in a humanitarian light while he still had the opportunity to do so.[53] The role of Roosevelt, and other world leaders, in regard to the Holocaust remains an area of research and widely differing views.

It was surprising that after the comments of Aubrey Williams concerning the "shocking appearance" of the president and his comments of the probability of Roosevelt not running for another term, there was no follow-up from the *New York Times*. In fact, William's comments were relegated to page thirty-five. This was in spite of the fact that his assertions were clearly contrary to the official often-repeated reassurance given to the public by McIntire about the excellent state of the president's health.

The next article appearing in the *Times* followed Roosevelt's physical examination by Bruenn. In his clinical notes following the examination, Bruenn recorded: "Accordingly, a diagnosis was made of hypertension, hypertensive heart disease, cardiac failure (left ventricular), and acute bronchitis."[54]

Meeting the press upon returning to the White House, the president chose to focus on the least serious item of the diagnosis. The first sentence in an article on March 29, entitled "Roosevelt Was Ill of Bronchitis, But Says That He is Feeling Fine," is clearly misleading the public:

> President Roosevelt, in a jovial mood and looking much better than he did last Friday, told his press conference this afternoon that he had been suffering from a mild case of bronchitis for the last two or three weeks. He then coughed and patted his chest to demonstrate.[55]

Reporters asked how he felt, and Roosevelt replied he "had bronchitis, but otherwise was fine." He told the reporters that he had been to Bethesda Naval

Hospital for an X-ray and added that the bronchitis was not very serious. Asked if he was alarmed, he replied that he "had been told that one out of 48,500 cases of bronchitis might develop into pneumonia, and so he thought he had a rather slim chance (of developing pneumonia). The same article ends with a replaying of earlier health issues—grippe in January, a wen (soft, painless, benign cyst) removed from his neck in February, a head cold in March, and Williams comments and McIntire's reassurance in January that Roosevelt "was in better health than at any time since he entered the White House."[56]

Two days later, the White House correspondents showed an aggressiveness not present before—they asked Early if he could make public the results of the president's physical examination at the Naval Hospital on Tuesday, March 28. Early replied that he thought that would be possible as soon as the report was received from the hospital.[57]

The pattern of cover-up continued to be reflected in the newspapers. On April 1, 1944, the *Times* reported that "President's Health Improving."[58] Again on April 3, the "President 'Definitely' Better"—"Vice Admiral McIntire said the bronchitis was well on the mend and the President's cough was better."[59] Although the news for public consumption was that the president was better, the fact remained that he was not able to keep his scheduled appointments. For example, on March 30, Metropolitan Opera soprano Lily Pons, and film director Cecil B. deMille were scheduled to visit with the president, but were received instead by Major General Watson, Roosevelt's military aide.[60]

The first indication that the *New York Times* staff did not totally accept McIntire's "satisfactory health reports" appeared in an article on April 5, 1944, that included the characterization, "Unique Report Made by McIntire." The earlier public diagnosis of bronchitis was expanded to include influenza or respiratory infection and a sinus disturbance. However, there was still no mention of heart disease, cardiac failure, or severe hypertension. Instead the admiral noted that "we have decided that for a man of 62-plus we had very little to argue about, with the exception that we have had to combat the influenza plus the respiratory complications that came along after."[61] This report by McIntire was probably in response to an early request by correspondents to see the results of the examination by Bruenn at Bethesda Naval Hospital.

McIntire said the checkup had been delayed and "strung out" because Roosevelt contracted a cold and bronchitis in the middle of the checkup. "Although he said that Mr. Roosevelt made only the one trip to the hospital, he left the impression that the other aspects of the checkup had been carried on some weeks at the White House."[62]

Up until this time, McIntire seemed to always place the best interpretation on Roosevelt's illnesses and recoveries, usually through acts of omission.

This seems to be the first time that he actually stated something that was not a fact—implying that bronchitis came after the examination and was not, in fact, the original diagnosis.

Eleanor Roosevelt, in discussing this period of her husband's life makes no mention of Bruenn's examination or his findings. She does mention Roosevelt's decision to go for a trip of relaxation in early April.

> Franklin seemed to feel miserable, which was not astonishing, considering that he had been through so many years of strain. Finally, on April 9, he made up his mind that he would go down and stay with Bernard Baruch at his plantation, Hobcaw, in Georgetown, South Carolina.[63]

The days at Hobcaw were restful, with a reduced workload and time for visiting with family and friends in the afternoon and evening. His hypertension continued, with somewhat higher levels in the morning than later in the day, the reverse of the usual diurnal change. Bruenn reported that prior to breakfast, the blood pressure was 230/126. Later, sitting up, the blood pressure was 210/126. Several days of intestinal discomfort began on April 28, with the blood pressure once reaching 240/130 mm Hg.

X-rays taken on return to Washington indicated a group of cholesterol stones in his gall bladder. However, by this time, the symptoms of abdominal pain experienced at Hobcaw had disappeared. On his return, the *New York Times* reported that

> FDR looked tanned, rested. . . . He returned to the capital with an improved color and with some of the tired seams smoothed from his face. . . . Traces of his bronchial congestion still were present ten days ago, but Admiral McIntire said they had disappeared now.[64]

The *New York Times* initially called Roosevelt's trip to Baruch's estate in South Carolina a two-week rest at an unspecified location in the South. It was extended, they reported, in quoting Mrs. Roosevelt, to four weeks to complete his rest. Details of his whereabouts were revealed only after his return to the White House, which was covered on the front page. *Life* magazine and the *Times* published photographs, captioned "Roosevelt Returns," showing him looking rested.[65]

As concern grew, political leaders jumped in and pronounced Roosevelt fit and ready to lead the nation, trying to quiet what Democratic National Chairman Robert Hannegan called malicious rumors. After Roosevelt's lowpoint in March, return from vacation in May, Hannegan appeared to have scooped the president by nominating him for a fourth term. Worse yet, a few weeks later he suggested Roosevelt should serve a fifth term if there were "comparable emergency."[66]

Dr. Harry Etter, a physiatrist (specialist in physical medicine and rehabilitation) and currently a retired U.S. Navy Rear Admiral, confirmed this positive view when he examined Roosevelt shortly after his return from Baruch's South Carolina estate. McIntire requested that Etter examine the president from the standpoint of his physical disability.

The president was in his swimming trunks at the side of the pool. Etter found Roosevelt to be "alert, keen and in a great mental state." The president was without the pallor, grayish cast, or cyanosis seen by Bruenn earlier in March. In an interview on April 9–11, 1996, Etter noted that he was aware, at the time, of Roosevelt's congestive heart failure and had seen the chest X-rays. A specialist in physical medicine, Etter did not do a general medical examination. He never examined the president again.[67]

When the president was visiting and recuperating in South Carolina, there continued to be concern about his health. One month after the president and his staff returned to Washington, McIntire met with reporters in the office of Stephen T. Early. He saw this briefing as fulfilling a promise made during the president's absence to give a complete report on the effect this holiday might have on Roosevelt's health.

McIntire continued to maintain that the trip was to recuperate from a severe attack of bronchitis. Mr. Charles Hurd, under whose byline the article appeared, noted:

> While Admiral McIntire refrained from technical descriptions in discussing Mr. Roosevelt's health, he stated and reiterated his conclusion the President's health was better than average for his age.... "I can tell you now," Dr. McIntire said, "that we gained everything we hoped to from our stay in South Carolina ... many physical checks had been made and all are well within normal limits." He added these were extremely satisfactory. When he was asked what was meant by normal limits, he explained that "different standards apply to men of different ages, that he was speaking of the President as a man in his sixties and that the President's health is for a man of his age, excellent."[68]

The vice admiral was claiming that all checks were within normal limits, at a time when cardiologist Bruenn was taking his blood pressure twice daily between April 9 and June 14, and the readings averaged about 196/112 mm Hg on awakening and 194/96 mm Hg in the evening.[69] Instead of sharing specifics about the president's health, McIntire was quoted at the conclusion of the article as observing that "right now his health is as good as any time in the last year." He recalled the president's visit to Teheran and said: "He never performed better in his life than on the Teheran trip, which was a wonderful example of what he can do physically."[70] Less than a week later, in speaking to the Auxiliary of the American Medical Society, McIntire stated that, "The President is in fine shape now; all fixed up now and he needs to be, with this war."[71] In so speaking, the president's personal physician completely ignored the most crucial medical findings of the American president. Perhaps the key phrase in the June report is the one that claims the president "needs" to be in fine shape because of the war. This is perhaps an indication that the president's role in leading the wartime effort was far more important than the right of the American people to know of his gravely impaired health. With the Normandy landing, Operation Overlord pending, there was no doubt that the country needed a strong, vigorous, and healthy leader.

Secrecy and the White House Physician

After Roosevelt's return from the Cairo and Teheran conferences, his health became a major issue for the president, his family, and his staff. What would now, in the words of modern presidential politics, be called a cover-up was composed of continuing fallacious reassurances and a lack of candor in communicating with the patient, his family, and the public of presidential health issues. With basic information not made available to explain his absences and increasingly haggard appearance, there might have been an assumption that something invidious was being concealed. When Bruenn published his "Clinical Notes on the Illness and Death of President Franklin D. Roosevelt" in 1970, he wrote that to his knowledge no factual clinical information regarding Roosevelt's health and illnesses in the 1943–1945 period had ever been published.[72] His notes were written to ensure the record of Roosevelt's health and the accuracy of that record.

Following the president's death, his medical records disappeared from Bethesda Naval Hospital. According to Bruenn,

> the original hospital chart in which all clinical progress notes as well as the results of the various laboratory tests were incorporated was kept in the safe at the U.S. Naval Hospital, Bethesda, Maryland. After the President's death this chart could not be found.[73]

In 1993, Representative Marge Roukema, of New Jersey, was requested to aid in the search for those records. Roukema was asked to contact both the Franklin D. Roosevelt Library and Bethesda Naval Hospital. The library did not have the records and the hospital did not answer the request. Given the importance of Roosevelt's leadership in World War II, Congresswoman Roukema was asked to contact various other nations' embassies to see if their governments had any information regarding Roosevelt's medical condition. Letters were sent to the ambassadors of Japan, Great Britain, France, Germany, and the Russian Federation. They all answered, but no substantive materials were provided by any respondents.

In an interview with Bruenn in 1990, Jan K. Herman, historian with the United States Navy, raised the question of the missing records. Bruenn commented in more detail:

> It's one of the strangest things. When I'd come back [from seeing the president at the White House], I would go to Dr. Harper's office [commanding officer of the Naval Hospital] or Dr. Duncan's office [executive officer of the Naval Hospital] and they would give me the chart and I would write a note for that day concerning what I'd found, return it to the administrative office, and then it would go back in the safe. After I wrote the final note, I never saw it again, never saw it. You might find it in your files, I'm not sure.[74]

Secrecy was so stringent at the time that trips to the White House by Dr. James Paullin, an internist and president of the American Medical Association, were not discussed even in superficial terms with his wife, family, or colleagues. Paullin's daughter, Caroline Minnich, stated that her father's absences from home were understood to have involved medical consultation regarding Roosevelt.[75] Nor did Paullin leave any memoranda, diaries, notes, or medical records related to his White House visits, although some of his visits are mentioned in the memoirs of McIntire.

The White House, through the comments of McIntire and Early, conducted a misinformation campaign with the press. It could be argued that McIntire committed deliberate errors of interpretation or omission. In the press conference promised upon Roosevelt's return from Baruch's Hobcaw plantation, the reporters had requested specific information. Comments related to blood pressure levels, abnormalities of lungs and heart, such findings as cyanosis, orthopnea (respiratory distress while lying in a flat position), EKG and X-ray abnormalities were entirely omitted, as was the duration or even the existence of the hypertension. McIntire would recall—erroneously—in his book *White House Physician* that Roosevelt's blood pressure was within normal range and there were no cardiac symptoms in early May 1944.[76] In contrast, Bruenn noted that between April 9 and June 14, Roosevelt's average blood pressure was exceptionally high.[77]

During the medical crisis in March, April, and May, McIntire implied that physical examinations of Roosevelt had been made prior to the March 28 exam by Bruenn, and publicly supported Roosevelt when he had claimed the major problem was bronchitis. Bruenn's report and diagnosis had been presented to McIntire, who chose to withhold it from the American public, but instead repeated assurances that the president was "in the best health ever."

When reviewing McIntire's role in the medical cover-up related to Roosevelt, it is difficult to sort out the optimism of a patriot, the lack of candor of a political operative, and the professional limitations of a physician who was an ear, nose, and throat specialist, not an internist or cardiologist. McIntire further omitted mention of congestive heart failure in his book *White House Physician.* He provided the results of the physical examination of May 10, 1944, but selectively omitted cardiac failure and hypertension which were known to him.

It was Bruenn's belief that McIntire's actions were politically motivated. He mentioned that a naval photographer took a picture of Roosevelt but included Bruenn causing (McIntire) concern, since the presence of a cardiologist would suggest a potential undisclosed medical problem.

> I had been warned to keep my mouth shut because wherever I might be, the President might be there too and they didn't want any unnecessary knowledge being spread around.[78]

Jonathan Daniels of the White House staff has also acknowledged that he took part in misleading the public, since he selected and carefully edited the photographs of the president for distribution.[79]

Roosevelt was a part of the campaign of secrecy, if not its leader. It could not have continued without his consent. It was Roosevelt himself who placed the emphasis on his bronchitis after Bruenn's examination in March 1944, choosing not to have asked about other diagnoses: hypertension and secondary congestive heart failure. Roosevelt earlier (January 1944) blamed the "flu" for his unprecedented failure to present the State of the Union address personally to Congress. Bruenn did not discuss the severity of hypertension with Roosevelt (but he did know of its existence), nor the complication of congestive heart failure, primarily because the president never asked.[80] He did inform Roosevelt's daughter, Anna, and Eleanor in general terms about the medical situation, with the admonition that they avoid adding to Roosevelt's presidential burdens. His memory of informing Anna in a limited way is reflected in her oral history interview for Columbia University.

> None of us knew exactly what was wrong with Father. . . . We knew he had high blood pressure, and that's all. . . . I never heard him discuss, and I know plenty of times when he could have, I never heard him discuss Father's death at all, so that I had absolutely no idea, until I met Dr. Bruenn again after Mother's death.[81]

Given Roosevelt's sense of responsibility, especially to those in combat which included his own four sons, the limited treatment available for his illness at that time, and the magnitude of the illnesses he was accustomed to experiencing over twenty years, it was logical that health considerations would have been peripheral in his thinking. Furthermore, he enjoyed his work in spite of his illnesses. Had the president devoted more attention to his health and sought more aggressive, earlier diagnosis and therapy in 1943–1944, as he had years earlier for his paralysis, it is likely that he would, by definition, have received more appropriate, effective care. Bruenn said that Roosevelt was one of his rare patients in fifty years of clinical practice to ask no questions. Clearly, he was either not interested in knowing or was actively interested in ignoring his condition. He was the leader of the world leaders and, hence, considered by many indispensable even if his health was profoundly impaired. It would be hard for any physician to be objective under these conditions.

Apart from McIntire's clearly incorrect reporting, the medical culture of the time generally promoted a lack of candor in discussing serious diseases. Illness or its progress was not customarily discussed with patients, unless they failed to comply with doctor's orders. Presidential health matters were assumed to be private, rarely reported frankly or with clinical detail. Only in later administrations would the approach become more forthcoming, reflecting the move toward greater openness in medicine and in society. In spite of the cultural changes over the past half century, a comparable military exigency with similar clinical problems could well lead to a cover-up even though the public is more sophisticated, the media more technically advanced, and privacy rights less sacrosanct. When asked whether he would have done anything differently, Bruenn stated that he would not, except that he would have been more pessimistic. When asked what he had recommended for senior naval officers with similar medical problems, he indicated that they were reassigned or discharged from service for health reasons. No physician, according to Bruenn, advised Roosevelt to decline renomination. Bruenn was quite relieved that his opinion regarding the fourth term was not asked. He exclaimed, "Thank God."[82]

The success, then, in misleading the public was based on a combination of wartime restraint, censorship, concern for the commander-in-chief's status as an alert and fit leader, the inherently uncertain prognosis of hypertension, and the medical/social climate of the era. It is probably inevitable that the excessive secrecy and patently misleading reassurances during the president's lifetime fueled speculation both before and after his death.[83]

~ 5 ~

Presidential Years 1944–1945: The Last Campaign

As the calendar moved toward the month of July and the anticipated Democratic National Convention, McIntire continued to reassure the American public that the president was in the best of health. On June 9 he was quoted in the *New York Times* observing that "right now his health is as good as at any time in the last year."[1] Again on June 14 the public was reminded that "the president is in fine shape now."[2]

However, not until the second week in July did Roosevelt clearly state his position regarding a fourth term, thus ending months of speculation. In a letter to Robert E. Hannegan, chairman of the National Democratic Committee on July 10, 1944, Roosevelt was very clear about his intentions and the reasons on which he based them.

> I feel that I owe to you, in candor, a simple statement of my position. If the Convention should carry this out, and nominate me for the Presidency, I shall accept. If the people elect me, I will serve.[3]

The motivation for his decision, in spite of the decline in his health and the likelihood of continued heavy burdens, reflected his intense sense of duty—to his country in wartime and to his political party. He wanted the chairman to see clearly that his decision was greater than merely his personal desire to continue as president.

> For myself, I do not want to run. . . . After many years of public service, therefore, my personal thoughts have turned to the day when I could return to civil

life. All that is within me cries out to go back to my home on the Hudson River, to avoid public responsibilities, and to avoid also the publicity which in our democracy follows every step of the Nation's Chief Executive. Such would be my choice.[4]

To Roosevelt there was no acceptable alternative but to continue. He still needed to complete his tasks, which he listed in the letter to Hannegan:

> To win this war wholeheartedly, unequivocally and as quickly as we can is our task of the first importance. To win this war in such a way that there would be no further world wars in the foreseeable future is our second objective. To provide occupations, and to provide a decent standard of living for our men in the Armed Services after the war, and for all Americans, are the final objectives.[5]

Perhaps his decision also reflected a long standing sense of competition. Roosevelt felt deeply about the family tradition of service. The history of his family, who arrived in New Amsterdam from the Netherlands in the early seventeenth century, their economic and social progress, the relation of service to the larger society, was the subject of an English composition in his sophomore year at Harvard College.[6] He saw the Roosevelts as a family with great virility and believed that "there was no excuse for them if they did not do their duty by the community."

Some biographers believe that Roosevelt used his famous cousin Theodore as a standard of comparison to measure his own career.[7] He may have felt that he was in the shadow of the twenty-fifth president. Theodore had volunteered for combat in World War I when he was in his late fifties, although President Woodrow Wilson rejected his offer. The competition between the two Roosevelt families had over the years divided the descendants of Theodore and Franklin, although there were many instances of cordial cooperation.[8] There is a possibility that the continuing conflicts and need for favorable comparison was a factor in the decisions Roosevelt made related to his career.

There are no specific indications that any physicians were consulted concerning Roosevelt's decision to run for a fourth term. In an interview in 1990, Bruenn said, "They all wanted him [Roosevelt] to run. . . . And he wasn't particularly anxious to run."[9] Indeed, in Bruenn's words, "[Roosevelt] was loathe to run and commented that his advice was not requested."[10]

Very few Roosevelt advisers suggested that there not be a fourth term. Benjamin V. Cohen, a distinguished attorney, early Roosevelt appointee, and adviser, suggested that instead of a fourth term, the president should accept an invitation to become the chief executive officer of the United Nations. The communication to Roosevelt included a lengthy argument emphasizing that although Roosevelt could be reelected, a fourth term might not be best for all concerned. However, Cohen did not make his argument based on the president's health problems. A friend of Cohen's would later note that the relationship with Roosevelt cooled after this suggestion was made. Roosevelt replied to Cohen: "You have only left out one matter—and that is the matter of my own feelings!"[11] Other staff members discussed the possibility of Roosevelt not running, but not because of ill health. In his diary, Secretary of the Interior Harold Ickes mentions a conversation with James Forrestal:

> Jim has the feeling that I have, that the chances are strongly in favor of the next Vice President, if he is elected with Roosevelt, succeeding to the Presidency. I feel this rather strongly. I don't necessarily mean that the president will die in office or become so incapacitated that he might not be able to carry on. He might very well resign. I believe that he is sick of domestic affairs and after the war would like to devote himself exclusively to the world situation.[12]

Other advisers believed that Roosevelt's health was such that he should run for a fourth term. Ickes also quotes a conversation with Bernard Baruch who believed that if the president would take care of himself, he could successfully complete the campaign and be elected.[13] Secretary of Labor Frances Perkins, in her biography of Roosevelt written approximately a year after his death, noted that no one in the cabinet had any fears about the president's health preventing his run for a fourth term.[14] Samuel Rosenman, presidential adviser, believed that there was no great concern among the White House staff about a fourth term—everyone seemed to take it for granted that the president would run and win.[15]

And always there were the positive words of his physician, McIntire. When he later considered the 1944 campaign in his book, McIntire addressed the question: "Could he [Roosevelt] stand up under the strain of four more years?" Although he claimed that his statements simply reported the findings of specialists and that the consultants had given a positive response to that question. He implied that he had given the president the advice:

> With proper care and strict adherence to rules, I gave it my best judgment that his chances of winning through to 1948 were good.[16]

Neither did any member of the family suggest that he not run for a fourth term. In all probability, this was due to the fact that the family was not aware of how dangerously ill the president actually was. Eleanor is quoted as saying: "I knew without asking that as long as the war was on, it was a foregone conclusion that Franklin, if he was well enough, would run again."[17] Bruenn would later comment that Mrs. Roosevelt had "tubular vision."[18] Anna

Roosevelt Boettiger, from her residency in the White House during this period, was aware that her father was not as healthy as he had been; he tired more quickly and she could see the loss of weight. She was instrumental in getting McIntire to arrange for the examinations by Bruenn. However, as noted in Chapter 4, in the interview for her oral history at Columbia University, she asserted that "None of us knew exactly what was wrong with Father. . . . We knew he had high blood pressure and that was all."[19] Her husband (their marriage occurred after these events), Dr. James Halsted, was quoted many years later as commenting that "on medical grounds alone, he should not have run in 1944."[20] There is no indication that any family members or government officials asked specific questions of the physicians concerning whether Roosevelt's health would permit a fourth-term campaign.

Writing later in 1959, son James Roosevelt would restate his long-held feelings about the fourth term.

> . . . I never have been reconciled to the fact that Father's physicians did not flatly forbid him to run. . . . None of us was warned that Father's life might be in danger.[21]

According to Bruenn, McIntire alone communicated with congressmen, cabinet members, or other leaders, although he (Bruenn) did meet with the family to suggest in general terms that Roosevelt avoid undue strain or pressure. The president's political colleagues were anxious for him to run again in 1944 for a combination of reasons. They believed that the nation still needed his leadership, but they also knew that their own careers depended on Roosevelt's staying in the presidency.

It was well known that James Farley, former postmaster general and campaign manager did not believe that Roosevelt should seek a fourth term.

> Anyone with a grain of common sense would surely realize from the appearance of the president that he is not a well man and there is not a chance in the world for him to carry on for four more years and face the problems that a President will have before him; he just can't survive another term."[22]

Even when he announced his support for Roosevelt after the nominating convention in Chicago, Farley recalled that, "I have been opposed on principle to a third or fourth Presidential term."[23] However, both he and Edward J. Flynn, Farley's successor as chairman of the Democratic National Committee, were concerned about Roosevelt's health as early as the end of his second term. Later, Flynn wrote that it was "obvious to me even then that the president's health was beginning to suffer."[24]

There was one major political figure who stated publicly his belief that

Roosevelt had serious health impairments. Edwin Pauley, secretary and acting treasurer of the Democratic National Committee, believed that the president would not live much longer and therefore felt compelled to make sure that Henry A. Wallace would not be the vice presidential candidate because he "was not a fit man to be President of the United States."[25] Writing to Jonathan Daniels, Pauley made clear his belief that Roosevelt would not complete a fourth term.

> I felt, therefore, that I could make no greater individual contribution to the Nation's good than to do everything in my power to protect it from Wallace during the war and postwar period. My pre-convention slogan was: "You are not nominating a Vice President of the United States, but a President."[26]

Others would express the same opinion, only later in retrospect. George Allen later wrote that everyone of their group "realized that the man nominated to run with Roosevelt would in all probability be the next President." Flynn is quoted as saying later, "I felt that he would never survive his term."[27]

If most of the political associates did not speak out concerning the possible inability of Roosevelt completing a fourth term, as the Democratic Convention began, *Time* magazine on the first page of the July 24 issue titled its story "Democrats: the Struggle" and plainly stated its belief that "the next vice-president may very possibly become President.[28]

Roosevelt's Prognosis

Indeed, Roosevelt should not, from a medical perspective, have run for a fourth term. Statistically, his chances of surviving an additional four years were remote. A publication of the Society of Actuaries states that the average blood pressure levels from 1935–1953 for males accepted for ordinary insurance were 130/79 mmHg (age 55–59), and 132/80 mmHg (age 60–64). Levels of 140/90 or higher were known to cause mortality varying from 3 percent to 28 percent per year at ages 20–29 and 60–69, respectively.[29]

The risk was known to increase further with still higher levels of blood pressure, as sustained by Roosevelt. Given a systolic pressure of 150–177 and a diastolic of 98–102, mortality was 304 percent greater than standard. Roosevelt's levels were usually in excess of these values from March 1944 to his death. In some instances, his levels were considerably higher than earlier dates—such as February 27, 1941, when his readings were 188/105.

What causes this increased likelihood of death? Several diseases including cerebrovascular accident (or stroke), renal (kidney) failure, and congestive heart failure have long been identified as complications of hypertension. A sixfold increase in mortality occurred in men with marked elevation defined as 148–177/93–102. This was based on an analysis of men accepted for ordinary insurance from 1935–1953 at age 25–69 when the policy was issued.[30]

The true increased risk of death for Roosevelt due to vascular lesions of the central nervous system was more than sixfold higher than for those with normal blood pressure, because his blood pressure levels were substantially in excess of those used as criteria for severe hypertension, and because he had experienced congestive heart failure. In 1943, the mortality rate for white males age 60 per 1000 per year was 29, assuming no particular risk factors.[31] With a sixfold increase, a mortality of 174/1000 per year would be experienced. Roosevelt had endured more than two decades of paralysis, the incessant pressures of World War II, and the four-to-five-year interval of significant hypertension—hence he was statistically at still greater risk each year, especially for a cerebrovascular accident.[32]

The presence of congestive heart failure diagnosed in March 1944 would further decrease the likelihood of survival. If Roosevelt's only risk was for vascular lesions to the central nervous system, such as the massive cerebrovascular accident (stroke) that he did sustain on April 12, 1945, the decrease in survival in succeeding years after 1941 is shown in Table 5.1. His risk of developing nephritis placed him in even further jeopardy (Table 5.2) The risk of developing heart and circulatory disorders was in fact realized, based on the belated diagnosis of congestive heart failure in March 1944. His survival probabilities are listed in Table 5.3.[33] Clearly the above analysis indicates that Roosevelt had far less than a 50 percent chance of surviving his fourth term based on complications of hypertension alone.

The complication of his congestive heart failure predicted a still more ominous prognosis. A median survival of 1.66 years was found in men following a diagnosis of congestive heart failure. The one-year survival rate was 57 percent and the five-year survival rate was 25 percent for men. This outcome matches Roosevelt's clinical course since he survived his diagnosed congestive heart failure by 13 months—March 28, 1944 to April 12, 1945— or more if one considers that recognition as delayed.[34]

There remains the role of poliomyelitis alone in Roosevelt's decreased survival probability. Its impact was much less severe than the hypertension with resulting heart failure and ultimately a stroke. Based on a 50 percent increase in mortality each year for a 39-year-old patient confined to a wheelchair beginning in 1921, Roosevelt would have survived for twenty-seven years, to 1948, at the end of his fourth term. If he had not been paralyzed, his life expectancy would have been thirty years.[35]

These grim analyses quantify the dire prognosis facing the president in 1943–1944. If the above tables were to be calculated from 1940 or 1941, Roosevelt's probability of survival would be remote at best. Starting as late

Table 5.1

FDR's Survival Probability—Central Nervous System/Vascular Lesion

Year	Percentage
1944	69
1945	55
1946	46
1947	37
1948	31

Source: Calculations based on data from *Statistical Bulletin* of the Metropolitan Life Insurance Company.

Table 5.2

FDR's Survival Probability—With Addition of Nephritis

Year	Percentage
1943	86
1944	74
1945	63
1946	55
1947	47
1948	40

Source: Calculations based on data from *Statistical Bulletin* of the Metropolitan Life Insurance Company.

Table 5.3

FDR's Survival Probabilities—Cardiac Disease

Year	Percentage
1943	92
1944	85
1945	78
1946	72
1947	66
1948	62

Source: Calculations based on data from *Statistical Bulletin* of the Metropolitan Life Insurance Company.

as 1941 when multiple elevated levels were recorded, the 31 percent chance of survival, assuming cerebrovascular hemorrhage alone and with no other complications, would be reached in 1948 as noted above. However, if the earlier elevations (162/98, April 22, 1937 and 178/88, November 13, 1940) were used as the starting points, the 31 percent survival would have occurred still earlier, in 1944 and 1947. These calculations demonstrate that Roosevelt's prognosis for survival was grim; his chances of living out his fourth term were limited.

An even more dire implication was the possibility of severe disability before death due to the effects of hypertension. Roosevelt's massive cerebral hemorrhage resulted in a rapid death according to Bruenn. This spared Roosevelt an interval of long suffering and disability and the nation the political twilight zone created by Woodrow Wilson's stroke. The chaos resulting from Roosevelt's disability in 1945 would have hampered national security with the war still raging in Asia, relations souring with the Soviets, the United Nations awaiting its initial meeting, and the decision to use the atomic bomb facing the chief executive.

What were Roosevelt's chances of developing a disabling but, at least for the moment, nonfatal stroke? Based on the findings of the landmark Framingham Study (which has provided research data for numerous complications of heart disease), he had at least a 3.6 times greater likelihood than the normotensive population of developing atherothrombotic brain infarction (stroke). Based on the age distribution of those studied and the criteria for severe hypertension, Roosevelt's outlook was clearly worse than even this risk. Furthermore, his likelihood of coronary heart disease was almost double that of normotensives (persons with normal blood pressure). For congestive heart failure, which was belatedly diagnosed in March 1944, the risk was more than four times that of the normotensive population.[36]

From July 1944 through January 1945, Roosevelt experienced several incidents of chest pain, likely angina pectoris, due to the effects of inadequate flow to the muscle of the heart (myocardium). On the morning of the day he would receive word of being nominated for a fourth term, July 20, a severe pain suddenly struck Roosevelt. He and his son James thought it was an acute digestive upset and had nothing to do with his heart.[37] A second attack occurred on August 10, 1944, in Bremerton, Washington, on the return trip from leading a conference with General Douglas MacArthur, Admiral Chester Nimitz, and Admiral William D. Leahy in Honolulu. Speaking from the fantail of a destroyer, Roosevelt experienced substernal oppression with radiation to the shoulders.[38] On the day of his fourth inauguration, Roosevelt experienced once again the same type pain he had experienced in San Diego, again in the presence of his son James.[39]

Specifically, in the first incident Roosevelt groaned, the color drained from his face, and according to his son James, said: "Jimmy, I don't know if I can make it; I have horrible pains." However, after a short rest he felt better and resumed his scheduled activity of observing a landing exercise of the Fifth Marine Division. James would later evaluate the incident and note that his father insisted that no one know of this episode because it would "cause unnecessary alarm and jeopardize his chances of re-election."[40]

The second attack was perhaps brought on by additional personal stress.

Only four days prior to the incident in Bremerton, his faithful friend and former secretary, Marguerite A. "Missy" Lehand, had died in Boston from a cerebral embolism.

The third episode—January 20, 1945, Inauguration Day—was even more alarming. According to James, his father "looked awful," "his color was bad," he was "terribly tired," and "short of breath."[41] The only staff member who would speak bluntly to James about his father's illness was Lieutenant Commander George Fox, Roosevelt's physical therapist. Roosevelt fought the pains with some bourbon so that he would be able to attend the reception following his Inaugural Address. The views of James are those of a loving son who feels that his father's physicians either underestimated the severity of his father's illness or lacked the will to tell the family. It seems that he assumed that if his father had been told he would not live out the fourth term, he would not have run. His supposition, in view of Roosevelt's strong determination to see the end of the war, is unlikely.

Of all the medical arguments against the fourth term, the most compelling is the nightmare scenario of a wartime president unable to speak, mentally incapacitated, and determined, even more than President Woodrow Wilson, to hold on.

The statistical analyses above were published years after Roosevelt's death, but the pernicious effects of hypertension were well known at this time. In general, the more prolonged the interval of elevated blood pressure, the greater the risk of death (see also Note 28, Chapter 4). An article appearing in the *Journal of the American Medical Association* observed:

> The progressive increase in mortality with each increment of blood pressure which has shown up in mortality studies is attributable largely to the fact that in a very general way the blood pressure tends to become more elevated with increasing duration of hypertension.[42]

The hazard to the nation paralleled his own medical risk. Yet, neither the risk to the nation or to himself were considered significantly dangerous by the president or those around him. In fact, the approach to his last campaign echoed his 1928 gubernatorial race. He emphasized his demanding schedule of speaking engagements, travel, and public appearances as a means of confirming his excellent health. For more than sixteen years, the health issue had intruded upon his political campaigns. To him it was familiar. He used it shrewdly.

The 1944 Presidential Campaign

As the 1944 campaign developed, the health of the president would become an increasingly important issue. And once again, Roosevelt would respond in ways that would minimize the issue for American voters. It would seem obvious that, given the precarious state of the president's health, the questions of vice presidential succession would be the most important issue. However, the president's counsel and close political adviser, Judge Samuel Rosenman, believed that the survival and unity of the party was the president's main concern.[43] Roosevelt believed that to renominate Henry A. Wallace would create a convention fight that would

> . . . split the party wide open . . . it may kill our chances for election this fall, and if it does, it will prolong the war and knock into a cocked hat all the plans we've been making for the future."[44]

This statement by the president would indicate that his priority was not his health, but the creation and structure of the postwar peace. Although James Farley would later state that "it was widely known among political leaders that he [Roosevelt] was a dying man," that comment was not made prior to the selection of the vice presidential running mate.[45]

The field of candidates was crowded. Vice President Wallace was the foremost name but even Roosevelt's political enemy, Joseph P. Kennedy, had a problem with naming Wallace as the president's running mate.[46] According to Kennedy biographer Michael R. Beschloss, Kennedy believed Roosevelt would be defeated in 1944 because Wallace was on the ticket:

> That will weaken the ticket because whether Roosevelt likes it or not, there's still an undercurrent of feeling that his health is not of the best and while he will keep that reasonably well concealed, they can't help but expect that there's a bare chance that if he were elected, he would find it necessary to resign to take some international job for health reasons, and the Vice President would become President—and certainly there are countless Democrats who could never accept Wallace as President.[47]

Other possibilities included former Supreme Court Associate Justice James Byrnes, Senator Alben Barkley, and Supreme Court Justice William O. Douglas. On July 10, 1944 Roosevelt had written Democratic National Committee Chair Robert Hannegan that he would accept the nomination if it was offered.[48] The next day, July 11, 1944, Hannegan; Frank Walker; Mayor Edward Kelly of Chicago; John Boettiger, the president's son-in-law; George Allen, an official of the Democratic National Committee and a friend of the president; and Edward Flynn, leader of the Democratic party in the Bronx, New York, and a long-time associate of the president, met with Roosevelt to discuss the vice presidency. Preoccupied with the war, Roosevelt did not devote much time to the selection of a running mate. He had a tendency to make each person interested feel that he was the one for the position. In this meeting he did understand that the nomination of Wallace would cause a tremendous battle within the party. Byrnes was just as quickly rejected, as a lapsed Catholic (who converted to Episcopalianism) and a southerner with segregationist views. Barkley was thought to be too old. Roosevelt seemed to be most enthusiastic about Douglas, while the others favored Truman. [49] The result of this meeting was a letter from Roosevelt to Hannegan saying he would support either Douglas or Truman. Truman was still not accepting the role of potential candidate, saying that he was nominating Byrnes. A telephone call from the president at San Diego to Hannegan at Chicago was used to persuade Truman to accept the nomination. [50]

William Hannegan (son of Robert Hannegan), later stated that no one in this group anticipated Roosevelt's death. It was assumed that he would complete this term as he had the previous three. However, in an unpublished interview, Robert Sherwood was told by Robert Hannegan that the president would be willing to step down once the war ended and the United Nations established. Though Hannegan may have felt that Roosevelt would not complete the term and Truman would accede to the presidency, it was not necessarily because Hannegan believed such would be caused by Roosevelt's health problems.

Edward Pauley's belief that the country would be choosing a successor president instead of a vice president was not shared by many of the other participants in the decision process. Newspaperman Robert G. Nixon, a correspondent with the International News Service from 1930 to 1958, covered the White House beginning in 1944. His oral history expressed the opinion of most people:

> There was a structure built about him (Roosevelt) that made people take for granted that he was going to live forever. I'm sure he thought so too. I don't think it ever crossed his mind—the shadow of death. Now this may be the key to it in a sense. [Samuel I.] Rosenman [Roosevelt's counsel and long-term associate] said something to the effect that it really didn't matter who was the choice for the vice presidency. What he was saying was that the president was the important man—not the vice president. The reelection of Roosevelt is the essential thing. His inference was that the choice was entirely political on the basis of here is a person with no strikes on his record, who comes from the Middle west where we need representation. It was just that simple. I don't think that it ever crossed Roosevelt's mind that a Vice President might succeed him. [51]

Professor John K. Galbraith recalls his participation in the 1944 Democratic National Convention. He had been in government service until autumn of 1943, when he left to join *Fortune* magazine. He believed that at that time there was no real reason to consider Roosevelt's health. While at the convention, he was unaware of rumors regarding Roosevelt's health and felt that Senator Truman was highly regarded but was not selected as a "successor." [52]

If Vice President Truman believed that his succession was imminent, he had abundant opportunity, while maintaining loyalty to Roosevelt, to discretely prepare himself for the issues he would have to face. However, nothing in Truman's letters to his wife Bess ever betrayed the slightest thought of succession. His letter to her regarding his highly publicized campaign preparation meeting with Roosevelt on August 18, 1944, on the south lawn of the White House under the Jackson magnolia tree indicated that it was routine both politically and personally. There was no hint of the president's serious illness, much less imminent death. Truman's daughter, Margaret, would remember her father's observing a tremor in Roosevelt's hands that caused him to spill his coffee at lunch.[53]

Margaret Truman Daniel believes that her father had not the slightest inkling that the vice presidential nomination would lead to the presidency. Had he been so advised, it is her belief that he would not have accepted the nomination in 1944. Truman was genuinely happy in the Senate, was popular with his colleagues, and enjoyed his role as a member of the "club." He had "made himself available" to potential delegates at state-level meetings for several months prior to the 1944 National Convention, but spent most of his time chairing a War Investigation Committee popularly known as the Truman Committee.

Mrs. Daniel believes that none of the Cabinet members or congressional leaders present in the White House on April 12, 1945 at her father's swearing in had anticipated this event. She emphatically noted that at no time was Senator, later Vice President Truman, advised, even in the most guarded terms, that Roosevelt was mortally ill. His selection as the vice presidential candidate was not made in anticipation of the president's death. She believes that Roosevelt simply lost confidence in Wallace and Byrnes, but did not select her father as a "successor."[54]

Although Truman was, at no time, advised of the president's deteriorating health, he did feel anxious at times that something was happening to Roosevelt. In the first draft of his memoirs he recalled:

> The very thought that something was happening to him (Roosevelt) left me in a cold sweat.[55]

A revision in the draft deleted the words "in a cold sweat" and inserted the words "very much worried." In the notes of an interview in the same file, Daniel Noyes (assistant to President Truman) asked Truman:

> I remember someone said to you at a press conference, "Are you keeping up with foreign policy. There is some indication, at least to this observer that the

time is not far off." I remember you saying and this is not exact: "I wake up every morning in a cold sweat dreading that it might be today." To which Truman replied: "I did. I said it in July after the convention in Chicago."[56]

Truman had several other concerns about assuming the vice presidency. His wife and sister had been on his senatorial payroll, an embarrassment likely to emerge in the national campaign of 1944, which it did without serious consequences. Far more sensitive was the death by suicide of his father-in-law, David W. Wallace, in 1903. Family friend William Hannegan, whose father Robert was Democratic National Committee chair, thought these might have been convenient rationalizations by a reluctant Truman because of his genuine satisfaction with his role in the Senate.[57]

Because the status of Roosevelt's health during the 1944 campaign was a major concern, newsmagazines such as *Time* provided much insight into his health. *Time*, although ardently pro-Dewey, attempted to be objective during the fall of 1944.

On the day following his nomination acceptance speech, Roosevelt left the San Diego naval base on a navy cruiser for a trip to Pearl Harbor to meet with his commanders in the Pacific—General MacArthur, Admiral Nimitz, Admiral William Halsey, and Lieutenant General Robert Richardson, Jr. According to *Time*, Roosevelt looked "tanned, gay and relaxed," upon his return from Pearl Harbor—a trip of twenty-nine days and 10,000 miles.[58] He was continuing to shrewdly use his health to forward his political fortunes. Such a trip would demonstrate his general good health and his ability to carry out the duties of the commander-in-chief.

Returning to the Bremerton Navy Yard, across Puget Sound from Seattle, the president reported to the nation from the bow of a destroyer. His speech was described in *Time* as "rambling, folksy," a surprisingly mild assessment, given its excessive length and poor delivery.[59] In any case, the audience did not respond favorably. Physical difficulties made him uncomfortable, thus distracting him and contributing to a substandard performance. Specifically, Samuel Rosenman suggested that a weight loss caused the braces to no longer fit, and the wind "increased the insecurity of the braces."

> The speech at best was a rambling account of his journeys and experiences during the past month, and he ad-libbed a great deal in a very ineffective manner. It was considered a dismal failure.[60]

Remembering the photograph taken of the president in San Diego—showing the president with glassy eyes, haggard face, and a weary expression—Rosenman felt that the president's health had changed for the worse: "I heard that speech delivered, and I too had a sinking concern that something must have happened to the president since I had left him in Hawaii."[61] George Elsey, a Navy officer assigned to the White House map room, would later express considerable concern about the speech as an indicator of the president's health. Elsey said that he had heard the Bremerton speech with dismay, thought it disastrous and that Roosevelt seemed much older and more tired.[62] He was among the last of the staff to see the president at the White House on March 29, 1945 just before his final trip to Warm Springs. Elsey felt that Roosevelt was in a very weakened condition, barely able to recognize Elsey or respond to his greeting.

According to Bruenn, who had accompanied Roosevelt on the trip, Roosevelt may have sustained an attack of angina pectoris at the time of the Bremerton speech. Although there were no changes on his EKG, Bruenn reported that the president experienced pain underneath the sternum or breastbone, which extended to both shoulders and lasted for fifteen minutes.[63] The health incident was not mentioned by the *Chicago Daily Tribune*, a staunchly anti-New Deal newspaper. To its editors the presentation was not a campaign effort; the paper reported that "No word of politics entered the president's speech."[64]

A week later, the report in *Time* was ambiguous. At the first press conference since his report from the Pacific, a major concern was how the president felt. The article on August 28, 1944, depicted Roosevelt's face as having "the thin and careworn look it has worn for months," but appearing as "lightly tanned, looking rested and fit."[65] The writer noted that he was at first querulous, then genial, and even jovial. The accompanying photograph with Senator Truman was reassuring, showing Roosevelt as alert and with the appearance of good health. A report on the week of September 4, noted that Roosevelt spoke with pauses and "a scarcely audible voice." It prefaced those remarks with a comment that his face was thin and deeply lined, but "he looked more relaxed than he had the previous week."[66]

Shortly after returning to Washington on August 17, 1944, Roosevelt told the press conference that he would soon see Prime Minister Churchill and others in Canada. Boarding the train, Roosevelt and his party arrived in Quebec, Canada on September 11. McKenzie King, Prime Minister of Canada, a participant in this and previous conferences with Churchill and Roosevelt, kept an extensive diary of the meetings in Quebec. Periodically in those diaries, he mentions his concern about Roosevelt's health. In his entry for September11, he records that "[Roosevelt] is genuinely tired and weary. . . . I should think he looks much thinner in the face and is quite drawn and his eyes quite weary."[67] Several days into the conference, Prime Minister King observes that he (Roosevelt) "still looks very weak. . . . I feel a great concern for him."[68]

These observations at Quebec are notable when coupled with the observation of Bruenn, who was accompanying the president. He mentions in his "Clinical Notes" that "the conference was noteworthy only in that his blood pressure tended to be higher than usual."[69] He was still receiving digitalis and one-half gram of phenobarbital three times a day, and his blood pressure ranged from 180/100 to 240/130 mm Hg.

As the campaign progressed into September, the Democratic party leaders were concerned that Roosevelt had to prove once again to the voters that he had the strength and stamina to complete the campaign and the term of office if he won. In order to convey this message, he had to be seen and heard. A series of speeches began with one to the Teamsters Union at the Statler Hotel in Washington, D.C. on September 28. The "Fala" speech was to become one of the best known political speeches of the twentieth century. First, there was the decision to present the speech while sitting down. Then after a rousing speech interrupted several times by cheering and clapping, Roosevelt arrived at the concerns of his dog Fala.

> These Republican leaders have not been content with attacks on me, or my wife, or on my sons. No, not content with that, they now include my little dog, Fala. Of course, I don't resent attacks, and my family doesn't resent attacks, but Fala does resent them. You know, Fala is Scotch, and being a Scottie, as soon as he learned that the Republican fiction writers in Congress and out had concocted a story that I had left him behind on the Aleutian Islands and had sent a destroyer back to find him—at a cost to the taxpayers of two or three, or eight or twenty million dollars—his Scotch soul was furious. He has not been the same dog since. I am accustomed to hearing malicious falsehoods about myself . . . but I think I have a right to resent, to object to libelous statements about my dog."[70]

Time's report of the speech glowed with praise. *Time* noted that "The Old Master still had it, Franklin Roosevelt was at his best." It further described the president as a veteran virtuoso with an actor's perfection of timing, tone, and assurance to an audience that roared with approval. The speech made it clear to the American voters that Roosevelt still had his magic— the Fala speech was described as a "haymaking right hook" delivered by the "champ."[71]

The speech showed the gifted public speaker and political leader, but it did not fully answer the questions related to Roosevelt's health and his ability to successfully complete the campaign. The magazine's compliments did not endure long. Only one week later, *Time* was again reporting Roosevelt's health in a negative way—that at his Friday press conference his voice had a hoarse, stopped up quality, indicating a head cold. And McIntire was also again reporting his belief that the president was well, that he had been "hit by the flu, hit hard . . . but he is right back in shape." This explanation, *Time* noted, was occasioned by the "acute national interest in Mr. Roosevelt's health."[72]

By the middle of October, there was still no announcement verifying campaign speaking engagements. The "Fala" speech so impressed Democratic Party Chair Robert Hannegan that he began making proposals for a series of similar events around the country—New York City, Pittsburgh, Chicago, and Cleveland. Suddenly, an announcement was issued from the White House that the president would not be making any more public appearances. It was not clear who had made the decision and immediately all the old questions concerning Roosevelt's health were stated by *Time*.

> But what everyone really wanted to know was whether or not the president was going to campaign; and if not, why not? One explanation advanced was that he was "going to do a Lincoln" (the Emancipator, 1864, made no speeches, did not register or vote). Another was the state of his health.[73]

Although "his physicians appear well satisfied with his general condition," the same issue included the observation that the president had "virtually abandoned the uncomfortable braces." Thus, it was the basic speculation of *Time* that the reason for Roosevelt's limited campaign in 1944 may have been "the state of his health."[74] It was an ambiguous assessment of the man guiding America toward the end of the greatest global conflagration in history.

As the presidential campaign began to wind down in October, the health issue was out in the open. Quoting the *New York Sun*, which it described as an "arch-Republican paper," *Time* introduced an essay on the six previous presidents who had died in office with the opening words, "Let's not be squeamish."[75] The *Time* writers were using the comments of the *New York Sun* and the *New York Daily News* to continue to raise the health issue:

> The *Sun* and the *News* were saying out loud what many have wondered about: is the president too old or tired to live out Term IV? Plainly Franklin Roosevelt's health was a political issue.[76]

A *New York Daily News* article, written by John O'Donnell, was devoted entirely to the political importance of the president's health. O'Donnell wrote:

> The life expectancy of Franklin Roosevelt is indeed a definite political handicap to his fourth term pretensions. The President is a tired and ailing and aged man. . . . Four years ago . . . he looked hale and hearty. Now he is drawn, haggard, and gray. In the future White House advisers are going to

insist on only profile shots because the changes wrought by illness in his feature are less shocking.[77]

Even Senator Truman, campaigning in Los Angeles on October 16, 1944, was confronted by questions concerning Roosevelt's health. At a press conference that morning he had been quizzed about the direction of his policies if he became president—to which he replied that the question was "improper." This happened after one reporter pointed out that six presidents had died in office. Another reporter asked if Truman would care to comment on "apprehension in Republican circles as to the president's health." The senator's reply was that such is "grossly exaggerated."[78]

As the Democratic leadership sought to deal with the increasing perception that Roosevelt would not campaign in his usual ways, they were faced with a major negative discussion of the health issue. The *Chicago Daily Tribune*, reflecting the staunchly anti-New Deal position of its publisher, Colonel Robert R. McCormack, printed a major editorial on October 17, 1944, entitled "Mr. Roosevelt's Health." The editorial virtually forecasted Roosevelt's death in office. His absences from office (some of which were concealed by censorship) had become more frequent. The deterioration in his appearance and "once magic" radio voice, and his use of a wheelchair in speaking at the Teamsters dinner were all bluntly noted. Roosevelt's health "is one of the principal issues of the campaign and cannot be evaded by false appeals to delicacy."[79]

The harshest words of this editorial were, however, saved for vice-presidential candidate Truman. It described him as "the pliant tool" of Boss Thomas J. Pendergast in looting "Kansas City's county government." He was further depicted as "the yes-man and apologist in the Senate for political gangsters." It was that paper's belief that if Truman was elected to office, he would have a greater possibility of succeeding to the presidency than any vice president had within the last century. As a political matter, the editorial questioned Truman's appeal to black voters because of his previous voting practice and the racial practices of his "border state." The editorial conclusion was that the Democrats thus found it necessary to soft pedal the president's health issue and keep Truman in the background. The final sentence asked the question: "Do decent citizens of America want to do business with Truman?"[80] This is especially ironic since as president, Truman would dramatically advance the civil rights agenda.

A few days later, the *Tribune* again focused on Roosevelt's use of a wheelchair in a proposed campaign stop in Pennsylvania. It reported that his physical condition had deteriorated to the extent that he no longer was able to stand with the aid of braces.[81] Coverage of the New York campaign by the *Chicago Daily Tribune* was critical, sharply contrasting with the *New York Times*.

On the same day—October 24, 1944—that the *Times* was reporting favorably on the New York campaign, the *Daily Tribune* carried another scathing editorial about Truman. At a press conference, Truman noted that if anything should happen to the president other people had told him (Truman) that he was qualified to be president. The editors took exception:

> What is more likely is that the state of Mr. Roosevelt's health is on his mind, just as it is on the minds of a great many others who have seen Mr. Roosevelt's recent picture and have heard his voice. . . . Mr. Truman considers himself qualified for the Presidency. On this record, do his countrymen? In voting for the fourth term they may well be voting for the Truman first term.[82]

If all of the *Chicago Daily Tribune's* coverage was not clear enough about its position on Roosevelt's election, the editorial headline on October 28, 1944, said it as bluntly as possible: "A Vote for FDR May be a Vote for Truman."[83] The forecast was not subtle. Twelve years as president had taken their toll. Roosevelt would be sixty-three years old and far from well at the fourth inaugural. The editorial pictures Senator Truman being ignored by the political bosses and being sent along the Chautauqua circuit and the milk trains. Mr. Kelly, political leader in Chicago, didn't want the voters to know that "in view of Mr. Roosevelt's age and brittle health, a vote for Roosevelt is very likely to be a vote for Truman for President."

Given the continuing negativity of the *Chicago Daily Tribune, New York News*, and *New York Sun*, the conclusion was reached by the Democratic leadership that the American people needed a report. McIntire was described as strolling into the presidential bedroom each morning and insinuating himself into the daily bull sessions, despite his heavy responsibilities as surgeon general of the Navy.[84] The *Time* essay of October 23 once again carried the reassurances of the president's good health, quoting McIntire at great length.

> He (Roosevelt) had a hard time shaking off that (cold) attack and it knocked out his reserve for a while (last winter). As a result he had some sinus trouble and bronchitis, and the coughing wore him down a bit. . . . Now he has recovered his reserve. . . . He hasn't been in the pool since going to Quebec . . . But he's going to start in the pool again now . . . He is a powerful swimmer. Nothing wrong organically with him at all. He's perfectly O.K. . . . The stories that he is in bad health are understandable enough around election time, but they are not true.[85]

McIntire was clearly still misleading the press. He was still referring to Bruenn's findings, in March, of heart failure and hypertension as bronchitis and sinusitis. The fact was indeed that Roosevelt had not been swimming and later when he attempted to swim at Warm Springs in November, blood pressure determinations taken before and after showed an alarming rise (260/150 mm Hg).[86] At a crucial time, American voters had not received accurate information revealing the critical nature of Roosevelt's continuing illness. *Time* and other media raised questions about the presidential fitness but also reported McIntire's reassurance that everything was satisfactory.

As the campaign was drawing to a close at the end of October 1944, Robert Hannegan was still concerned that voters would perceive that Roosevelt was not healthy enough for a fourth term. After previously announcing a series of national rallies, Hannegan had the embarrassment of having the White House state that the president would not be making any more public speeches. It had now been decided that most of his speeches would not be made from public rostrums, but from dining tables equipped with microphones. When the decision was made for the president to tour New York City, Hannegan was quoted in *Time:* "After the people have seen him, they can make up their own minds about his vigor and health."[87] There is no doubt that this was the chief purpose of the trip—it was reflected in the reporting. The *New York Times* confirmed that the tour had a major goal of combating rumors that the president was not in good health. That goal was reflected in the title of its front-page story: "President Defies Rain To Let New York See Him." The article explained carefully how the tour accomplished its goal:

> The two facts of Mr. Roosevelt's ride through the rain and his standing at Ebbets Field are counted on to put to rest the rumors that the president was in bad health and that he is unable to stand. These have been in circulation since he made his opening campaign address to the International Brotherhood of Teamsters in Washington without once rising to his feet.[88]

Two days later, the paper would carry the customary reassurance of Roosevelt's staff under the title "President All Right after Ride in Rain." The short front-page article quoted Early, presidential secretary, as saying that the president had shown no signs of having caught cold, and McIntire "isn't a bit worried about him."[89]

Time magazine reports of this final campaign trip through four boroughs of New York City noted that in all his campaigns "it had never rained more incessantly and gloomily than now." In this dismal rain, the commander-in-chief was met by 40,000 workers at the Brooklyn Army Base, then by more than 35,000 workers at the Brooklyn Navy Yard, then went on to Ebbets Field (Brooklyn Dodgers stadium), Queens, the Bronx, Harlem, to mid-Manhattan, and down Broadway. The entire crowd was estimated between 1.5 and 3 million. He was described by reporters as smiling "with a pink glow to his face." But at other times, he was reported to be sallow, tired, and with heavy lines on his face. Barely six hours later he appeared at the Waldorf Astoria Hotel for a dinner of the Foreign Policy Association. Media reports were mixed. Roosevelt, silently and unsmilingly ate his meal, and "his weary face looked seamed and haggard." But when the floodlights indicated that it was time to speak, the reporters noted that "in an instant the president was his old broad-smiling self, waving gaily as the diners applauded."[90] Roosevelt had been wheeled to the dais and did not stand during his speech. However, there was nothing to indicate to the 2,000 people present that the speaker had a life-threatening illness.

The numerous photographs of the president appearing in the metropolitan papers during his visit to New York gave the appearance of a man in favorable health. Paul R. Fitzpatrick, New York state Democratic chairman, pronounced Roosevelt in good health: "He looked even better than he did four years ago when I rode with him on his inspection tour in Buffalo."[91]

In the final analysis, the New York City tour, coupled with his stunning performance in the "Fala" speech, quieted concerns about Roosevelt's health just before the election. In the final few days of the campaign, health concerns continued to recede. Thomas Dewey also avoided the issue of the president's health, at least overtly. One Roosevelt biographer stated that Dewey did not use the health issue because it might possibly create sympathy for Roosevelt.

> . . . [H]e (Dewey) might have said that Roosevelt was on his deathbed, unable to deliver a speech standing up and unfit to run, but that too could create sympathy for the president, who in the last month of the campaign had completely disregarded his regimen of rest and was out on the hustings.[92]

Time continued its coverage of the campaign in its November 6 issue with a very positive cover story about Truman. However, the second article in this issue was entitled "The Strangest Campaign." The health issue had continued to recede, but *Time* illustrated how shrewdly Roosevelt dealt with it. The issue did not carry any discussion of the president's health problems or its political implications. Yet, when the campaign train arrived at Fort Wayne the president left the train to address approximately 24,000 people. Roosevelt knew that many wanted to reassure themselves about his health, and he said:

> I am in the middle of a war, and so are you. . . . It is quite a job, but I am perfectly able to take it and so are you.[93]

The continuing concern over the president's health was not reflected in the result of the election. Early in the campaign Roosevelt had made a prediction regarding the election—giving himself 335 electoral votes, Governor Dewey 196. The final vote was 432 to 99. It would seem that the voters could not risk changing presidents in such a critical time of international conflict, regardless of adverse health predictions. On election eve as the president and his staff waited in Hyde Park for the returns, among those waiting was McIntire. The media noted that he would not leave until the returns were substantially in Roosevelt's favor—perhaps an indication that he was still concerned about the toll the campaign had taken on the president's health.[94]

In summary the issue of Roosevelt's health was raised by *Time* magazine on an almost weekly basis during the presidential campaign of 1944. However, any long-term negative effect on the president's reelection life was avoided by his vigorous but brief campaign, and by McIntire's totally misleading reassurances that were often parroted by Robert Hannegan, the national party chairperson.

Life magazine, like *Time*, another Luce publication, formally supported Dewey for president and argued its position in a series of three well-reasoned editorials. Shortly after the national Democratic convention, *Life* bluntly but hypothetically considered the consequences to the Democratic Party if Roosevelt, after reelection, were to die in office—an unusually harsh proposition on which to base hypothetical surmises. [95] It is interesting to note that *Life* had not commented on Roosevelt's appearance in July when he accepted the nomination, even though a photograph taken at the time triggered widespread concern.

The *Life* writers did not amplify the health issue during the campaign. It did report, however, that penicillin was used to irrigate Roosevelt's sinuses,[96] a claim that was never substantiated. However, the magazine also published a number of favorable photographs, especially those taken during the "Fala" speech. Just prior to the election, *Life* described Roosevelt as cheerful, ruddy, and tanned but also as thinner, haggard, with a deeply lined face.[97]

Despite the persistent undercurrent of concern about Roosevelt's health which often found expression in the media's coverage of the 1944 reelection campaign, there is no indication that officials in Washington and elsewhere, not even Roosevelt and Truman, anticipated the president's death in office.

Perhaps there would have been concern and anxiety if there had been common knowledge of Roosevelt's health status just after the election. On November 18, 1944, Bruenn noted that "the patient" had lost more weight and his appetite was poor.[98] His blood pressure was recorded as 210/112. The blood pressure recorded the last week in November just after a swim at Warm Springs reflected an alarming rise, from the November 18 reading—it was now 260/150 mm Hg.[99]

Historians continue to speculate on what was known at the highest levels of government about Roosevelt's health in his last year. Of particular concern was the question: What was Roosevelt's own view? Two recent studies explore this question. One addresses the question in the context of the president's foreign policy,[100] the other does so in terms of the selection of Truman as running mate in 1944.[101] Each study depicts the president as terminally ill in his last year, but they provide contradictory assertions about the president's view of his own mortality.

Robert Ferrell's *Choosing Truman* presents a Roosevelt who believed that he would continue in the White House "for not merely a fourth term but a fifth, maybe more."[102] To the contrary, Amos Perlmutter's *FDR and Stalin* argues that the president must have known that the Yalta Conference in February 1945 "would be his last great summit, a farewell appearance on the stage of history."[103] It is said that he had been told that he (Roosevelt) had only three months to live. Perlmutter adds that Robert Duncan, executive officer at Bethesda Naval Hospital, conducted a thorough examination of Roosevelt in December 1944. Such an examination could not be confirmed by Bruenn, nor is there any reliable evidence of such an examination occurring.[104]

When Roosevelt was speaking with his son James on Inauguration Day, January 20, 1945, the topic about which he was the most interested was the proposed trip to Yalta. There was nothing in that conversation, as reported by James, that hinted at any contemplation of death. He had not even at this date revised his will (it had been last revised on November 12, 1941),[105] even though substantial sums were involved and at least one provision, for his friend Marguerite A. LeHand who had died in 1944, was out of date. Roosevelt continued to anticipate a heavy schedule through the time of his death.

His son James, writing in 1959, recalls the plans and dreams that Roosevelt had for his fourth term. His first job would be to secure real peace, to fulfill the dream of Woodrow Wilson, and attend the opening session of the United Nations in April. There were plans to visit England, the king and queen, and Winston Churchill. He wanted to visit the North African desert, and also to travel the seas in a slow freighter.[106] In addition, he was planning events in details for 1945 and 1946, and preparing the broad outlines of his program for the remainder of his term.

However, the one thing that he was not doing was preparing his successor. It would be logical to note that if Roosevelt had a conscious belief in his impending death he would have been preparing Truman more thoroughly.

The clinical outcome of the four candidates for president and vice president in 1940 illustrates the difficulty of prognostication even for a four-year interval. In fact, the medical outcome was a paradox. Had the electorate based their vote solely on apparent health, Wendell Willkie, the Republican candidate, would have emerged victorious. He was a decade younger (48 years old) than Roosevelt and seemingly vigorous, robust, and vibrant. However, Willkie would have died in office during World War II, presumably running for reelection, for his death was on October 8, 1944. As president, the wartime stresses of office that Willkie would have experienced might have led to an even earlier demise. Succeeding to the presidency would normally be the vice president. However, his choice for vice president, Senator Charles McNary, died eight months before Willkie, on February 24, 1944. Thus, the vice presidency would have been left vacant. The nation was without a constitutional procedure for replacement of a vice president at that time. The line of succession to the presidency would have reached the secretary of state. As part of a wartime coalition effort, a prominent Democrat, conceivably Roosevelt himself, might have occupied this position.[107] Hence, a purely medical decision in the 1940 presidential election would have led to the death of both president and vice president in the midst of global conflict and a national election.

The preponderance of evidence shows that Roosevelt, although certainly aware of his own mortality, did not consider his death to be imminent although he had been diagnosed as having heart failure and hypertension.

The Fourth Inauguration

After years of illnesses reported by the media, followed by recovery and/or reassurances of his good health, the American public, the government, and even Roosevelt, were eager to put the best appearance on reports of his health problems. However, in spite of all efforts, troubling observations continued. As Inauguration Day approached, Budget Director Harold G. Smith noted that the president was tired and more stooped than usual. Although Smith thought he needed to relieve Roosevelt of as many burdens as possible, there were never the slightest suggestions in his diary that he foresaw the president's death.[108]

The fourth inaugural address was the shortest since George Washington's, a five-minute speech from the South Portico of the White House, without any of the pomp and circumstance customarily associated with inauguration festivities. In the words of the *New York Times:*

> No parade could have been more dramatic than yesterday's inaugural, which was kept as simple as it possibly could be. . . . Whoever assumed the Presidency at this moment would take up a burden heavier than any American has borne since Lincoln's first inaugural.

The editorial states, "on this day above all others, the president is the symbol of the Constitution which he swears to preserve, protect and defend."[109]

A major concern of many who attended was the physical appearance of the president. In discussing the inauguration later, many persons commented on Roosevelt's health. In the biography of his father, James Roosevelt described a scene very much like the one in San Diego, July 1944, where Roosevelt had an attack of angina.[110] John Gunther had last seen Roosevelt at the Foreign Policy Association speech in October. Seeing him again at the time of the inauguration, Gunther was shocked at the change in appearance:

> His face was gray, gaunt, and sagging and the muscles controlling the lips seems to have lost part of their function. . . . I felt certain he was going to die."[111]

At a cabinet meeting the day before the inauguration, Frances Perkins noted in her biography of Roosevelt,

> When he came in I thought he looked badly, and this was the first time I had ever thought so. . . . His faced looked thin, his color was gray, and his eyes dull.[112]

A biographer of Perkins relates a comment that Mrs. Woodrow Wilson made at the luncheon following the Inauguration: "He looks exactly as my husband did when he went into his decline."[113]

Samuel Bookatz was a Navy portraitist and artist assigned to the White House during World War II. His knowledge of human anatomy was exceptionally thorough. He noted a progressive decline in Roosevelt's appearance. The president was thinner, more sallow in complexion, and clearly fatigued. Up to the time of the inauguration and prior to leaving for Yalta, in his view the changes were gradual.[114]

Storm Whaley, an announcer of that era, attending the Radio Correspondent's Dinner honoring Roosevelt on January 11, 1945, sat close enough to the president to have an unobstructed view of him. He recalled that Roosevelt initially displayed a death-like gray color and a slack mouth. Later, during dinner, Roosevelt recovered his usual liveliness. During a brief toast to the men and women in uniform, "his voice was as strong as ever and he was transformed into the newly elected president of 1933." Hence, even in a brief interval of a few hours, Roosevelt's apparent state of well-being changed dramatically.[115]

The person with the most continuing professional concern for the president's health, Bruenn, attended the inauguration, noting that Roosevelt gave the speech without difficulty, using his leg braces for the first time since August 1944. He concluded his diary entry with the observation that "at the reception that evening he [Roosevelt] appeared to be in excellent spirits."[116] Evidently, he had become accustomed to the haggard look of Roosevelt that others continued to find of concern.

And always there were the views of McIntire, placing a positive "spin" on any comments related to the president's health. On the day of the inauguration he once again exulted that Roosevelt was in "fine shape" as he started a fourth term and "he went through the campaign in fine shape and right on through the following months." When quizzed about recurrent rumors related to tooth extractions, operations, and other ailments, McIntire declared that "all that stuff is just talk and there's nothing to be done." A number of reporters mentioned that apparently Roosevelt's hearing was not as good as it might have been because he didn't seem to hear press conference questions as readily as he once did. McIntire's explanation was that Roosevelt's left ear always had been "a little down" and maybe an auditory check might be in order.[117]

Perhaps political victory improved the manner in which reporters saw the president. John Crider, in the *New York Times* the day after the fourth inauguration, reported that "A Grim Roosevelt Begins New Term." However, the subtitle reads "Though Changed, the President Appears in Good Shape to Carry On His Job," and further notes that "he shows no outward signs of illness, and after a rest looks as well as he did several years ago."[118] Roosevelt himself, in typical humor, at the outset of his fourth term, wise-cracked "The first 12 years are the most difficult." Editorially the *New York Times* was more prophetic than it had imagined when it stated, "We expect of him, as of every President, in times of crisis, almost more than it is humanly possible to give."[119] The "News of the Week in Review," in the Sunday *New York Times* on that same day, portrayed Roosevelt as noticeably aged since his previous inaugural but not more than expected over a four-year span.[120] Clearly the optimism of the *Times* and its reporters was based solely on its interpretation of Roosevelt's appearance.

Only two days after the inauguration, the president and his party left Washington en route to the Yalta Conference. Yalta, a town in the Crimea, was the scene of the second wartime summit conference between Churchill, Roosevelt, and Stalin. This was the time for focusing on postwar plans. Roosevelt sought Soviet participation in the war against Japan. Churchill was concerned with the postwar settlement in Europe—securing a vote for France in the occupation of Germany, and preventing a possible dismemberment of Germany as a political unit. Stalin was particularly concerned with the establishment of the postwar boundaries of Poland.

Arriving at Norfolk they boarded the heavy cruiser USS *Quincy* for the trip to Malta. During the travels by airplane to Livadia Place near Yalta, during the conference itself, and on the extended return trip by sea to the United States, many persons had occasion to observe the president.

Commander William M. Rigdon, serving as the president's assistant naval aide during the Yalta trip, noted that "Roosevelt had lost much weight and that his face was drawn, but it did not occur to me that he was seriously sick." In 1962, when he wrote of his experiences, he believed "it is incredible that many of us who were with Roosevelt daily did not see that he was declining. . . . Photographs I took then show plainly he was a sick man."[121] Movies were shown on board each evening. According to Rigdon, "Some of us noticed, but without concern, that his lower jaw often hung down as he watched the pictures."

Douglas MacArthur II, a career diplomat serving with the American Embassy in Paris, met Roosevelt approximately one week (February 18, 1945) following the Yalta Conference on the *Quincy* in the captain's quarters where he debriefed the president for perhaps thirty to thirty-five minutes on the French reaction to the Yalta agreement. It was MacArthur's impression that the president was dazed, pale, looked to be ill; and he was not certain that the president was really registering much of the debriefing. MacArthur recalled Roosevelt sitting in the chair—he was not unconscious, there was no abnormal movement or other overt sign of illness, but he felt that Roosevelt was dazed throughout the interval. After the meeting, MacArthur spoke to Admiral Leahy and commented that the president was "a very, very sick man." Leahy did not deny nor confirm this, but obliquely referred to the fact that Roosevelt was having a bad moment.[122]

Also taking part in the meetings aboard the *Quincy* was future Quaker Oats CEO Robert A. Stuart, Jr. In 1945, Stuart was serving as an assistant secretary in the office of General Walter Bedell Smith, Eisenhower's chief of staff. Smith detailed Stuart to accompany Ambassador Jefferson Caffery to Algiers to meet with Roosevelt en route from his return from Yalta. A young major, he was enthusiastic about meeting the president and commander-in-chief.

> To this day, I remember feeling a sense of shock and dismay. The President was sitting at a desk in his stateroom. He looked white as a sheet and was covered with perspiration. He appeared to have some difficulty in focusing on Ambassador Caffery and me as we were introduced. . . . I was shocked by his appearance seeming both exhausted and sick.[123]

Tony Hiss, a well-known journalist, the son of Alger Hiss (State Department official, Yalta conference participant, later convicted of perjury in the Whittiker Chambers case), recalls that his father felt that Roosevelt was in total command of his faculties throughout the Yalta Conference. He was fatigued, even haggard at the outset, but less so as the conference progressed.[124]

Bruenn would later write that Roosevelt generally appeared to be stable physically, but that during the discussion of Poland he was worried and upset and experienced pulsus alternans—an evenly spaced alternation of strong and weak cardiac beats which can occur in patients with congestive heart failure, especially due to hypertension.[125]

Robert Hopkins, the son of Harry Hopkins (principal presidential adviser), was the official Signal Corps photographer at all international conferences from Casablanca through Cairo, Teheran, and Yalta. He kept many photographs taken at Yalta. In some which were widely circulated, Roosevelt appears to be drawn, haggard, and weary. In others, he appears quite animated. Hopkins felt that the president was very lively, interested, and completely in command of his facilities. Hopkins felt that the president's appearance was in general rather good at the Yalta conference, although a few of the photographs would show otherwise.[126]

Edward R. Stettinius, Jr., represented the United States at Yalta as secretary of state. In *Roosevelt and the Russians*, Stettinius recalls his concern about Roosevelt's health just prior to the delegation leaving for Yalta.

> I had been concerned over the president ever since his inaugural address on the porch of the White House on January 20. That day he had seemed to tremble all over. It was not just his hands that shook, but his whole body as well. By the time he reached Malta he seemed, however, to be cheerful, calm and quite rested.[127]

He further found the president to be mentally alert and "fully capable of dealing with each situation as it developed." While writing of the discussion related to membership in the proposed United Nations General Assembly, Stettinius believed Roosevelt's strong participation furnished "excellent proof that he was alert and in full command of his faculties."

Charles E. "Chip" Bohlen, assistant to the secretary of state and translator, was also concerned with the state of the president's health in the days leading up to the Yalta Conference. Bohlen made a distinction between physical health and mental status. He concluded that even though Roosevelt's physical appearance was disturbing and not up to normal, his mental and psychological well-being were not affected. He suggested that the president's refusal to hold extensive discussions with the British prior to Yalta might have been explained by the state of Roosevelt's health. He further noted: "Our leader was ill at Yalta, but he was effective. . . . I so believed at the time and still so believe." He concludes that the outcome of the conference was in no way related to Roosevelt's health.[128]

James F. Byrnes, a member of the American Delegation, made observations similar to Bohlen's when he noted that Roosevelt did not effectively use the intensive file of studies and recommendations which had been prepared for the president by the State Department.[129]

And as usual McIntire's observations, though recorded later in 1946, related that Roosevelt was worn out but "never once was there a loss of vigor and clarity." He was still able to deflect concern about Roosevelt's health by suggesting that much of it was the result of the way in which photographers took shots of Roosevelt. It was the flashlights that provided such a "ghastly pallor and accentuated the thinness of his face."[130] Never once was there a suggestion from the president's physician that Roosevelt was becoming increasingly ill.

Upon the return from Yalta, Judge Samuel Rosenman joined the president's party at Algiers to work on Roosevelt's address to Congress. When he arrived aboard the ship Rosenman was "disheartened by his physical appearance." He described the president as "listless and apparently uninterested in conversation—he was all burnt out."[131] Secretary of Labor Perkins had known Roosevelt even longer than had Rosenman, since Roosevelt's days in the New York state Senate in 1911. In her biography she recalls the man she greeted upon his return from Yalta. He looked "fit and fine." At the first cabinet meeting, his "face was gray, his eyes were bright, his skin was a good color again . . . I remember saying to myself . . . he gets tired but just give him a little rest and he comes right up again."[132]

As might be expected, those who idolized Roosevelt generally saw him as healthy. Those with major differences in policy objectives felt he was incapacitated. *Life* magazine, in its editorial of February 26, 1945, following the Yalta Conference, proclaimed that "almost everywhere the Yalta Conference was received as good." However, it was pointed out by Walter Lippmann, a widely quoted columnist, in that same editorial that there were exceptions—"the chief exceptions to the general joy are the Vatican, the London Poles, and of course the Germans, who called it an unlimited triumph for Stalin."[133]

Within a few short years, as America advanced into the Cold War era, criticism of the Yalta Conference agreements became the explanation for changes in Eastern Europe, which were particularly favorable to the Soviets. In 1948, *Life* would change its editorial stance and with a picture of the conference print a bitter caption, "High Tide of Appeasement Was Reached at the Yalta Conference." In the same issue, a former governmental colleague, William C. Bullitt, would charge:

> At Yalta in the Crimea, on Feb. 4, 1945, the Soviet dictator welcomed the weary President. Roosevelt, indeed was more than tired. He was ill. Little was left of the physical and mental vigor that had been his when he entered the White House in 1933. Frequently he had difficulty in formulating his thoughts, and greater difficulty in expressing them consecutively. But he still held to his determination to appease Stalin.[134]

Others present at Yalta, including Churchill's physician Lord Moran, expressed the belief that Roosevelt's health adversely affected his performance in the Yalta discussions. Robert Ferrell's study, *The Dying President*, noted that Moran was proposing a medical and a political diagnosis. He observed that "the president appears to be a very sick man . . . I give him only a few months to live." He believed that the Americans were purposely blinding themselves to the issue: "Men shut their eyes when they do not want to see, and the Americans here cannot bring themselves to believe that he is finished."[135]

On March 1, 1945, Roosevelt reported to Congress, wanting them to understand just what had been accomplished at Yalta. He apologized for not standing to address the Congress and explained that it was easier to sit than to carry around the ten pounds of steel braces on his legs. Eleanor Roosevelt would write later that when Roosevelt sat to give his address it signaled that "he had accepted a certain degree of invalidism."[136]

Roosevelt's speech writer and counsel, Judge Rosenman, listened as the president gave this final report to Congress. He was disappointed and dismayed "at the halting, ineffective manner of delivery."[137] Rosenman believed that in spite of the delivery Roosevelt accomplished the key goal of his address: "I come from the Crimea Conference with a firm belief that we have made a good start on the road to a world of peace." Roosevelt had spent part of the previous day at Arlington Cemetery, in a heavy rain and sleet storm, for the burial of his military aide, Major General Edwin M. Watson. The distinguished health economist, Professor Eli Ginzberg, who was an adviser to the War Department at the time, thought Roosevelt looked "half-dead" on his return from the Yalta conference and was hence not surprised at the president's passing six weeks later.[134]

The next day, the *New York Times* reported that the Yalta address to Congress won favorable bipartisan and international raves with only a few disclaimers. It described Roosevelt's tone as "friendly, intimate."[139] An editorial in *Life* on March 12, 1945, also described the address in very positive terms, noting that the speaker was sure of himself. The reporting in the *Chicago Daily Tribune* reflected a negative position, noting the address as rambling and given in a mechanical tone, and with a show of hesitancy. Roosevelt's frequent ad-libs were disparaged, especially the indiscreet reference to DeGaulle as a prima donna. Several senators were quoted in the *New York Times* with their view of a tired president, but one who appeared much better than when he had left for Yalta.[140] The reporting, however, was far more cautious than in the past about forecasting Roosevelt's demise. Perhaps the reelection for a fourth term continued to temper their previous blunt style about his health issues.

The blatantly misleading reassurances of McIntire were published without probing questions, or even a hint of doubt during these critical months.

Specific medical documentation was not forthcoming, and the journalists of that era probed no further. The *New York Times* and the *Chicago Daily Tribune* were equally deceived by Roosevelt's personal physician and permitted their editorial policies to distort news coverage. Walter Trohan, a reporter for the *Chicago Daily Tribune*, was not deceived.[141] It was his contention that McIntire knew that the president was dying in the summer and fall of 1944. He believed that the president had lost most of his cognitive ability—there would be long pauses and often inappropriate responses at press conferences.

For public consumption Roosevelt's physician once again reiterated that "his health was excellent." McIntire was joined by Jonathan Daniels, a presidential assistant, who responded to reports that the president had been ill on the trip to Yalta, but "I can set them at absolute rest, I have never seen him looking so well."[142] McIntire's final published reassurances were identical with those of the previous eleven years. Through the end of his life, the severity of Roosevelt's hypertension and heart failure was overlooked in these pronouncements. The public continued to be deceived.

One reader of the *New York Times* was aware of the enormous gap between official reassurances to the press and the grim, indeed ominous, medical realities. Bruenn was "appalled," a strong term for this cautious, discreet physician to use in describing his superior's entirely misleading optimism in speaking to the press and the public.[143] As a naval lieutenant commander, Bruenn could not confront, much less contradict in public, his superior officer, McIntire. Aside from professional constraints, Bruenn had been sworn to secrecy by the FBI. Only twenty-five years later, in April 1970, with the consent of the family, if not at their insistance, did even limited public disclosure become possible with the publication by Bruenn of his clinical notes in the *Annals of Internal Medicine*.

Shortly after the Yalta address to Congress, Roosevelt's friend Prime Minister MacKenzie King of Canada arrived at the White House for a visit. During a talk on Saturday, March 10, some of the topics of conversation indicated that Roosevelt believed he would complete his term. He mentioned to King that "three years from now when I am through here, I am thinking of getting out a newspaper. . . ."[144]

King continued to be concerned with Roosevelt's health:

> The visit has left the impression on me that the president has distinctly failed. . . . There are certain signs of failure of memory which are quite noticeable, such as repetition of stories and incidents. He is fond of talking continuously. He does listen and take in points, but links everything too much to a personal point. The point is no human mortal was ever meant to possess the kind of power these three men (Roosevelt, Churchill, Stalin) have come to have today.[145]

Roosevelt appeared better than in his photographs, but had "distinctly failed," was very tired, "hardly in shape to cope with problems," and showed signs of failure of memory. Paradoxically, he clearly was planning to speak at the first meeting of the United Nations at San Francisco in May.[146]

Even more demanding was an extended European trip planned for June which would take him to Buckingham Palace, Chequers (Churchill's estate), to address the Parliament, visit the men on the battlefield, and then to visit Queen Wilhelmina in Holland and stay at the Hague. This assumed that the war in Europe would be over before June (in fact the case) and Roosevelt's trip was going to provide a triumphal close to the war.

King was a guest at Roosevelt's press conference of March 13. There was no intimation of impending death. In fact, Roosevelt's conversations with King displayed a clear grasp of pending military and political issues.

Two weeks later (March 23) an understated but ominous note from Moscow appeared in the *New York Times* in an article entitled "Moscow Stresses Desire for Peace."

> Many Soviet figures have expressed interest in President Roosevelt's health. Mr. Roosevelt is known as a friend of the Soviet Union and the Russians have shown concern over occasional rumors that he was suffering from strain.[147]

The Soviets were also said to be interested in knowing the views of Vice President Truman.

If the Russians thought that President Roosevelt was suffering from strain, they were probably correct, although not realizing that their political stances were a major cause of that strain. On March 8, 1945, Churchill sent a message to Roosevelt in which he stated that Stalin should "be informed of our distress at the developments which led to the setting up by force of a government in Rumania of a Communist minority."[148] He also mentioned that Molotov had a different view from us as to how the Crimea decision on Poland would be put into effect. Roosevelt replied that he did not know what Churchill meant by a "divergence between our governments on the Polish negotiations."[149] This only illustrates the stress Roosevelt felt in trying to keep the agreements together given the conflicts between Churchill and Stalin.

Edwin H. Friedman (well-known Rabbi and author) proposes a relational view of stress. He speaks of emotional triangles in which individual symptoms can be a function of one person's relationship to two other people.

Stress occurs in a leader when that leader is caught in a position of responsibility for the relationship of the other two, Friedman explains:

> The position that is most dangerous to a leader's health is what I call the togetherness position. The together position is one in which the leader feels responsible for keeping a system together. The leader in that position is most likely to burn out, dysfunction, or suddenly die at the point when forces pulling in opposite direction have stretched the leader's capacity to hold things together to its breaking point.[150]

Friedman contends that the Churchill/Stalin conflict over Poland after Yalta could have had a very negative effect on Roosevelt's health after the conference. Roosevelt's stress "might well have been escalated by the triangle between Churchill and Stalin in which he (Roosevelt) was trying to hold an alliance together."[151]

Following the president's death, the *New York Times* reported that a week earlier Pope Pius XII had conveyed his blessings and asked that Roosevelt be told that "I am praying for him and especially for his health."[152]

By the end of March, the president had begun to ignore the rest periods recommended. According to Bruenn's notes, Roosevelt's color was poor, and he appeared to be very tired. It would seem that a period of rest would be in order. Eleanor wrote that her husband had become less willing to see people for any length of time.[153] This observation was confirmed by Robert Sherwood (playwright, Pulitzer prize winner, FDR speechwriter), who said, after visiting the president, that he was put in the strange position of carrying the conversation with Roosevelt by himself.[154]

The White House Usher's Diaries show that during March of 1945 the president was keeping an average of 5.1 appointments per day. It is a rebound when compared with March of the previous year when the average was 2.9 appointments per day, but less than several prior years. With the few appointments each day and his wife's observation that he had become less willing to see people, a trip to Warm Springs seemed to be in order.

Audiotape and Newsreel Analysis

Research included reviewing a number of speeches, including Fireside Chats and videotapes (transposed from contemporary newsreels), made in the months prior to and following Roosevelt's inauguration for a fourth term, as well as all public addresses from the start of his presidency. This review is limited by the technical limitations of the newsreel tape, variable weather conditions, and the possibility of editing to enhance the audio tape. It appears that none of these speeches reflects previous or progressive neurological disease.

In his after-dinner speech to the Foreign Policy Association on October 21, 1944, and in his brief remarks to a large Washington crowd greeting him in a heavy rainstorm following the election, his voice was strong and his use of humor typically ironic.

In his final Fireside Chart, January 6, 1945, there is no indication of any stumbling or weariness. He told the nation that he was looking forward to many positive developments in 1945.

However, there is a marked difference between the sound of the president's March 1, 1945, address to a joint session of Congress about Yalta and his appearance on film. He sounded much better than he looked. The speech has been described in negative terms by journalist Jim Bishop, by the president's secretary William Hassett, and by Rosenman. The address lasted fifty-five minutes and was notable for both content and delivery. Roosevelt's initial comment, in which he explained his need to be seated, was given in an off-hand, factual way without complaint or self pity. In its coherence and delivery, the address may even have been somewhat better than the brief fourth inaugural. The president did seem to wander a bit, even digressing into a description of villas in Yalta destroyed by Germans. He spoke under his breath of the need to keep the length of the speech to under one hour and slipped on a few words, but there was no stammering.[155]

The purpose of the address was to help smooth the transition to postwar political, economic, and military realities. He modified the controversial "unconditional surrender" declaration proclaimed at the 1943 Casablanca Conference to apply only to the Nazi leadership and militarists, but not to the average German citizen. He pledged not to destroy Germany after the war, but to ensure that there would be no remilitarization under a temporary government comprised of the four Allies. He emphasized the need for bipartisan support of the nascent United Nations and suggested that the fate of nations such as Greece, Yugoslavia, and Poland was still under consideration. There were moments of wit, hope for the future peace of the world, and for the avoidance of the errors that followed the close of World War I. The speech was interrupted by applause several times and, where appropriate, laughter.

While the audiotape conveys a logical, comprehensive overview of the political-military situation and a speech well organized and delivered, the few moments of newsreel film available present an entirely different perspective. The president appears distracted, fatigued, and somewhat ill-at-ease. The visual component may in large part have contributed to the negative views of this address by those in attendance. It is possible, however, that technical problems exaggerated the president's haggard appearance. The camera crew failed to adjust the lights to accommodate a speaker who was seated rather than standing. Roosevelt later complained that the lights were shining directly in his eyes distracting him and preventing him from seeing the prepared text clearly.

This was the case during the 1944 campaign and afterwards into the spring of 1945—the visual images of Roosevelt played a major role in how those about him perceived his health. Hardly ever were the negative perceptions of his health based on medical knowledge. The close circle of doctors around Roosevelt—Bruenn, McIntire, Lahey, and others—were the only exceptions.

~ 6 ~

"The Day of the Lord, April 12, 1945"

On March 1, 1945, Roosevelt addressed Congress to report on his trip to Yalta and the agreements reached with Churchill and Stalin. The weeks in March were a time when the imminent San Francisco Conference of the United Nations was a major focus of Roosevelt's. Earlier, Roosevelt and Churchill had agreed to Stalin's request to support a proposal giving the Ukrainian Soviet Republic and the White Russian Soviet Republic representation in the Assembly of the United Nations. On March 29, Roosevelt met with Assistant Secretary of State Archibald MacLeish and White House Press Secretary Jonathan Daniels to approve a statement that noted:

> . . . [I]f the United Nations organization agreed to let the Soviet Republics have three votes, the United States would ask for three also.[1]

March continued to be filled for Roosevelt with concerns related to the implementation of the Yalta agreements. In addition to the furor over the Allied agreements for multiple representation in the United Nations Assembly, other Yalta agreements increased the stress being felt by the president. Molotov and Stalin were insisting that the reorganization of the Polish government would essentially be limited to the Lublin (communist) government and not representative of a larger multiparty group as agreed upon at Yalta. In Rumania, the Soviets refused to call a meeting of the Allied Control Commission—shortly a pro-Communist government was appointed by their King.[2] Stalin had informed Roosevelt that he would be sending Ambassador Gromyko instead of the more senior Foreign Minister Molotov to the initial meeting of the United Nations in San Francisco. All seemed to be indications that the Yalta agreements were in grave danger. Historian James McGregor Burns has written "while Roosevelt looked on dismayed and almost helpless, everything seemed to come unhinged."[3]

On March 29, the president cabled Stalin to express his concern that the hopes and expectations resulting from Yalta were being dashed. He sought once more to undergird the unity of the Big Three:[4]

> Having understood each other so well at Yalta I am convinced that the three of us can and will clear away any obstacles which have developed since then.

Even as he attempted to bolster the Russian relationship, there is evidence that he no longer had faith in the ability of the Russians to keep the arrangements made at Yalta.[5] These concerns had begun to affect his health once more. After Yalta, although his appearance was not good, his blood pressure readings were elevated, but stable. Bruenn noted that by the end of March Roosevelt had begun to "look bad." His color was poor and he appeared very tired.[6]

On March 29, the president left Washington for Warm Springs. In his memoirs, McIntire reflected on the state of the president's health as he left for Warm Springs for his last visit. Even after Roosevelt's death, McIntire would still deny that he was critically ill.[7]

> His heart, quite naturally, was our principal concern. . . . Time proved our fears were groundless, for that stout heart of his never failed. . . . As for cerebral hemorrhage, it was and is unpredictable. There are some conditions, of course, in which we think we can predict it, such as extremely high blood pressure and advanced general arteriolosclerosis although there is no certainty. President Roosevelt did not have either of these. His blood pressure was not alarming at any time. . . .

Consequently, McIntire did not go to Warm Springs on this last trip but left the president in Bruenn's care. Bruenn's clinical notes contradict much of McIntire's memories of this time. According to Bruenn, the president's blood pressure ranged from 170/88 to 240/130 mm Hg.

Arriving at Warm Springs on March 30, Roosevelt began to feel its magical effects. His appetite was good, he rested well, and he increased his activities. Bruenn noted that Roosevelt was in excellent spirits taking motor trips each afternoon, and planning to attend a weekend barbecue and minstrel show. His blood pressure fluctuated widely from 170/88 to 240/130. However, those closest to the president knew that nothing had changed. In his diary, Bill Hassett recalls a conversation with Bruenn on the evening of March 30 after they had arrived in Warm Springs. He mentioned to Bruenn: "He [FDR] is slipping away from us and no earthly power can keep him here.

He recalled that he had mentioned something similar to Bruenn when they had last been in Warm Springs in December of 1944. Hassett mentioned that Roosevelt's signature was "feeble," but Bruenn replied that his "condition was not hopeless," and that he could be saved "if he could be shielded from mental strains and emotional influences"—a condition that Hassett believed could not be met.[8]

Part of that stress was surely related to Yalta. However, even there in Warm Springs, the post-Yalta world would continue to intrude. In March, the German commander in Italy met in Zurich with Allen Dulles, the OSS chief in Switzerland to discuss possible German surrender in Italy. When told of the meetings Stalin was highly agitated, believing that this would enable Germany to move additional troops to the Eastern front. There followed a blizzard of messages between Roosevelt and Stalin, in which Stalin expressed his anger that the Allies would take actions that would be detrimental to the Soviets. In spite of Roosevelt's reassurances, two days after he arrived in Warm Springs there was a telegram from Stalin—a telegram which one historian characterized as "one of the most insulting communications ever addressed by one chief of state to another, in which he accused the president of being a liar or a dupe of his aides."[9]

The exchange heated up and two days later on April 5, Roosevelt responded to Stalin:

> Frankly, I cannot avoid a feeling of bitter resentment toward your informers, whoever they are, for such vile misrepresentations of my actions or those of my trusted subordinates.[10]

On April 7, a final message was received from Stalin concerning Poland.

Just recently Roosevelt had been asked by Churchill what should be communicated to Parliament about Poland. On the morning of April 12, 1945, Roosevelt sent Churchill this message:

> I would minimize the general Soviet problem as much as possible because these problems, in one form or another, seem to arise every day and most of them straighten out as in the case of the Bern meeting. We must be firm, however, and our course thus far is correct.[11]

Thursday, April 12, began as any other day at the "Little White House" at Warm Springs. Roosevelt was signing papers, and doing the necessary chores in a room where his cousins were keeping him company (Laura Delano was arranging flowers and Margaret Suckley was crocheting). An artist, Elizabeth Shoumatoff, was working on a portrait while Lucy Mercer Rutherfurd watched. But the day that began as any other, was not to end as others. In the words of his secretary, Hassett:

Today the great and final change. In the quiet beauty of the Georgia spring, like a thief in the night, came the day of the Lord. The immortal spirit no longer supported the failing flesh, and at 3:35 p.m. the President gave up the ghost.[12]

The final day of Roosevelt's life resonates in counterpoint with his first day as president. His first inauguration was held on a cloudy, dim Saturday—March 4, 1933—in the depths of the Great Depression. On that day, his radiant inaugural address dispelled the gloom of the greatest crisis faced by the nation since the Civil War. The pervasive despair and hopelessness of the early 1930s had intensified the economic paralysis that threatened the well-being, indeed the very life of the nation. With Roosevelt's inauguration came new hope that America would endure, revive, and prosper under his courageous leadership. That day marked a turning point for Americans, as did Roosevelt's final day. The day of the president's death was a warm, golden, sunny day across the eastern seaboard. However, with his passing it seemed that the optimism of the nation also departed. Suddenly, it seemed that his optimism, buoyancy, and humor had only been on loan to the American public.[13]

Roosevelt died in Warm Springs, Georgia, at the Little White House where he had gone to rest and recuperate, as had been his custom many times. It had been a working holiday. After much insistence, Sergio Osmena, the president of the Philippine Commonwealth, had gained a short conference with Roosevelt. The meeting ended with a press conference. The conference was routine with no hint of illness or distress. On April 11, Roosevelt edited his Jefferson Day Address, which was to be given April 13 on nationwide radio, following an introduction by Truman from Washington. His last photograph was also taken on that day by the well-known portraitist Elizabeth Shoumatoff, showing Roosevelt looking reasonably well and less haggard than White House photographs of mid to late March. On the evening of April 11, Henry Morgenthau came to dinner at the Little White House, and was shocked at the haggard appearance of the president. Reports of the dinner noted that Roosevelt's hands shook, he knocked over glasses when he poured, and he was constantly confusing names.[14]

April 12 was a Thursday and the staff was anticipating an evening barbecue with musical entertainment provided by Chief Petty Officer Graham Jackson, one of Roosevelt's favorites. Bruenn saw the president at 9:20 A.M., shortly after he had awakened. Even though he seemed to have a pain in his neck he did not ask Bruenn any questions, and Bruenn volunteered no answers. He found the president to be in good spirits. Roosevelt seemed to be rebounding from the fatigue that had led him to take the rest. Afterwards, Bruenn made his telephone report to McIntire—blood pressure was 180/110–120, the "heart action was the same, an enlarged organ limping along with a murmur."[15]

At approximately 1:15 P.M., the president complained of a terrific occipital (the back of the skull) headache, pressed his hand behind his neck and leaned forward. As his body sagged in the chair his cousins held him to keep him from falling. While Margaret Suckley instructed the telephone operator to find Bruenn, Arthur Prettyman, valet, and Irineo Esperancilla, household staff, carried the president to his bedroom.[16] After reporting to his supervisor McIntire earlier that morning, Bruenn had left the Little White House just before lunch to enjoy the warm Georgia sunshine at the pool, only five to ten minutes away. It was there that he received the emergency call to attend the president who had just collapsed.[17]

For Bruenn, the timing of his patient's massive cerebral hemorrhage came as a complete surprise, a "bolt out of the blue."[18] Totally devoted to Roosevelt, yet clearly an objective clinician, Bruenn knew that the president's general outlook was bleak, but was surprised that it happened at this time. The Secret Service agents who had daily contact with Roosevelt were also caught by surprise. James J. Rowley, who later was in charge of the White House Secret Service detail during the Truman and Eisenhower administrations, expressed surprise when told by Mike Reilly, agent in charge, of the president's death.[18] Other agents on night duty had heard Roosevelt giving a persistent, hacking cough for almost an hour in the early morning hours of April 12; then the president apparently went back to sleep. Agent James Griffith said, that in spite of this, he was surprised at Roosevelt's death a few hours later, but not astounded.[19]

In his "Clinical Notes," Bruenn provides a detailed account of the last hours and minutes of Roosevelt's life.[20] When he arrived at the president's cottage, Bruenn found Roosevelt "pale, cold, and sweating profusely." His heart rate was 96/min. The systolic blood pressure was over 300 mm Hg; diastolic pressure was 190 mm Hg. Believing that the president had suffered a massive cerebral hemorrhage, Bruenn immediately called McIntire, who replied that he would call Dr. James Paullin in Atlanta. After an hour and a half, the blood pressure had fallen to 240/120 mm Hg. After two hours, the blood pressure was 210/110 mm Hg; with the heart rate at 96/min. At 3:31 P.M. breathing stopped and heart sounds were not audible. Paullin arrived and administered adrenalin to stimulate the heart, which had no effect. At 3:35 P.M., Bruenn pronounced Roosevelt dead. McIntire's notes indicate that "Both Dr. Paullin and Commander Bruenn were in agreement that the cause of death was a massive intracerebral hemorrhage which, in all probability, had ruptured into the subarachnoid space."[21] Bruenn had not anticipated, nor had he any medical reason to anticipate that Roosevelt's passing would occur on the afternoon of April 12. He remained optimistic and Roosevelt's condition was stable that morning. Roosevelt himself had reassured his wife just a few days before that he was feeling better, and she agreed that he looked better. In the moments before the fatal hemorrhage, Roosevelt's conversations were entirely lucid and appropriate. He had signed papers which were flown to him that morning, commented on the design of a new postage stamp, and kidded good naturedly with his cook. Bruenn was naturally profoundly saddened by this fatal outcome. However, at the moment of death he felt, in a sense, relieved that at least his "patient" and the nation would be spared a long, lingering interval of disability as had occurred in the case of President Woodrow Wilson.[22]

It is important to note that even at the very moment of Roosevelt's collapse, political constraints and the need to ensure control of medical information were dominant. There were at least three physicians in Warm Springs just minutes from the Little White House—internist H. Stewart Raper, physiatrist Robert Bennett, and orthopedist Edwin Irwin. None had treated Roosevelt for anything beside the effects of paralysis, but all were qualified to assist immediately in this emergency.[23] Instead McIntire, after receiving the call from Bruenn relating the seriousness of the situation, called Paullin in Atlanta and asked him to go to Warm Springs.[24] Paullin, with Frank Lahey, a reknowned surgeon, had examined Roosevelt several times in the spring of 1944 at the request of McIntire.

Raper noted that Paullin contacted Homer Swanson, a neurosurgeon in Atlanta, to accompany him to Warm Springs. However, it was not clear to Raper why a neurosurgeon would be consulted—it seemed that there was no medical role for Swanson at this time at the Little White House.[25] Mrs. Raper related that Swanson disclosed his trip to Warm Springs at a dinner party in 1989, although he had not spoken of it earlier.[26] Swanson's name is omitted from contemporary accounts of the day and in later histories. His widow recalls that Paullin had asked Swanson to come to Warm Springs and "to bring his instruments." She, like Raper, was not clear as to why the instruments would be needed or why a neurosurgeon would be consulted.[27]

Other sources of possible emergency medical assistance were hospitals in LaGrange and Columbus, Georgia. Yet the staffs there were not called, nor was the transfer of the president to either location contemplated.

Even the death certificate omitted the major contributory cause, namely, hypertension. Instead, arteriosclerosis is listed by Bruenn (Appendix A).

In Washington, the Senate had concluded its business at 4:56 P.M., recessing until noon of the following day. Truman proceeded to the offices of Speaker Sam Rayburn. Upon arriving he was told by Rayburn that Steve T. Early, press secretary, had called and requested that Truman return the call as soon as possible. Truman was advised to come to the White House from the Capitol as quickly and quietly as possible. He did so without the recently assigned Secret Service escort, other than the agent who was his chauffeur. Arriving at the White House at 5:25 P.M. he was ushered into the presence of Eleanor Roosevelt who informed him that the president had died.[28] Vice President Truman reacted with shock and grief, mirroring the emotions of the nation and the world. Earlier that day he had written a letter to a relative in Missouri saying, "It looks as if I have more to do than ever and less time to do it." He was unable to sign the letter until after he had been sworn in—at which time he added a note at the bottom: "This was dictated before the world fell in on me. . . . But I've talked to you since and you know what a blow it was. . . . But, I must meet it."[29]

Shock and confusion delayed the passing of power. The president died at 3:35 P.M. However, assembling leaders of government, including the principal congressmen and cabinet members, bringing the wife and daughter of the vice president to the White House, locating the chief justice, and finding a Bible on which the oath of office could be administered, delayed matters until about 7 P.M. The International News Service flash, sent immediately after Truman took his oath had been timed at 7:08 P.M.[30] The formalities of presidential succession had taken almost two hours to complete. The photographs of the new president's induction, which appeared on page two of the *New York Times* of Friday, April 13, reflected disbelief in the face of reality and succession.

The new president was described as being in a state of shock by Secretary of State Edward R. Stettinius, Jr. who was responsible for organizing the swearing-in. A young correspondent from North Carolina, David Brinkley, noted Truman to be walking about the East Room in a daze. Tears were seen in his eyes according to *Life* magazine. Truman himself would tell Budget Director Harold G. Smith, the week later, that he had never expected to be there as president.[31]

Fortunately, there were no military or domestic crises requiring presidential attention that day. The war was progressing well. In the Pacific, there were reports of a daylight bombing raid on Tokyo. In Europe the American Ninth Army reached the Elbe River. The dawn of the nuclear era was only two months away. Successful testing would occur in July and atomic bombs were detonated on August 6 (Hiroshima) and August 9 (Nagsaki). Secretary of War Henry Stimson following the first cabinet meeting immediately after the swearing-in gave the new president's first and most urgent briefing. It dealt with the development of the atomic bomb. There is evidence that Roosevelt, had he survived, would have agreed to detonate the bomb, as did President Truman.[32]

Systematic, comprehensive preparation for succession to the presidency did not exist in 1945. It remained lacking until later, when the more complex, nuclear era made contingency planning necessary. The fact that the new president did not know of the atomic bomb development reflected Roosevelt's personality, the manner in which he dealt with his associates, and the extreme secrecy of this project. According to Roosevelt's counsel Samuel Rosenman, he never told his staff any more than he had to tell them. This ensured that he was the only one who would know the whole picture on any subject.[33] Historian Robert Ferrell discusses this characteristic of Roosevelt in his study, *The Dying President: Franklin D. Roosevelt, 1944–1945.* This characteristic was evident in the way Roosevelt handled his medical history with the voters and with his staff. The relationship between Roosevelt and Truman was a reflection of Roosevelt's approach to sharing information. It was also perhaps a reflection of the theory that vice presidents were only peripheral members of the administration, rarely consulted by the president on major issues.

Levels of Grief, Levels of Knowledge

"Shocked," "sudden," "unexpected," "tragic" were words used again and again when Americans heard the news of Roosevelt's death. On the morning of April 13, a full banner headline in the *New York Times* proclaimed "President Roosevelt Is Dead; Truman to Continue Policies; 9th Crosses Elbe, Nears Berlin." Just beneath that banner Americans were informed that "End Comes Suddenly at Warm Springs."[34]

Many prominent government officials, senators, members of congress, clergy, and other well-known persons shared their surprise and sorrow with the *New York Times:*

- Governor Thomas E. Dewey: "With a deep sense of tragedy the nation learns of the loss of Franklin Delano Roosevelt."
- Bishop Manning: "The President's sudden death is a shock beyond words."
- Senator Alben Barkley: "I am too shocked to talk."
- Secretary Harold Ickes: "All of us will help him [Truman] realize the ideals of the great general who has gone down facing the enemy."
- Secretary of State Edward R. Stettinius, Jr.: "A great leader has passed on into history at an hour when he was sorely needed."
- Jesse Jones, former Secretary of Commerce: "We were not prepared for the shock of President Roosevelt's death."
- Henry J. Kaiser: "A sorrowing America and a grateful mankind will hold his memory in reverence."
- Harry Hopkins: "I am so terribly sorry."
- Senator Arthur Vandenberg: ". . . his untimely death."
- Speaker Sam Rayburn: ". . . too shocked and flustered."
- Ambassadors from Italy (Alberto Tarchiani) and Soviet Union (Andrei A. Gromyko): "Shocked."

News of Roosevelt's death affected servicemen such as Captain David Selin, Thirteenth Air Force, Fighter Division, stationed in the Philippines. He and his fellow officers were stunned and remained silent for several minutes. Their first thought, after this entirely unanticipated announcement, was that the war would be prolonged for several additional years. Specifically, the loss of Roosevelt's leadership would undermine the war effort. Four to five days later, when the shock wore off, the servicemen went about their business as usual and realized that his death would not have the effect they initially feared. Captain Selin and other officers did not know who the new president was, nor did they know of the development of the atomic bomb.[35]

Editorial writers around the nation joined the writers and editors of the *New York Times* in expressing shock and sadness at the president's sudden passing. Even the normal conservatism in language most often used by the *New York Times* disappeared on this day.

> ... [I]n that dark when a powerful and ruthless barbarism threatened to overrun the civilization of the Western world. . . . It was his leadership which inspired free men in every part of the world to fight with great hope and courage.[36]

The *New York Times* emphasized the unexpected nature of Roosevelt's death as it proclaimed on its front page in large headlines: "Even His Family Unaware of Condition as Cerebral Stroke Brings Death to Nation's Leader at 63."[37] There is no doubt that Roosevelt's daughter was aware of the general state of his health. However, there was a likelihood that none of the family knew of the seriousness of his condition earlier on this day.

Jim Bishop, author of numerous books, including *The Day FDR Died* relates an incident that occurred on April 12 about 2 P.M. Anna was leaving the White House to go to Bethesda to be with her sick son, a patient in the naval hospital, when McIntire stopped her. He told her that Roosevelt had had "some sort of seizure" and was unconscious. This happened minutes after he had received the information from Bruenn that the president had suffered a massive cerebral hemorrhage. When pressed by Anna, McIntire continued his typical cover-up by responding that he did not believe the seizure would affect Roosevelt's brain. Anna proceeded to try to gain more information from Bruenn, who knew that his superior officer, McIntire, had been minimizing the president's serious health problems for a long time. McIntire did not tell her of the hemorrhage, nor did Bruenn. She proceeded to Bethesda. It is difficult to define any reasonable cause for withholding information from the president's daughter. This was another reflection of McIntire's need to cover up the medical truth even from those who were near and dear to the president.[38]

In explaining how unexpected the death of the president was, Arthur Krock wrote in the *Times's* lead article on April 13:

> How unexpected was President Roosevelt's death despite the obvious physical decline of the last few months is attested by the circumstance that no member of his family was with him at Warm Springs, no high-ranking associate or long-time intimate, and that his personal physician, Rear Admiral Ross McIntire was in Washington, totally unprepared for the news. [39]

McIntire once again refused to be open and honest with the press, emphasizing that there was nothing that would lead them to expect this cerebral hemorrhage. The *Times* recorded McIntire's response to the press:

> The Admiral, in answer to questions from the press today, said "this came out of a clear sky," that no operations had been performed recently on Mr. Roosevelt and that there had never been the slightest indication of cerebral hemorrhage. His optimistic reports of the late President's health, he declared, had been completly justified by the known tests.

It was amazing that he could answer the press in this manner, knowing that only a few days earlier, on April 6, the president's blood pressure had reached 240/130 mm Hg.

Almost obscured in the many pages of biography and photographs printed in the April 13 edition of the *New York Times* was one column buried on page nine entitled "Roosevelt Health Long Under Doubt." Over years and months, the *New York Times* had reported the opinions of McIntire as he continually reassured the public that the president's health was at least acceptable. Even in March of 1944 when McIntire, and his patient Roosevelt, told the press that Roosevelt had acute bronchitis—while not mentioning the finding of cardiac failure—the *New York Times* and other newspapers did not question the medical reports. Now, on the day after his death, the *Times* subtitled this article, "Official Reports of Condition At Times Seemed at Variance with His Appearance." After reporting the fact that correspondents seemed to think that Roosevelt appeared in greater decline than might be attributed to his advancing years, the writers proceeded to explain why the paper did not raise questions at earlier dates:

> Factual accounts of his health, however, could be based on the official statements of Vice Admiral Ross T. McIntire, the President's official physician, and White House Secretaries. When he looked badly, news reports could so say, but when he came home tanned and looking refreshed, they reported that also. [40]

At *Life* magazine, the editors asked their international correspondents about the reactions of the common people. The world's newspapers carried the eulogies of the politicians and statesmen. But Roosevelt had articulated for many the hope of a better world and now the correspondents heard them speak in cities over the world.[41] In Britain, Walter Graebner chronicled the ringing of bells and the quietness of bars. In Russia, Craig Thompson wrote that the people on the street stopped Americans saying, "What a pity." Theodore White wrote from Chungking that one "coolie" walked away muttering, "It was too soon that he died." In Rio de Janeiro, a beggar told Eileen MacKenzie, "Senhora, I am desolated." Around the world people tried to articulate their sadness and loss.

Former Governor Harold Stassen (Minnesota), a member of the UN delegation, met with Roosevelt twice in March 1945 and had seen him on various occasions over the previous years. In an interview he related that he was at a meeting in the editorial offices of the *San Francisco Examiner* when five bells sounded, followed by the news. Stassen had felt that Roosevelt was in fine spirits, alert, and active although tired ("all of us were tired" he noted) just a few weeks before, and was absolutely astonished at the news of Roosevelt's death.[42] Robert Weaver was a senior administrator in the Department of the Interior and the U.S. Housing Authority during the presidential terms of Roosevelt. He was another government staffer who was shocked by the news, although he had been aware of the deterioration in Roosevelt's health. In an interview, he stated his belief that at no time did Roosevelt's health problems endanger the interests of the nation.[43] Most world leaders shared general feelings of complete surprise if not incredulity.

The outpouring of emotion was an intensely felt mixture of shock, grief, and fear. The shock and grief are more easily understood for they are experienced at the death of any loved one. The feeling of fear is more complex. The editorial that best dealt with this topic appeared in *Life*, illustrating the way in which Americans had accepted his leadership:

> He was the one American who knew, or seemed to know, where the world was going. The plans were all in his head. Whether one liked this or that policy or not, one knew that he would do what he would do. It was easier to let him worry for the whole country, (but now Americans) know they will have to take more political responsibility for themselves from now on.[44]

The editorial also saw that mixture of grief and fear around the world, where it was shared by even the common person. "And in their mourning was a whisper of fear. Without him [FDR], was America their friend?"[45]

Roosevelt was the seventh president to die in office, and there were similarities in the public response to each of these deaths (Table 6.1). The public response was often distinguishable from the greatness of the president. A biographer of Warren G. Harding, Francis Russell, observed "an ephemeral sense of national unity in the aftermath of his death," along with "anxiety for a lead-

Table 6.1

Succession to the Presidency

President	Age at death	Successor	Year
William H. Harrison	68	John Tyler	1841
Zachary Taylor	65	Millard Filmore	1850
Abraham Lincoln	56	Andrew Johnson	1865
James Garfield	49	Chester A. Arthur	1881
William McKinley	58	Theodore Roosevelt	1901
Warren G. Harding	57	Calvin Coolidge	1923
Franklin D. Roosevelt	63	Harry S. Truman	1945

Source: Adapted from *Statistical Bulletin,* Metropolitan Life Insurance Company, March 1976, p. 2.

erless future" and even "feelings of guilt." Russell's reason for the feelings of guilt was "The President, political salvator mundi died for us . . . we are unworthy of his sacrifice."[46] As with Roosevelt, the initial response to Harding's death was one of profound sorrow. Even considering only what little was known of Harding's administration prior to his death, before the broad corruption by senior levels of his administration was perceived, there was no factual basis for such hyperbole.

Each of the recently deceased presidents was awarded instant apotheosis, regardless of the attitude of politicians and the public during their lives. Twenty years prior to Roosevelt's death Sigmund Freud discussed this phenomenon:

> Towards the dead person . . . take up a special attitude, something like admiration for one who has accomplished a very difficult task. We suspend criticism, overlook his possible misdoings . . . and set forth in the funeral oration and upon the tombstone only that which is favorable to his memory.[47]

An example is found in the words of Winston Churchill addressing the House of Commons at the time of Roosevelt's death: "In Franklin Roosevelt there died the greatest American friend we have ever known, and the greatest champion of freedom who has ever brought help and comfort from the new world to the old."[48] Inevitably, it takes months for the wound to heal and much longer to evaluate the president's place in history. In the case of Roosevelt, the initial shock and the subsequent mourning process was heightened by radio and newsreel coverage of his death.

Denial and Deception

The widespread and prolonged reactions that greeted the death of Roosevelt were a social and psychological phenomen. His twelve years in office had

107

been marked by the most profound changes in all dimensions of American culture. The Depression and efforts to provide relief, the preparations for war and the global military campaigns, brought pervasive, permanent structural changes to American society. From the theater to the stock market, banks to agriculture, all aspects of American life were profoundly altered by Roosevelt's New Deal. The tangibles of post offices, roads, hospitals, schools, and murals all would endure, as would social security, wage and hour regulation, union rights, rural electrification, the Tennessee Valley Authority, and insured bank accounts. The one constant in all these changes, for both those who deified him and those who demonized him, was Roosevelt himself. The illusion of permanence, of "immortality" was almost inevitable. In other countries, Roosevelt was so identified with these changes and the conduct of the war, that many people relied on him, not on America. Aid such as Lend Lease was often thought of as a personal gift from Roosevelt. After his death, correspondents in Italy wrote of small children dressed in clothes "which Roosevelt sent us from America" and earnestly said their prayers "for their benefactor."[49]

This sense of permanence related to the person of Roosevelt produced two basic approaches to the news of his death—denial and deception. In his study of "Reactions to the Death of President Roosevelt," social scientist Harold Orlansky provides an approach to understanding why many chose denial.[50] Because of the belief that Roosevelt might live forever, this conviction of immortality was the basis for the belief that death was only an intrusion on the natural order of life—such as an "accident."[51] Thus, the first reaction of most persons was to deny the news, or to show a strange inability to accept it. On CBS radio, the announcer (Bob Trout) spoke: "The news is known, but the brain does not quite grasp it," while Mayor LaGuardia of New York was quoted as saying". . . it is extremely difficult for one to realize fully what has happened."[52] To the average American the news was so unexpected and sudden that to deny it was the best possible approach to handling such a momentous event.

Orlansky makes the point that the Roosevelt of infancy, youth, and early adulthood had become hidden in the mists of time. The image of Roosevelt that the public carried was the president in his adult form and that form was fixed in our minds by the "stereotyped, glamorized handling of the publicity media."

> His public words were formal, weighty or, at times, witty, but never the banal little trivia that all men speak in unposed moments. . . . To think of this man whose voice yesterday rang out across the land, lying now stiff and silent in coffined death was a task too great for consciousness.[53]

The common image of a vital man in the office of the president led people to deny the fact of death.

Denial was not just a result of a lack of knowledge. In the last year of his life and his presidency, his tremors, his loss of weight, his pale color, his instances of memory loss, and lack of energy were observed by many of those who had occasion to see him on a regular basis. His failing health seemed to be well recognized by his staff and other government officials. In his diary, William Hassett, secretary to the president, recalls his conversations with Bruenn, indicating that he (Hassett) had felt for more than a year that the president was dying.[54]

Those with the most detailed day-to-day information, his staff and members of the Secret Service, clearly were aware of Roosevelt's physical decline. After his death, *Time* magazine reported that those men who guarded the president were given specific information about his physical condition.

> In January, U.S. secret servicemen were told by their superiors that the President was in serious ill-health . . . about March 1 the Truman bodyguard was told that President Roosevelt might go at any time.[55]

Several Secret Service agents protected Roosevelt.[56] All confirmed that Roosevelt was intellectually intact. Jim Griffith saw the president nearly every day during this last three years, and Floyd Boring saw him daily for a year before his death. Interviewed independently, they agreed that the president's death was shocking because it was not anticipated at the precise time it occurred, but they were not astounded. Another agent, Neal Shannon, confided to Agent Griffith, that Roosevelt's hacking cough heard while both were on duty in the early morning of April 12 was like a "death rattle." However, it was not their responsibility to report their observations to the medical staff.[57]

George Elsey was in the U.S. Navy and assigned to the White House staff from 1942 to 1945, except for seven months overseas in 1944. He observed Roosevelt frequently. On the last day that Roosevelt was at the White House, March 29, 1945, he came into the library where Elsey was working to select some books to take to Warm Springs. Roosevelt was exhausted and did not even recognize Elsey although he knew him well. Elsey rose when the president was wheeled in, but there was no response to his greeting. The president merely glanced around the room, did not select any books, and then motioned to his attendant to wheel him out.[58]

In retrospect, many of the president's intimates have stated that they worried about Roosevelt's impending death, or that they should have seen it coming, but that they brushed those worries aside. Merriman Smith, a correspondent with United Press, recalled being summoned urgently with two of his colleagues from a picnic in preparation to the Little White House. He assumed the reason was that the war in Europe had ended, or that other major military developments had occurred. Only in retrospect, on the funeral train, did he speculate that Roosevelt's medical condition had been perilous for some time in spite of the reassurances of the president's physicians.[59] His emotions had been denying what his eyes had been observing. In an oral history interview for the Harry S. Truman Library in 1971, Judge Marvin Jones recalls his attendance at the fortieth wedding anniversary of President and Mrs. Roosevelt on March 17, 1945. He remembered that Mrs. Roosevelt carried most of the conversation and the president would sometimes "brighten up for a moment and then . . . his head would drop down." Jones was bothered, but did not mention it to anyone at the time. Later, Jones was speaking with Mrs. Robert Jackson, wife of Justice Jackson, and asked her if she remembered.

> She remembered how he looked. And she had reached the same conclusion that I had that he couldn't last long. It was too bad but, of course, I didn't mention it at the time to anybody, and she didn't either, I suppose.[60]

Even world leaders would not easily accept the fact that the man had died from critical medical reasons. Stalin would term his passing "premature," even suspecting foul play and demanded a post-mortem examination.[61]

Harry Easley was a friend of Harry S. Truman since 1932 and was highly involved in the political campaigns in Missouri. Interviewed for the Oral History Project at the Harry S. Truman Library in 1967, he recalled a conversation between the two of them:

> He [Truman] told me that the last time he saw him [FDR] that he had the pallor of death on his face and he knew that if he lived that he would be President before the term was out.[62]

When his memoirs were published, Truman omitted the first paragraph of his original draft, which read:

> Long before it was whispered in Washington circles, I already sensed that Franklin Delano Roosevelt was mortally wounded. During the first few weeks of his fourth administration, I could see what the long years in the Presidency had done to him. These were fateful years. They were years of the killing responsibility of wartime leadership and the burdens of the heroic days of reconstruction from the great depression of the "Thirties."[63]

His first paragraph in the published version modifies and tempers these dire observations and speaks only in general terms of Roosevelt's condition. The second paragraph started provisionally, "The very thought that something was happening to him left me in a cold sweat." In the published version, this was modified by inserting the words, "very much worried," as a replacement for "in a cold sweat."[64]

Thus, even ten years after Roosevelt's death, Truman softened the expression of his feelings. He, like many others, sought to emotionally deny what was happening: "I did not want to think about the possibility of the President being seriously stricken. . . . What rumors there were, luckily, were confined to few circles, or they could have brought on panic and damage."[65]

Daniel Noyes, who assisted Truman with his memoirs, asked him if he remembered saying: "I wake up every morning in a cold sweat dreading that it might be the last day." Truman replied that he had said those words in July 1944 after the convention in Chicago. He added: "I watched him very carefully, and from this point on I was worried to death (in a later draft he deleted the words "to death" and added "very much worried") each time I saw him."[66]

Richard L. Miller, a Truman biographer, notes that in late 1944 Truman kept friends awake long into the night asking for advice and reassurance.[67] Easley was one of those friends and in a conversation Truman said, "He was going to have to depend on his friends. . . . He was talking about people like me, he said." Easley's conclusion was that "he [Truman] knew that he was going to be the President of the United States."[68]

Margaret Truman comments in her biography of her father that although he tried not to think about Roosevelt's health, there were times when he could not avoid the unpleasant truth that the president was continuing to decline. She recalls that Roosevelt looked terribly weary during what some felt was a lifeless and rambling speech to Congress on March 1, 1945. She made the distinction between denial and deception as they related to the president's health issues. To her, Roosevelt was not involved in deception, perhaps only in denial: "The President was deluding himself. . . . No one including President Roosevelt himself was aware of how sick he was." This was the same "patient" that, after being diagnosed with heart failure, hypertension, and severe bronchitis, insisted his only medical problem was one of severe bronchitis. Margaret Truman would assume that Roosevelt was not deliberately deceiving people, but was just denying the truth about his health, for he surely must have been aware that critical physical changes had been taking place in early 1944.

There is no doubt in Margaret Truman's mind however concerning the role of McIntire, whom she wrote "deliberately deceived the president about his true condition."[69] In his diary, Harold Ickes relates a conversation with Roosevelt's son-in-law, John Boettiger, in late February 1945.[70]

... [John] does not think that the President gets proper medical attention. He particularly deprecates Ross McIntire as a physician.

However, there is no evidence that he mentioned this feeling to the president or any of his staff.

As the presidential party was leaving Washington, D.C., for Warm Springs on March 29, 1945, Alonzo Fields, a chief usher, overheard the doorman saying to McIntire, "I know it is none of my business but the President looks bad to me. . . . Don't you think you should have gone with him?" McIntire replied: "I don't think he will need me. . . . I am sure he will come back a different man . . . fit as a fiddle."[71]

Even as McIntire was responding to reporters at the time of Roosevelt's death, he declared that his optimistic reports of the late president's health had been completely justified by the known tests. And in the words of a Navy White House staffer, (Elsey) a feeling of deception was clear:

> McIntire's book [*White House Physician*] I found then gravely deficient, sloppy and full of errors. It was ghostwritten by someone who didn't know the situation very well and I think Ross McIntire did himself and FDR an injustice by painting too rosy a picture.[72]

Much of the "denial" before Roosevelt's death, and the recovered memory later may have been due to the illusion that Roosevelt could be president indefinitely. The first question at his press conference following his reelection in 1944 was, "What are your plans for a fifth term?" Although the reporters and Roosevelt broke up in hearty laughter, there was a serious undertone. It may be that observers reviewed him with a selectivity which excluded the reality of severe physical decline and inevitable death. A wish that the commander-in-chief remain at his post in the midst of a global war may have superseded an awareness of his impending mortality. For those observing him continuously over long periods of time, the deterioration would appear incremental. Anyone seeing him for the first time, or those comparing his photographs of 1941–1942 with photographs taken at Cairo-Teheran and later, would be deeply shocked by the magnitude and speed of the deterioration. Yet, the president beguiled the country, as well as seemingly his physicians, with his history of prior recoveries, his blithe spirit, and political and military imperatives. As Bruenn would repeatedly say with awe, "He could charm the birds out of the trees."[73] Only in retrospect was the likelihood of death absolutely clear.

Intimate Portraits

Unpublished diaries by two of Roosevelt's most intimate companions, cabinet secretary Harold Ickes and close friend Dorothy Suckley, give inside perspectives of the president's health and the extent of the cover-up. Ickes served as secretary of the interior throughout Roosevelt's entire administration. He directed the Public Works Administration for six years, spoke out early and forcefully against Hitler, and encouraged Roosevelt to run for a third term in 1940. Nicknamed "Honest Harold," Ickes gained a reputation as blunt and incorruptible. When it came to Roosevelt's health, however, Ickes's diary presents an unrealistic image indicating he did not perceive the gravity of the president's illness.

The entries in his diary typify the success of the continued cover-up, the misleading diversions plainly contradicted by the President's increasingly haggard appearance, unavailability for discussion of serious issues, and variable ability to focus on major problems. These contemporaneous entries reflect concern. Rumors had replaced reality. Forecasts of Roosevelt's death came from two of the most senior officials yet Ickes was surprised when learning that the President died. "The President came down with an intestinal disturbance that seems to have caused a great deal of trouble; the result has been that for 10 days to 2 weeks he was in bed and practically no one could see him."

This diary entry of May 17, 1941, coincided with significant hemorrhage due to hemorrhoids and resulting in anemia so severe as to require blood transfusions. Even as close as Ickes was to Roosevelt he was unaware of the true nature of the illness, a pattern which continued to the president's death and thereafter. Ickes was clearly disappointed in Roosevelt's leadership at this time and faults him for not more assertively championing support for England in her struggles against Germany.

One year earlier on January 27, 1940, Ickes wrote that Roosevelt let intimates know that he was "very tired and really looking forward to retiring at the end of the year."

Ickes relied heavily for information on McIntire, who served as a major insider and confidant. Ickes quoted him on numerous occasions of relaying Roosevelt's views on senior officials, prospective presidential appointments, who were in favor, and who was not, as well as on policy issues. He was included in the tightest of inner circles and was a regular at Roosevelt's poker playing evenings, and cruises on the presidential yacht. This political role appears to have transcended that of his medical function. Ickes more often refers to him as "Ross" than as "Dr. McIntire."

Ickes's diaries reflected the party line which denied a serious medical condition. "A head cold" was noted on October 24, 1943 and hence Roosevelt is "not accessible." Likewise on January 2, 1944, Ickes was disappointed that he could not meet Roosevelt to discuss important petroleum matters since the president "took to bed with a common cold—no temperature at first." By April 9, three months later, Ickes still had not been able to obtain an appointment, in spite of his sense of urgency. Clearly, Roosevelt's belatedly diagnosed hypertensive congestive heart failure was continuing to limit his appointments. At a cabinet meeting, Roosevelt was tired and strained, ostensibly due to the flu or bronchitis. Ickes gave no hint of anything more ominous and the president appeared to be fully in charge of a "contentious" discussion.

"Ross" covered up the grave nature of the president's illness in the entry of April 29. Ickes was surprised that Roosevelt was at "Bernie Baruch's place (Hobcaw) in South Carolina," but was assured by Ross that he was "much better" with clearing of his lungs, bronchial tubes, and sinuses. There was not the slightest hint given to Roosevelt's favorite and staunch supporter of anything serious, and the tone was misleadingly casual. The entry of May 13 was simply that Roosevelt's health "has been greatly improved," but the appointment was still delayed. Anna Boettiger was candid at least in revealing that her father would just sit, or lie down, without trying to do anything during his "vacation" at Hobcaw, not even working on his stamp collection. Baruch himself advised Ickes that only if the president "takes care of himself" could he go through the coming campaign and be elected.

Finally meeting with Roosevelt, Ickes was plainly disappointed. "The interview was not satisfactory," he wrote on May 20, and he wanted a second meeting. The matters were important, but Ickes with uncharacteristic understatement felt that "He [Roosevelt] did not seem disposed to take a deep interest in any matter." There was a medical comment by the president mainly about Harry Hopkins, but also about "his own physical condition." However, Roosevelt does not disclose the role of his new physician, Bruenn. His name would appear only posthumously in Ickes's diaries with an incorrect first name.

On June 4, Ickes was blunt. While recently appointed Secretary of the Navy James Forrestal felt that the next vice president would succeed to the Oval Office, Ickes tempered the pessimistic view. Roosevelt would "not necessarily" die or become incapacitated, but rather would resign and devote himself exclusively to the world situation in which he "would be the most influential man."

Roosevelt's photos showed him to be a "sitting ghost." There was an advisory to Ickes from Thomas Corcoran, one of the original New Dealers, that Roosevelt's health was not good. Ickes was "disturbed," he wrote on August 6. Five days later he heard that his health had "taken a turn for the worse." Sam Rosenman, presidential counsel and speech writer, had just flown back with reassuring words that Roosevelt "was in excellent health." The "party line" continued. The rationalization was that the one bad photograph of July 20 was distributed to the public and not the five or six others in which he looked well. The president had been photographed on July 20 while re-reading his acceptance speech broadcast from San Diego to the convention in Chicago. The single photograph selected showed him with his mouth open, eyes glassy, haggard, and weary.

Ickes confirmed that Truman had *not* wanted the vice presidential nomination, but had been pressured by the "city bosses" who had in turn pressured Roosevelt. The Bremerton speech played to mixed reviews. Some were concerned that Roosevelt "was not a well man," Ickes wrote on August 10, or at least that he had had "one cocktail too many."

One month later, (September 24) Ickes concluded that Roosevelt should be good for four more years "unless something should strike him pretty hard." At lunch, the president was keen, alert, but very thin with dark patches under his eyes attributed to the wear and tear of the past eleven and a half years.

Drew Pearson, the columnist and radio commentator, conveyed that there was a "good deal of apprehension about the President's health" in the country. When Ickes confronted McIntire, he denied "the heart story," thus continuing the blatant cover-up. However, Ickes wrote on October 6 that McIntire advised the president to lose weight, thereby reducing the "strain" on his heart. He denied the rumors of intestinal cancer or the need to operate on the "prostate gland."

Even after the election, rumors of the need for a "serious operation" abounded. The president himself had "run some risks" in campaigning in bad weather, Ickes noted on November 16, but had needed to dispel the rumors beyond McIntire's official denials. On February 24, 1945, just a month after Roosevelt's fourth inauguration, Ickes wrote that "Jimmy Byrnes has been spreading rumors about the President's health," which Ickes felt highly improper. Byrnes would resign as director of the Office of War Mobilization a few weeks later. Furthermore, one of Ickes's sources deprecated McIntire as a physician.

Ickes's frankest concern appeared shortly before Roosevelt's death. He warned Anna Boettiger that her father's health continued to be of concern to the country, that he "did not seem to understand at times what people were saying to him and he seemed to forget quickly." Drew Pearson again "expresses concern" about the president's health.

"The President's death was entirely unexpected." Ickes wrote on April 28. "I saw Dr. McIntire as usual that morning and he knew nothing to disturb him." Ickes then described the circumstances of the cerebral hemorrhage, and asserted that "it was the best possible way for him to go." Howard Bruenn's name appeared for the first time. His first name was garbled as "Harold."

Meeting McIntire for lunch, four months later, Ickes noted the vice admiral's remark "the President's death had surprised him."[74] "The bolt from the blue" line that McIntire had offered the press on April 12 and would

115

detail in his book *White House Physician*, published in 1946, was restated. Further misleading is his rationalization, "I have wondered if the President's heart had given way under the great pressure of the load he was carrying," but that there was no way of predicting Roosevelt's death. Not a word of the hypertension, its severity, duration, or associated congestive heart failure was mentioned by McIntire.[75]

Dorothy Suckley, a distant cousin and close companion, provides fascinating new insights into Roosevelt's own perceptions of his declining health. In her diary, recently published in *Closest Companion*, edited by Geoffrey Ward, she revealed that the president was well aware of his blood pressure problem. He commented to her that his diastolic and systolic pressure levels were not working properly in unison and that his diurnal cycle was the opposite of what would normally occur. Specifically, he was aware that his readings were higher in the morning and lower later in the day (although specific values recorded during his stay at the Baruch estate in April and May 1944 do not reflect this). In May 1944 he questioned hypothetically whether or not he would be able to carry on for another four years and offered an alternative presidential candidate, Henry J. Kaiser, the industrialist.

Several days before his death, Roosevelt spoke with his companions, including Laura Delano, at Warm Springs, of retiring in 1946, thus suggesting that he himself did not believe that he would be able to carry on for the entire term. Laura worried that he was killing himself by slow degrees and might not be fulfilling his job. Delano also commented to Suckley, on April 7 that Roosevelt was working too long and that his "b-p" was a little higher.

On April 8, Suckley added that he was "slowly improving each day . . . is happier" and on April 9 "looks splendidly." Indeed, just before his death "his color was good and he looked smiling and happy and ready for anything."

Suckley's concerns about Roosevelt's health were paramount starting in the autumn of 1943 with many symptoms, such as fatigue and headache, ascribed to the "flu." By March 20, 1944 her worry escalated with good reason. Roosevelt had not bounced back from the "flu" of December. He needed "a complete rest," and was having "a miserable day." On March 26 she reported Roosevelt confiding that they will be "experimenting" on him again at the Bethesda Naval Hospital. The president's initial comment was that they found "nothing drastically wrong, but one sinus clogged up." By April 4 he "sounds as though he were depressed and worried too," although he acknowledged only being "bored," feeling tired, and having pneumonia (even that diagnosis was denied to the press). By April 8 he seemed to have rebounded, being more cheerful and full of confidence. The recovery was uneven and in spite of a prolonged vacation, she wrote on May 22, 1944, Roosevelt was worried, tired, with color "not good."

As an incidental point, Roosevelt had frequent nightmares and would recall them with clarity and alarm the next morning. Suckley wondered why
Secret Service agents did not enter his bedroom when he cried out, but they
were apparently accustomed to these episodes. Roosevelt's depression in the
summer of 1943 was associated with being dangerously tired, exhausted,
and in need of rest and sleep. By March 25, 1945, the president "looks terribly bad—so tired . . . every word seems to be an effort. How much longer
can he keep going this way."[76]

This volume reveals that Roosevelt clearly knew he was hypertensive and
was aware that he might not survive the fourth term. His relationship with
Suckley was so close that he could discuss these matters openly with her,
and apparently no one else. She herself was very sensitive about health matters and had her own ideas about appropriate therapy. The descriptions of
Roosevelt's depression and nightmares are remarkable since their occurrence
have generally been denied.

The diaries of Ickes and Suckley show different levels of knowledge regarding Roosevelt's health and reveal that the cover-up was complete. Despite his intimacy with the president, Ickes neither recognized nor inquired
about the seriousness of his illness. Although he saw Roosevelt with some
regularity and commented on his worsening appearance, he did not seem to
grasp that the president was mortally ill. Suckley, on the other hand, seemed
far more aware of the president's declining health and suggested that he was
too. Taken together, the Ickes and Suckley diaries present an inside portrait
of Roosevelt's condition and, although different, suggest how smoothly the
cover-up went.

~ 7 ~

Lessons for
the Twenty-First Century

The Medical Legacy of Franklin D. Roosevelt

More than a half century has passed since the death of Franklin D. Roosevelt. The military and political decisions of his time have profoundly impacted current affairs and will do so for generations to come. During Roosevelt's administrations, the foundation for a vibrant, just economy had been laid and a new world order dedicated to achieving and maintaining peace was established so firmly that it would withstand future crises and challenges. His successors have stood in his tall shadow. His presidency set the standard for the measurement of their abilities and achievements.

Roosevelt felt that all life is a battle. We have been fortified by the recollection of his own deeply personal struggle with paralysis. Even at the midpoint of the twentieth century, it had become clear that the cultural memory of Roosevelt and the events of his time had made an indelible mark on our public consciousness, and that his example would sustain future generations. President Bill Clinton remarked on the power of Roosevelt's memory at the dedication of the Roosevelt Memorial:[1]

> [Roosevelt] said over and over again in different ways that we had only to fear fear itself. We did not have to be afraid of pain or adversity or failure, for all those could be overcome. He knew that, of course, for that is exactly what he did. And with his faith and the power of his example we did conquer them all—depression, war, and doubt. . . .

The mysterious cycles in human events described by Roosevelt in his speeches would recur and new generations would have their own rendezvous with destiny. Yet, his unique contributions born of his own faith, his vision, and his fortitude would offer a bright beacon of hope and achievement.

Roosevelt remains an enigmatic figure, enshrouded in clouds of rumor and exaggeration despite a multitude of attempts to analyze his life, his career, and the challenges posed by his paralysis and other health problems. His medical history illustrates a dilemma that arose from a confluence of global forces and the presence of a seemingly indispensable wartime leader. The year 1944 was unique in the annals of the presidency, a time when an extraordinary personality and years of achievement became intertwined with a perilous medical condition. In his terms prior to 1944 Roosevelt had redefined the presidency in a profound, unparalleled, and enduring way. His dramatic use of the radio, extensive travels through the United States, Latin America, and overseas during World War II in pursuit of military and political goals established his worldwide leadership status.

The effect of New Deal policies, combined with his wartime leadership, made his candidacy in 1944 compelling even in the face of severe, unremitting ill health, and what should have been recognized as a limited life expectancy. He had achieved celebrity status in his lifetime, but this was part of the problem and explains why, even now, his medical issues remain unresolved. A terminally ill president, rationalizing his unique qualifications, surrounded by loyal staff, cabinet members and physicians, enveloped in wartime secrecy, struggled to continue in office. Faith in his invincibility dwarfed reason. The public was misled and the patient incompletely informed, probably in part at his own insistence. This scenario could happen again, with consequences that would be far worse than those related to Roosevelt's last year in the White House.

The preceding chapters have illustrated the failure of medicine in the context of extraordinary celebrity and national need. There was ignorance, denial, a deliberate campaign of misinformation, and a level of medical treatment below what would have been provided another citizen. The medical history of Roosevelt offers paradoxes, enigmas, and conflicts which parallel, and are interwoven, with the larger tapestry of his presidential career.

Medical judgment and advice, which would be routinely offered to virtually any other patient, even high-ranking military and civilian officers, were not provided to Roosevelt because "he was the President." After his examination of Roosevelt on March 28, 1944, Bruenn had recommended that "the patient should be put to bed for 1 to 2 weeks with nursing care." He records that his recommendations, including the one prescribing bed rest, were rejected "because of the exigencies and demands on the

President."[2] Bruenn further acknowledges that any other 62-year-old hypertensive patient showing the level of fatigue, pallor, tinge of cyanosis and other findings of severe congestive heart failure exhibited by Roosevelt on physical examination would have been hospitalized for further study and therapy.[3]

Normally, target organs would have been monitored—especially the heart. This was not done. Nor were laboratory tests, X-rays, EKGs, or other studies required by his symptoms systematically performed in the several years interval prior to Bruenn's examination.[4]

If a "conspiracy of silence" abounded, its leader was the patient. Even a poorly informed patient can lead a conspiracy of silence. When there was said to be not even a superficial inquiry by Roosevelt, no physician or informed layman felt the need to level with him regarding his diagnosis and prognosis. Delayed recognition of the significance of his hypertension, noted as far back as 1937, is inexplicable. The congestive heart failure, which was unmistakable in late March 1944, was apparently overlooked for several prior weeks or even months. The only diagnosed illness that Roosevelt and McIntire mentioned was bronchitis. Treatment of both conditions, congestive heart failure and hypertension, was delayed, and the grave prognosis was not communicated to the patient's family, designated successor, or other associates.

Roosevelt's medical history, while in the office of the presidency, raises serious questions about the role of the White House physician, and the accountability of that person as well as the quality of care provided.[4] What is the appropriate role for a physician to the president, especially in times of crisis? Roosevelt's attending physicians were all military officers who related to the patient as their commander-in-chief.[5] On March 31, 1944, the group met again to consult on the progress of treatment. In addition, two civilian consultants to the Navy were also present—Dr. James Paullin and Dr. Frank Lahey. However, after their initial participation, their roles appear to have been limited. Official reassurances about the president's health were always issued by McIntire and Early, the president's press secretary. These official assurances represent the primacy of political and military considerations over the physician's medical knowledge and responsibility to the patient and his family. Even if the compromises reached were thought to be reasonable, the outcome raises basic questions about the accountability of the medical staff. Deliberate deception is a recognized wartime strategy, but whether it can be extended to presidential health issues, particularly during a campaign for reelection, is a critical issue with which the voting public should be concerned.

The issue of the presidential physician's role provokes many specific questions. Should there be regular screening of the president by an objective panel of physicians? What are the parameters of the public's right to know?

What do those people surrounding the president need to know. How might such medical judgments affect a transfer of power under our constitution?

The Need for Medical Screening

The physicians surrounding Roosevelt shared much of the reverence, even the idolatry, of the public. A Roosevelt biographer characterizes McIntire as a doctor who "viewed his patient as superhuman, without flaw, capable of anything."[6] Their clinical judgments became distorted, subordinated to the political will, and the national mandate to win the war. Certainly the political and military situations in 1944 created an anomaly, making hazardous any extrapolation to subsequent elections. However, the scenario that played out across the nation and the world sends a clear warning for the future. Events evolved favorably in 1944–1945, but may not always in the future. Not every outcome of an ongoing health crisis in the White House may be as successful as Truman's succession to the presidency after the death of Roosevelt.

Presidential illness has been blamed for failures of leadership in the past. The most clear-cut example of leadership failure in the White House was Woodrow Wilson's stroke in October 1919, which left the ship of state adrift until the inauguration of his successor Warren G. Harding in March 1921. Routine executive functions were delayed and decisions deferred. The vacuum was filled, without constitutional or other legal sanctions, by Mrs. Wilson and Admiral Cary Grayson, the president's physician. Such a situation was appalling, but not as dangerous as in the nuclear era.

The medical histories of Roosevelt and Wilson should stimulate discussion of possible reforms. Some feel there is a need for regular and periodic independent medical examination of the president, and of presidential and vice presidential candidates, by nonpartisan, nongovernmental physicians. The regularity of the examinations is crucial. As illustrated in the case of Roosevelt, a panel of experts brought in on an emergency may have neither detailed knowledge of the patient nor the independence to perform objectively.

The right of the electorate to receive full, relevant disclosure from a presumably neutral group of physicians would seem to be requisite in the nuclear era, an epoch initiated by Roosevelt. Many medical and lay historians urge such examination and disclosure. The medical parameters and procedural ground rules, however, are vague and the role of mental health testing especially ambiguous.[7]

The rigors of the long political campaign in numerous primaries are themselves considered to be an almost Darwinian screening process. By definition, the campaigns exclude the less physically and emotionally fit. Such selective forces, however, cannot substitute for careful medical evaluation, especially for detection of asymptomatic or minimally symptomatic conditions. There is a tension created by public fear of illness and by political circumstances of the moment that make objective distinction between relevant and irrelevant medical data difficult, if not done by carefully designed criteria and an independent body of examiners. Consider some examples.

A national or international crisis occurring during a campaign works to the advantage of the incumbent since he appears more "presidential," above the campaign issues and struggle, and less partisan than in calmer times. In 1956, Dwight D. Eisenhower faced a reelection campaign that would be complicated by his medical history. On September 23, 1955, he had suffered a heart attack after a golf match and was effectively in a state of convalescence until November 22, 1955 when he held his first staff meeting at Camp David.[8] After the decision to run for reelection was made in the spring of 1956, Eisenhower required surgery for ileitis (Crohn's disease) on June 9, and did not begin even an abbreviated schedule of office work until mid-July.[9]

The needs of the presidential campaign and Eisenhower's health in the summer of 1956 are reminiscent of Roosevelt's campaign and health problems in the fall of 1944. Roosevelt's advisers had argued that he must be seen by the voters and the result was the much publicized tour of New York City. In August of 1956, Eisenhower's advisers argued that he would have to behave in a similar manner—motorcades, open cars, cheering crowds.

His questionable health status was raised as a major issue by his opponent for the presidency, Governor Adlai Stevenson, who suggested that Eisenhower would probably not survive a second term. The *New York Times,* on November 6, 1956, reported on page one about Stevenson's election eve speech in which he raised the "specter" of a Nixon succession to the presidency.

> . . . [A] Republican victory tomorrow would mean that Richard Nixon would probably be President of this country within the next four years.[10]

Little advantage was gained by involving the health issue and it possibly may even have backfired against Stevenson.

During October, two international crises provided the opportunity for Eisenhower to appear "presidential" and above the campaign issues of health problems. On October 23, antigovernment demonstrations began in Budapest as revolutionaries sought liberation of their country from Soviet domination. Although Eisenhower did not authorize direct military aid, the United States "mounted a massive propaganda attack in the United Nations and elsewhere upon Soviet actions."[11] Also in October, Israeli armed forces invaded the Gaza strip and the Sinai peninsula. Anglo-French paratroopers sought to respond in order to control the Suez Canal. Eisenhower forced a cease-fire and a withdrawal of British, French, and Israeli troops was scheduled for November 5, the day before the election.

The fear of a boomerang effect (similar to that received by Governor Stevenson in 1956) limited Governor Thomas E. Dewey. He spoke vaguely of "tired, old men" in his 1944 campaign against Roosevelt. The issue was whether the interests of the United States were advanced more by an experienced but ailing commander-in-chief in the midst of a global conflict, than by a healthy opponent with only county and statewide responsibility and who was not conversant with military or foreign affairs. The late Herbert Brownell, campaign manager for Dewey and subsequently attorney general in the Eisenhower administration, offered his insights when interviewed. Some in the campaign wanted to emphasize Roosevelt's presumed illness. Others, including Brownell, were more cautious. They were concerned that if their forecast was in error, and Roosevelt's health was adequate, his gaunt appearance, notwithstanding, the boomerang effect against the Republicans would be overwhelming and enduring. Reticence in discussion of illness, one's own, or that of others, was expected in that era. Hence, the Republicans had a dilemma in 1944 and chose the safer course. Some of the campaign staff quietly left over this issue, according to Brownell.[12]

In an era of escalating negative campaigning, candidates, especially relatively unknown challengers, would run the risk of being unfairly stigmatized for medical conditions which have no relevance to their fitness for office. The election process for presidents is subjective based on such imponderables as culture, symbols, spiritual values, and communications on a highly personal, emotional basis. The process cannot be defined in objective, quantitative, or scientific, much less medical, terms.[13] Disease when associated with a candidate may conjure weakness, and worse, acts of Divine Providence, and the punishment of sins.

An independent medical screening authority would have the responsibility for providing relevant information, which the electorate could use as one factor in evaluating a presidential candidate. Disclosure raises significant problems, however. Physicians may have honest, informed differences regarding the significance of abnormalities on physical examination, EKGs, laboratory testing, X-rays, and other imaging studies. The possibility of Eisenhower sustaining rupture of the left ventricle or aneurysm was emphasized by some of his doctors, but others doubted this outcome. [14] The course of hypertension, even severe and unremitting as was Roosevelt's, is difficult to forecast for an individual patient although it escalates risks for cerebrovascular accidents (strokes), myocardial and other infarctions, and kidney failure.

As new medical testing is introduced, such as positron emission tomography, new standards of screening candidates will evolve. Indeed, a candidate may score points by voluntarily submitting to such tests if rivals decline. Interpretation of such newer studies will be even more speculative than in those of classic, well-known tests. In spite of apparent excellent health initially, the stress of the presidency and inevitable effects of the passing of time may well change the medical picture drastically.

What frequency of subsequent testing would be appropriate for the incumbent? Should testing and disclosure be required of candidates for vice president, speaker of the House of Representatives, and the president pro tem of the Senate, who are in the immediate line of succession? The problems cited would be multiplied and the electorate would be awash in an avalanche of medical detail which would cloud the pertinent issues of intellect, experience, ideology, and other characteristics leading to voter preference or rejection.

For the reasons discussed above, guidelines for disclosure would require meticulous drafting and execution to avoid contaminating the election process and the course of a president's administration. If the public truly has a "right to know" about a person's medical history, then all candidates for president and vice president, as well as others in the chain of succession, should be required to submit to independent objective examination with agreed-to guidelines frequently revised to reflect progress in medical practice. The likelihood of intervals of incapacity, pain, surgery, sensory impairment, side effects of therapy, and immediate and long-term prognosis, would require concise but complete, nonpartisan exposition which could be readily understood by a lay public. Clearly written protocols reflecting the highest ethical standards are needed to protect the patient's privacy rights and to ensure comprehensive, accurate reports, an especially challenging goal in the environment of a highly competitive presidential campaign. This approach should ensure that the public would receive needed understandable information, other than selective, anecdotal, fragmentary, and misleading data.[15]

The procedural innovation of medical screening is justified because use of nuclear weapons has been entrusted solely to presidential discretion, and because presidents, as commanders-in-chief, have the authority in emergency situations to send troops into harms way with little or no role for the Congress initially. The nightmare scenario of a disabled president, such as Woodrow Wilson, confronted with potentially cosmic decision-making responsibilities to assume in national crises, like the Cuban missile crisis, is fortunately improbable in the post–Cold War era. However, international tensions continue and many smaller nations, prone to internal political instability, have nuclear capability. As the public's perception of America's vulnerability to nuclear attack has dimmed, the stimulus to develop a screening and disclosure protocol has dulled. Advocacy by physicians and political scientists alone is unlikely to create a compelling environment for change. However, this may change in light of the terrorist attacks.

More attention is being focused on the Twenty-fifth Amendment, which deals with sitting presidents, the potential incapacity of a president, and rules for the transfer of power. There are also abundant ambiguities and problems with the amendment, when it is viewed from the perspective of Roosevelt's medical history.

Roosevelt's Health and the Twenty-fifth Amendment

The Twenty-fifth Amendment to the Constitution was proposed on July 6, 1965 and declared ratified on February 10, 1967. This was the fourth time that Congress had sought to clarify the problems of presidential succession. On February 21, 1792, the first Presidential Succession Act passed the House of Representatives (31–24) after passing the Senate (27–24). The act provided that in case of the removal, death, resignation, or disability of both president and vice president, the President pro tempore of the Senate would succeed; if there were no Senate president, then the Speaker of the House. It was the desire of Thomas Jefferson to have the secretary of state next in line, but this was defeated.[16]

Not until 1886 did Congress seek to clarify the vagueness of the original act of 1792. On January 19, 1886, a new Presidential Succession Act was ratified. It provided that in the event of removal, death, resignation, or inability of both president and vice president, the heads of the executive departments, in order of the creation of their offices (starting with state and treasury), should succeed to the duties of the office of the President.[17]

This was the law in effect at the time of Roosevelt's death. On the morning of April 13, a short article appeared in the *New York Times* with the title "Stettinius Heads List in Line of Succession."

> Edward R. Stettinius, Jr., as Secretary of State, would take office as President in the event of the death of President Truman under the law of Presidential succession. As Secretary of the Treasury, Henry Morgenthau, Jr. is next in line, followed by Secretary Henry L. Stimson as Secretary of War. Senator Kenneth McKellar of Tennessee will become president of the Senate, in the light of his election last January 6 as president pro tempore.[18]

In 1947, at President Truman's urging a new Presidential Succession Act was passed. The Speaker of the House and President pro tempore of the Senate were next in line after the president and vice president.

As the United States and its former ally the Soviet Union moved toward the mid-point of the twentieth century, the problem of presidential succession continued to concern the president. After a heart attack in September 1955, Eisenhower's concern for orderly succession grew and he requested Attorney General Brownell to lead a team of experts in preparing an amendment on succession for submission to Congress. After subsequent illnesses, ileitis surgery (June 1956) and a stroke (November 1957), Eisenhower drafted a letter to Vice President Richard Nixon outlining his understanding of the terms of succession. This practice has been continued in all succeeding administrations with the contents not revealed to the public.

Finally, in the tenure of Lyndon B. Johnson, the Twenty-fifth Amendment to the Constitution was passed in 1967.

An Amendment to the Constitution of the United States of America Article XXV
(Proposed July 6, 1965; ratified February 10, 1967)

Section 1: In case of the removal of the President from office or of his death or resignation, the Vice President shall become President.

Section 2: Whenever there is a vacancy in the office of the Vice President, the President shall nominate a Vice President who shall take office upon confirmation by a majority vote of both Houses of Congress.

Section 3: Whenever the President transmits to the President pro tempore of the Senate and the Speaker of the House of Representatives his written declaration that he is unable to discharge the powers and duties of his office, and until he transmits to them a written declaration to the contrary, such powers and duties shall be discharged by the Vice President as Acting President.

Section 4: Whenever the Vice President and a majority of either the principal officers of the executive departments or such other body as Congress may by law provide, transmit to the President pro tempore of the Senate and the Speaker of the House of Representatives their written declaration that the President is unable to discharge the powers and duties of his office, the Vice President shall immediately assume the powers and duties of the office as Acting President

Thereafter, when the President transmits to the President pro tempore of the Senate and the Speaker of the House of Representatives his written declaration that no inability exists, he shall resume the powers and duties of office unless the Vice President and a majority of either the principal officers of the executive department or of such other body as Congress may by law provide, transmit within four days to the President pro tempore of the Senate and the Speaker of the House of Representa-

---

tives their written declaration that the President is unable to discharge the powers and duties of his office. Thereupon Congress shall decide the issue, assembling within forty-eight hours for that purpose if not in session. If the Congress, within twenty one days after receipt of the latter written declaration, or, if Congress is not in session, within twenty-one days after Congress is required to assemble, determines by two-thirds vote of both Houses that the President is unable to discharge the powers and duties of his office, the Vice President shall continue to discharge the same as Acting President; otherwise, the President shall resume the powers and duties of his office.

Approximately six years later, the amendment was used for the first time; facing a charge of federal income tax evasion, Vice President Spiro Agnew resigned his office on October 10, 1973. Acting upon the procedures (Section 2) of the Twenty-fifth Amendment, on October 12 President Richard M. Nixon nominated House Minority Leader Gerald R. Ford to succeed Agnew. Ford was confirmed on November 27 by the Senate and on December 6 by the House of Representative, taking office the same day. With Nixon's resignation on August 8, 1974, had earlier succession procedures been operative, hypothetically, the Democratic speaker of the House would have been next in line for the presidency, instead of Ford. That is, there was no mechanism to fill a vice presidential vacancy until the Twenty-fifth Amendment was enacted. Section 2 was again used by President Ford to nominate Governor Nelson A. Rockefeller of New York to succeed him as vice president. Sections 3 and 4 have never been invoked.

The Twenty-fifth Amendment may not solve the problems related to a situation in which an incumbent president is unable to discharge his powers and duties. Suppose a president does not, or can not, perceive the extent of his own physical or mental disability? Even if he does, but denies its impact on his capacity to meet his responsibilities, what mechanism is there to resolve the issue? Section 3 of the amendment does not provide for independent medical review of the president's health, nor is there a mechanism to initiate such a review. Roosevelt obviously knew that he was ill. However, he apparently did not entertain thoughts that this might interfere with his capacity to deal with Churchill and Stalin. To the contrary, he gave every indication that he felt he could meet his responsibilities. The role of the media has been substantially enlarged since Roosevelt's presidency, but the protective mechanisms shielding any president remain formidable, even in peacetime.

An additional difficulty related to the president's ability to discharge his duties is what may be referred to as an "inherent conflict of interest." The officials most likely to observe the deterioration of a president are his own appointees whose careers generally depend on his incumbency and who can be summarily dismissed by the president. They may be the only persons who would perceive the onset of irrational behavior, changes in level of consciousness, or episodic physical impairments. They have no rational recourse to resolve their dilemma. Even McIntire alluded to the problem of the president's entourage:

> I had not been in the White House for any length of time before I discovered that I did not have just one patient but a family. Not a small one either, for aside from the secretariat and the workers in the executive offices, there were the Secret Service men, the White House police, the ushers, the domestic help, and so on.[19]

Roosevelt's staff had to assume that McIntire had the medical situation under control. Only when the deterioration reached an extreme state, reflecting continued unremitting decline, did the family and staff insist on a "head-to-toe" examination in March of 1944. If questions did arise related to the disability of the president to discharge his duties, could a physician and/or staffer so close to the president give an objective evaluation without considering his or her own future?

Section 3 fails to define the criteria for inability to "discharge the powers and duties of the office." Neither the severity, nor likely duration, of such disability is considered. The worst case scenario is one in which the inability is mental alone, or combined with physical illness; the very nature of the illness may preclude self-recognition of its severity. That Roosevelt was physically ill in his last year in office is accepted by almost all historians and, to widely varying degrees, those who had firsthand knowledge. Several also observed what they express as mental impairment. At Yalta, Churchill's physician, Lord Moran, commented on Roosevelt's health:

> ... [H]e sat looking straight ahead with his mouth open, as if he were not taking things in. ... He has all the symptoms of hardening of the arteries of the brain in an advanced stage. ... [20]

Ambassador William Bullitt noted that frequently Roosevelt "had difficulty in formulating his thoughts, and greater difficulty in expressing them consecutively."[21] The Roosevelt described by these two observers would not have had the ability to recognize the severity of his illness. Dr. Robert Joynt, writing in the *Journal of the American Medical Association*, suggests that the great problem with the disability procedures of Section 4 of the Twenty-fifth Amendment relate to dementia or depression.

> One of the hallmarks of early dementia or depression is the loss of insight. Thus, affected persons often do not recognize their own problems with mood,

memory, and cognition, and they may angrily object if these defects are noted by others. Even with all our technological advances, there is no diagnostic test or biologic marker for a definitive diagnosis . . . it may also be difficult to recognize major mood alterations in a person constantly beset by stress and confrontation.[22]

Arthur S. Link, the late professor of history at Princeton University, and Dr. James Toole, neurologist at Bowman Gray School of Medicine, in their study on presidential disability suggested that Woodrow Wilson's cognition and behavior were so affected by his stroke that he was unable to compromise with his political opponents thus preventing ratification of the Treaty of Versailles, and preventing the United States from being a member of the League of Nations.[23]

Section 4 of the Twenty-fifth Amendment potentially provides a prescription for disaster. An alienated vice president and cabinet could, by a simple majority, initiate a declaration of presidential disability. President Harry S. Truman, in 1957, advocated that disability as related to the president should be decided by a vote of Congress

> . . . [W]hen a president is stricken with an illness . . . there should come into being a Committee of Seven composed of representatives of the three branches of the Government. . . . This committee would select a board of leading medical authorities drawn from top medical schools of the Nation. . . . This board would then make the necessary examinations, presenting their findings to the Committee of Seven. Should the finding of the medical board indicate that the President is unable to perform his duties and that he is, in fact, truly incapacitated . . . then the Committee would inform the congress. Congress would then have the right to act and by a 2/3 vote of the full membership declare the Vice President as President.[24]

The criteria, either medical or psychiatric, are not stated. The magnitude, duration, and prognoses of disorder are unspecified. None of the officials are likely to be physicians and even if one or two were, they would not be the president's own physician. Again, there is no independent panel of examining physicians. The most productive approach would be to have such a group composed of clinicians in current active practice with no governmental or partisan affiliations, nor other impediments to objectivity, and who are acceptable to the "patient" and his family.[25] This approach was supported by President Jimmy Carter in an article written for the *Journal of the American Medical Association* entitled "Presidential Disability and the Twenty-fifth Amendment.

> The great weakness of the Twenty-fifth Amendment is its provision for determining disability in the event that the president is unable or unwilling to certify to impairment or disability. . . . At this time the determination is made by the

president's personal physicians who must try to balance patient confidentiality and personal interest vis-à-vis the nation's interest. We must find a better way. This might be by creating a nonpartisan group of expert representatives of the medical community who are not directly involved in the care of the president.[26]

A disabled president could have his return to the Oval Office blocked by the same nonmedical, entirely political group comprised of the majority of the Cabinet and the vice president. Such a group could notify the President pro tempore of the Senate and the speaker of the House of their opinion that the president remains disabled. This must be done within four days, a requirement which may pose a practical limitation on their ability to respond to the president's self-evaluation of recovery. The president's return is somewhat protected if a difference arises regarding his capacity, because his opponents must muster a two-thirds vote of both Houses to preclude the president's return. If a two-thirds majority is obtained, what happens to subsequent efforts of the president to return? As before, there are no medical criteria to determine resolution of the disability, or its continuation. Only government officials have the responsibility and authority to decide the question.

The twenty-one day interval allowed for congressional debate and decision may prove catastrophic if national crises or foreign threats emerge, or if they existed before. The prolonged lack of clear "title" to the office, the primacy of political over medical conditions would cause national vulnerability both domestic and foreign. The role of commander-in-chief in particular demands absolute legitimacy of office rather than the ambiguity and doubt created by this section of the amendment. Yet, still other ambiguities abound. The term used in the Twenty-fifth Amendment, "principal officers of the executive departments," may mean the Cabinet and related personnel. Hence, the composition of such a vital group is unclear. Could an "acting" secretary vote if there were no secretary available? Who would be included in the related personnel category?

Roosevelt's health problems could have created problems under the provisions of Section 4 of the Twenty-fifth Amendment. The vice presidents during Roosevelt's third and fourth terms were entirely loyal to him. However, their predecessor, John Nance Garner was philosophically opposed to the New Deal.[27] If Section 4 had been in effect in Roosevelt's first and second terms and had his health declined at this earlier time, this amendment might have been implemented. What would have been the effect of this constitutional crisis on measures designed to cope with the Great Depression and to prepare the nation for possible military conflict?

How would the amendment have been implemented if Roosevelt had initially survived the cerebral hemorrhage of April 12, 1945, but with serious impairments of intellect, reason, memory, and judgment? Vice President

Truman would not have wished to be seen as grasping power from a stricken, but still living Roosevelt. The Cabinet's loyalty was to the president only. Just as they had displayed unrealistic optimism before Roosevelt's death on April 12, they would likely have maintained a positive view, hoping for recovery and precluding an "Acting President." The impasse resulting would have had the gravest consequences for the alliance, the remainder of the war, the United Nations, and the decisions related to the atomic bomb.

One clear occasion in which the Twenty-fifth Amendment, with all its flaws, might have been potentially helpful was the episode of paralysis experienced by President Woodrow Wilson following his stroke in the autumn of 1919, and continuing until his successor's inauguration, March 4, 1921. Wilson had summarily dismissed Secretary of State Robert Lansing because Lansing had called a Cabinet meeting without Wilson's prior agreement. In the midst of illness, a president might dismiss one or more Cabinet members before they met to consider his disability. Such dismissals of selected Cabinet officers could make Section 4 become inoperative. At least for the moment there would be only those "principal officers" who the president knew would support him regardless of disability. Unless a president were impeached he could effectively evade even the constructive features of this amendment.

There may be no acceptable medical solution to the issue of disability at the presidential level. Serious considerations of death and disability are culturally anathema. Leaders by definition are, at least at the time of their election, "strong and healthy." They are at least as vulnerable as other executives, but because of their status as icons, it is difficult to envision disease and death while in office.

Another important issue arising from Roosevelt's health history is that "access to care" does not necessarily lead to high quality care. In the case of celebrities generally, and presidents in particular, substandard and even potentially dangerous levels of care have been rendered. Jerrold Post and Robert Robins illustrate this point with the suicide of James Forrestal, secretary of defense in the Truman administration.[28]

> Forrestal's case illustrates two important principles. The first is that high status poses a danger to the proper medical treatment of any leader. Because of his special status, James Forrestal received less than optimal treatment. Had he been treated as an ordinary patient, confined to the psychiatric ward under the supervision of a highly skilled psychiatrist able to employ the full range of possible treatments and to control the environment, Forrestal might have recovered from his severe depression. . . .

After Bruenn's complete physical examination of Roosevelt in March of 1944, McIntire requested a memorandum of recommendations. Bruenn would recall later that McIntire, after reading the recommendations which included bed rest, diet, and so forth, said, "You can't do that. This is the President of the United States!"[29] Any ordinary citizen, having just been diagnosed with acute congestive heart failure, would have been immediately hospitalized.

The avoidance of such misadventures and the provision of objective, high quality, nonpolitical, medically comprehensive examination and treatment is a necessity in the dangerous and fast-paced world of the twenty-first century.

Research into Roosevelt's health and its impact on his presidency may have reached an impasse, unless unknown information is found in the papers of a hospital or government agency. Documents, especially Roosevelt's medical records which have been missing for more than a half century, are unlikely to appear. The few survivors have apparently said all that they recall or choose to recall.

Primary sources have been virtually exhausted. Their views predictably parallel the political and personal biases of their authors. Observers then and now see Roosevelt subjectively and selectively. Secondary sources, appropriately synthesized and interpreted, have generally been more informative than some of the primary ones. The *New York Times* provided the starkest divergence between glibly reassuring press releases which it was not in a position to question and the dire medical reality of Roosevelt's health.

Had the events of 1944–1945 occurred today, the results would probably have been different. Cable television, satellites, instant worldwide communication, a narrow range of privacy for presidents, candidates, and their families, and a high level of investigative reporting would make a cover-up of this magnitude very unlikely. The often questionable taste, the lack of discretion, and reporting which sometimes approach crudeness in current journalism are balanced by the rapid, usually accurate, detailed information, especially of medical conditions, that are transmitted to the public. The dangerous situation fomented by a disregard for, or denial of, the probable medical consequence would be all but assuredly prevented.

However, there is still some cause for concern as experiences with recent presidents indicate. Eisenhower's heart attack and surgery for ileitis were perhaps understandable by the public. However, his stroke raised the possibility that he could be impaired in speech and/or other mental functions. On July 2, 1955, while still the majority leader of the U.S. Senate, Lyndon B. Johnson suffered a severe heart attack. Professor Robert Gilbert suggests that his wife wanted Johnson to run for vice president because it would protect his health more than being the majority leader.[30] John F. Kennedy was highly medicated most of his adult life and suffered from Addison's disease, although his staff continued to deny it.

The public's right to know the facts of high-risk illness in a chief executive should be paramount, transcending the "privacy rights" of the president or presidential candidate. The potential consequences of future cover-ups are likely to be more devastating than those of Roosevelt's presidency. It is important to note that Roosevelt did not experience continuing mental disability in those days but could have as a result of the extreme hypertension. The Act of Presidential Succession operative in 1945 was not written in a manner to respond to mental disability.

The Future

Implementation for medical screening and a higher level of medical care for the president could be attempted, but relying on a medical solution alone is unrealistic. The health status of candidates may not accurately forecast subsequent illness and, in any event, public disclosure of physical or emotional problems may violate legitimate privacy rights. A political remedy would be more effective. Reorganization of the executive office to reduce the enormous burden and tension, to share responsibilities, avoid minutiae, and reduce gratuitous intrusions, would create a healthier climate for the president. The public and media need to reevaluate the excessively detailed, overly personal scrutiny to which presidents and their families are increasingly exposed. It may be time to restore a more reasonable perimeter of privacy for the president.

Without a shift in expectations to a more realistic plane, many presidents will, by definition, "fail" as the demands of the office continue to spiral beyond individual human capacity. Political consequences pale in comparison with the potential human toll, with disease and even death as almost inevitable outcomes. A systematic failure requires a systemic cure; mere fine-tuning will not do.

Issues related to presidential health and succession can be resolved only in a nonpartisan and creative fashion. The Twenty-fifth Amendment may be succeeded by a more practical plan of succession which will protect the nation in emergency situations, either by a new constitutional amendment or more feasibly by legislative action further defining and clarifying the existing amendment. Excluding politics from the medical examining room is a formidable challenge, but it must be met to prevent potential disasters due to illness sustained by the chief executive. Hopefully, these issues will soon be resolved by physicians, historians, administrators, attorneys, and spirited public citizens. There is a need for systematic interchanges between physicians' and medical researchers' interest in public policy, the political science community, and practicing politicians.

Such a multidisciplinary group of attorneys, scholars, physicians, historians, and others, has made recommendations regarding presidential disability. The group met three times: January 26–28, 1995 at the Carter Center of Emory University, Atlanta, Georgia; November 10–12, 1995, at Wake Forest University, Winston-Salem, North Carolina; and December 1–3, 1996, at the White House Conference Center, Washington, D.C. A publication of their opinion is available.[31]

Appendix A
Death Certificate of
Franklin D. Roosevelt

STATE OF GEORGIA
DEPARTMENT OF PUBLIC HEALTH
T. F. ABERCROMBIE, M.D., DIRECTOR
ATLANTA

CERTIFIED COPY

DEPARTMENT OF COMMERCE
BUREAU OF THE CENSUS

CERTIFICATE OF DEATH
GEORGIA DEPARTMENT OF PUBLIC HEALTH

State File No.
L. R. File No.

1. Place of Death
(a) County *Meriwether*
(b) Town *Warm Springs*

2. Usual Residence of Deceased
(a) State
(c) City or Town *Washington D.C.*

Full Name *Franklin Delano Roosevelt*

PERSONAL AND STATISTICAL PARTICULARS

MEDICAL CERTIFICATION

Sex *Male* — Race *White* — Marital Status *M*

Give Name of Spouse *Eleanor Roosevelt*

Age: Years *63*

Date of Birth *1-30-82* Birth Place *Hyde Park, N.Y.*

Usual Occupation *President of United States*

Industry or Business *of America*

Father *James Roosevelt*

Birthplace *Hyde Park, N.Y.*

Mother Maiden Name *Sarah Delano*

Birth Place *Newburgh, N.Y.*

Informant's Own Signature *F.W. Patterson*

Informant's P.O. Address *1016 Spring St. N.W.*

Burial, Cremation or Removal *Burial* Date *April 15, 1945*

P.O. Address or Place of Burial *Hyde Park, N.Y.*

Signature of Person Burying Body *H.M. Patterson & Son*

Undertaker, Address *Atlanta, Ga.* Date Filed with L.R. *April 17, 1945*

Registrar's Own Signature

Date of Death *April 12 1945* Time *3 35 P.M.*

I hereby certify that I attended the deceased who died on the above date.

I last saw him Alive on *April 12 1945*

Primary Cause of Death *Cerebral Hemorrhage* Duration *2 Yrs*

Contributory Causes *Arteriosclerosis*

Operation *none*

Diagnosis: Clinical — Lab. X-Ray (Check) Was Autopsy Performed? *No*

Physician's Own Signature *Howard G. Bruenn*

Physician's P.O. Address *U.S.N.H. Bethesda, Md.* Date Signed *4/13/45*

THIS IS TO CERTIFY THAT THE ABOVE IS A TRUE AND CORRECT COPY OF THE ORIGINAL CERTIFICATE, WHICH HAS BECOME A PERPETUAL RECORD IN THE ARCHIVES OF THE GEORGIA DEPARTMENT OF PUBLIC HEALTH. (NOT VALID UNLESS COUNTERSIGNED IN THE DIVISION OF INFORMATION AND STATISTICS.)

DATE *4-18-1945*

T.F. Abercrombie
DIRECTOR, GEORGIA DEPARTMENT OF PUBLIC HEALTH

DIVISION OF INFORMATION AND STATISTICS

ORIGINAL RETIRED FOR PRESERVATION

Appendix B
Clinical Notes on the Illness
and Death of
President Franklin D. Roosevelt

Howard G. Bruenn, M.D., F.A.C.P., New York

Reprinted from Annals of Internal Medicine *72:579–591, 1970*

Until the past 15 years the illnesses of a President of the United States had not been exposed in the public press. Indeed, in most instances not only have the details been obscure but the very fact that illness existed has been not infrequently denied. In the case of President Franklin D. Roosevelt, rumors about the state of his health began to be bruited about as early as 1936, 9 years before his death.[*] These speculations continued throughout the remainder of his life and rose to a crescendo of debate and uncertainty after his death. To my knowledge, no factual clinical information regarding his health and illnesses and the events leading to his death has ever been published. For the record and its accuracy, these notes are presented. The original hospital chart in which all clinical progress notes as well as the results of the various laboratory tests were incorporated was kept in the safe at the U.S. Naval Hospital, Bethesda, Md. After the President's death this chart could not be found.

Examination in March 1944

I first saw President Roosevelt professionally in March 1944. I was then an officer in the U.S. Naval Medical Corps (Reserve) stationed at the U.S.

---

[*]High S: "Is President Roosevelt a well man today?" *Liberty Magazine*, June 27, 1936.
Note: For electrocardiogram readings, see original article in *Annals of Internal Medicine*.

Medical Hospital, Bethesda. My position on the staff was consultant in cardiology to the National Naval Medical Center and to the Third Naval District. I was also in charge of the Electrocardiograph Department of the Hospital. Surgeon General Ross McIntire was the personal physician of the President.

The President was brought to the hospital on March 27, 1944, for a checkup at the suggestion of Dr. McIntire. As part of this examination, I was asked to see him. He was brought to the office in his wheel chair and lifted to the examining table by attendants. (It was common knowledge that a very severe attack of poliomyelitis in 1921 had resulted in total paralysis of both legs to the hips.) I obtained the following history:

During the latter part of December 1943 he had had an attack of influenza with the usual signs and symptoms—fever, cough, and malaise. After this he had failed to regain his usual vigor and subsequently had had several episodes of what appeared to be upper respiratory infections. There had been occasional bouts of abdominal distress and distension, accompanied by profuse perspiration. Since the attack of influenza he had complained of unusual and undue fatigue. One week before being seen he had developed an acute coryza, which was followed 2 days later by an annoying cough with the production of small amounts of thick, tenacious, yellowish sputum. Past history included a severe attack of poliomyelitis in 1921, with severe and permanent impairment of the muscles of both lower extremities to the hips. There was also a history (in the chart) of the development of a severe iron deficiency anemia in May 1941, with hemoglobin of 4.5g/100ml. This was evidently due to bleeding hemorrhoids, and the anemia responded quickly to ferrous sulfate therapy. There were no cardiac symptoms at that time.

Physical Examination

Physical examination on March 27, 1944, showed a temperature of 99° F by mouth, pulse of 72/min, and respiration of 24/min. He appeared to be very tired, and his face was very gray. Moving caused considerable breathlessness. He was in good humor but obviously moved with difficulty. He coughed frequently during the examination but produced no sputum. He was comfortable in a low position on a Gatch bed but appeared to be slightly cyanotic. There was no venous congestion. The ocular fundi showed occasional arteriovenous nicking but no hemorrhage or exudates. The chest was broad and deep. Expansion was good and equal on both sides. There was no impairment of resonance on percussion of the lungs, and tactile fremitus was not increased. Breath sounds were heard throughout and were accompanied by numerous sibilant and sonorous rales. The lung bases appeared to be clear. The apical impulse of the heart was not visible. There were no palpable thrills.

Percussion showed the apex of the heart to be in the sixth interspace, 2 cm to the left of the midclavicular line, suggesting an enlarged heart. The heart rhythm was regular. There was a blowing systolic murmur at the apex. The second aortic sound was loud and booming. The pulmonic second sound appeared to be increased over the normal in intensity. There were no murmurs over the base of the heart. Blood pressure was 186/108 mm Hg. (Previous blood pressures as recorded in the hospital chart were 7/30/35, 136/78; 4/22/37, 162/98; 11/30/40, 178/88; and 2/27/41, 188/105 mm Hg.) The radial pulses were full and the arteries only moderately thickened. The liver was not palpable, and there was no peripheral edema.

Other Findings

An electrocardiogram showed sinus rhythm with deep inversion of the T waves in leads I and CF_4 (only one precordial electrode position was used) with ST segment depression in the latter lead. The T waves in lead II were of low amplitude. Previous electrocardiograms recorded on November 14, 1936, September 16, 1937, and May 23, 1939, were reported to be within normal limits. A tracing taken in 1941, which was available, showed low amplitude of the T waves in leads I and V-4, of a degree that could be considered abnormal.

Fluoroscopy and X rays of the chest showed a considerable increase in the size of the cardiac shadow, as measured in the anterior-posterior position. The contractions along the left border in this view were limited, although more vigorous pulsations were noted posteriorly in the left anterior oblique position. The enlargement of the heart was mainly to the left ventricle. The great-vessel shadow was also increased in size. This enlargement was apparently due to a diffusely dilated and tortuous aorta, including the ascending, arch, and thoracic portions. The pulmonary vessels were engorged.

Diagnosis and Recommendations

In view of the continued low-grade pulmonary infection and cough and dyspnea on effort, it appeared that these symptoms might well be due to early left ventricular failure. Accordingly, a diagnosis was made of hypertension, hypertensive heart disease, cardiac failure (left ventricular), and acute bronchitis.

These findings and their interpretation were conveyed to Surgeon General McIntire. They had been completely unsuspected up to this time, and a memorandum of recommendations was requested. It was suggested that:

> The patient should be put to bed for 1 to 2 weeks with nursing care.

Digitalization should be carried out: 0.4g of digitalis every day for 5 days; subsequently, 0.1g every day.

A light, easily digestible diet. Portions were to be small, and salt intake was to be restricted. Potassium chloride in a salt shaker could be used as desired for seasoning.

Codeine, ½ grain, should be given for control of cough.

Sedation should be taken to ensure rest and a refreshing night's sleep.

A program of gradual weight reduction.

This memorandum was rejected because of the exigencies and demands on the President. Accordingly, he was placed on modified bed rest and given a cough syrup with ammonium carbonate and codeine.

Further Observations

When I saw the President at the White House on March 28, 1944, the physical signs were essentially unchanged. However, the cough was less tight. The next day, March 29, 1944, his color was better, and he appeared more rested. The lungs showed considerably less musical and sibilant rales, but moist rales were heard, particularly at the base of the right lung. The heart was regular at 64 beats/min. The blood pressure was 180/104 mm Hg.

The situation was discussed by Drs. McIntire, Capt. John Harper (Officer in Command, Naval Hospital), Capt. Robert Duncan (Executive Officer of the Naval Hospital), Capt. Charles Behrens (Officer in Command, Radiology Department of the Naval Hospital), Dr. Paul Dickens, and myself. At this meeting the following suggestions were made.

Limitation of daily activity must be emphasized.

Cigarettes were to be curtailed.

Trial of aminophylline, Grains, iii 1 tablet, enteric coated, three times a day, after meals.

Avoid, if possible, irritation and tensions of office.

Phenobarbital, Grain, ¼ of Thesodate®, three times a day.

Period of rest for 1 hr after meals.

Light passive massage.

Dinner in quarters at the White House.

A minimum of 10 hr sleep.

No swimming in the pool.

Diet: 2,600 calories, moderately low in fat.

The use of mild laxatives, if necessary, to avoid straining.

I saw the President on the morning of March 30, and he appeared to be somewhat better. There was no dyspnea with moderate elevation of the Gatch bed and no evidence of venous engorgement. The percussion note was clear throughout. Rales, however, were heard at both bases, more on the right than on the left. They cleared somewhat with cough, but some persisted, particularly at the right base. The heart was grossly enlarged to the left, with a heaving systolic impulse palpable at the apex. It was regular in rhythm and rate (74/min). At the apex the fist sound was poor in quality and was followed by a systolic blow. The second sound was relatively louder than the first sound in this area. At the base, second aortic sound was accentuated, but the pulmonic sound was also well heard. No diastolic murmurs were heard.

Results of the laboratory tests were as follows: basal metabolic rate, +15%; circulation time, 22½ sec; breath holding, 35 sec (time that maximum inspiration could be held); and urine: specific gravity, 1.014; sugar, 0; albumin, 1+; numerous hyaline casts; WBC, 6 to 8 per high power field (hpf); RBC, 0 to 6/hpf.

On the basis of the history, physical findings, and the few functional tests performed, it seemed apparent that some degree of congestive heart failure was present, and digitalization was again suggested to the Surgeon General and urged as an essential form of therapy.

Group Consultation; Progress

A meeting was held on March 31, with the two honorary medical consultants of the Navy, Drs. James A. Paullin and Frank Lahey, in attendance. Also present at this meeting were Drs. McIntire, Harper, Behrens, Duncan, and myself. At this time Drs. Lahey and Paullin were acquainted with the history and physical findings, and they were shown the X rays, electrocardiograms, and the other laboratory data concerning the President. There was much discussion. That afternoon the President was examined at the White House by Drs. Lahey and Paullin. Another meeting was held the next morning, and, again, there was much discussion. Dr. Lahey was particularly interested in the gastrointestinal tract but submitted that no surgical procedure was indicated. He did, however, indicate that the situation to his mind was serious enough to warrant acquainting the President with the full facts of the case in order to assure his full cooperation. Dr. Paullin was fully in accord with the diagnosis but did not believe that congestive heart failure was present of sufficient degree to warrant digitalization and advocated no specific therapy at this time. I stressed, however, that [1] because of the physical limitations of the patient the usual history of a diminished myocardial reserve was not obtainable; [2] the patient himself gave a rather vague but suggestive history of orthopnea and was objectively noted to have dyspnea; [3] the size of the heart, the hilar congestion in the X ray, and the physical examination were highly suggestive; and [4] the results of the few functional tests performed all indicated the presence of definite congestive heart failure.

After discussion of these points, Dr. Paullin interposed no further objections, and it was decided to proceed with the proposal for digitalization. I suggested further that a trial of ammonium chloride followed by an injection of mersalyl (Salyrgan®) might be helpful, both diagnostically and therapeutically; but it was decided by the group that in view of the complexity of the situation as little medication as possible be used at this time. Digitalization was to be accomplished first, and this was to be checked by the electrocardiogram. Fluid intake and output charts were to be kept, as well as successive measurements of weight. (It was found impractical later to record fluid intake and output and impossible to accurately weigh the patient.) The plan of digitalization was agreed upon, that is, 0.5 g digitalis leaf the first day, (March 31, 1944); 0.4 g for the next 3 days; and 0.2 g on the fifth day. In other words, a total of 1.9 g of digitalis leaf was to be given in 5 days (1.4 g as the digitalizing dose) followed by a maintenance dose of 0.1 g each day. It was arranged to have another meeting of the same group 2 weeks later, at which time the President's condition would be reassessed.

On April 1, 1944, I examined the patient at the White House at 10 A.M. He did not appear as well as he had. His color was poor, and he looked tired. The patient stated that he had had a "fairly good night" but could not elaborate on details of any particular discomfort. He had several paroxysms of nonproductive cough just before the examination of the chest. There was no dullness at the bases, but moist rates were detected again at both bases. Blood pressure was 192 to 200/106 to 108 mm Hg. Urine concentration was 1.008 to 1.026. He was seen the next day by Drs. McIntire, Lahey, and Paullin. Among other suggestions, restriction of tobacco was stressed.

The patient had a very refreshing night's sleep (10 hr) on the night of April 2, and had to be awakened on the morning of April 3. There was no dyspnea on lying flat, and his color was good. He did not cough during the entire examination. The lungs were entirely clear. For the first time a distinct apical impulse could be observed in the sixth interspace in the left anterior axillary line. The first sound at the apex had a much better tone than formerly, but the systolic murmur persisted. A soft systolic murmur was heard at the base. The blood pressure was 208 to 210/108 to 110 mm Hg. An electrocardiogram showed less deep inversion of the T waves in lead I but this type of change was particularly striking in the precordial leads.

The next day the patient said the night of April 3 had been excellent. He had no complaints except that he felt he had been eating too much and thought he was getting fat. (Diet was reduced to 1,800 calories.) There was no gastric discomfort. He had cut down appreciably on his tobacco (6 cigarettes a day) and appeared to be much better. His color was good, and there was no dyspnea. The lungs were clear, the heart was unchanged, and the blood pressure was 222 to 226/118 mm Hg.

On April 5, 1944, he was in excellent spirits. He had slept well the night before. There was no cough or gastrointestinal complaints. He said he felt fine. On physical examination he looked very well. The lungs were clear. The first sound at the apex was normal in tone and louder than the second in this area. Apical impulse was vigorous. There were apical and basal systolic murmurs as before. No diastolic murmurs were heard. Blood pressure was 218/120 mm Hg. Phenobarbital therapy, ¼ grain, was started twice a day (morning and noon).

He said the night of April 5 had been very good. On April 6 he complained of a little nausea, which he had noticed late in the afternoon of the day before. When questioned, he dismissed it as of no account. He had eaten dinner the previous night and his breakfast in the morning with good appetite. He had no cough. Physical examination was unchanged. Blood pressure was 210/120 mm Hg. X ray of chest and electrocardiogram were done, and sedimentation rate and blood chemistries were measured.

On April 7 he said he had gone for an automobile drive the previous afternoon which he keenly enjoyed. Digitalis had been omitted on April 6 because of questionable gastric discomfort.

X rays of the chest taken 2 weeks after starting digitalis treatment showed a definite decrease in the size of the heart and marked clearing of the lung fields. All blood chemistries were normal. An electrocardiogram at this time showed changes toward normal, that is, less deep inversion of the T waves in the precordial leads. The second meeting of the Naval Consultants was convened at this time, and these results were shown. It was agreed that digitalis treatment should be continued. The diet was modified according to the original recommendations, including salt restriction and small portions; weight reduction was to be promoted.

The President's crushing schedule of daily appointments was restricted, and, where possible, a period of an hour or two was set aside in the afternoon for relaxation. This included time spent floating and swimming in the White House pool, which the President enjoyed greatly. No fatigue or discomfort was experienced with this mild type of exercise. Finally, it was arranged with his consent, that, when possible, a period of 1 or 2 weeks was to be spent outside of Washington for rest and relaxation.

A Stay in South Carolina

From this time on I saw the President three to four times a week while he was in residence at the White House. The visits were usually made in the morning between 9 and 9:30 AM, after he had had his breakfast and while he was still in bed. Included in these visits was an inquiry into his state of well-being; an examination, including the heart and lungs; and a determination of his blood pressure. At no time did the President ever comment on the frequency of these visits or question the reason for the electrocardiograms and the other laboratory tests that were performed from time to time; nor did he ever have any questions as to the type and variety of medications that were used. Although the President continued to improve, it was decided that it would be wise to provide a period of rest and relaxation away from Washington. He had originally intended to go to Guantanamo Bay for this purpose, but because of the War, the state of his health, and other considerations it was deemed desirable that he stay within the continental limits of the United States. Accordingly, arrangements were made for that purpose through Mr. Bernard Baruch, who offered the use of his estate, Hobcaw, in South Carolina. Members of the party included the President, Admirals William Leahy and Wilson Brown (Naval Aide), General Watson (Army Aide), Admiral McIntire, Mr. Bernard Baruch, and myself. In addition, there were the usual Secret Service detail, communications crew, and Lt. William Rigdon, who acted as secretary to the President.

At Hobcaw the weather was excellent, although a little cool, and the President followed a very simple regimen. He usually awakened about 9:30 AM. He had breakfast in bed, and I attended him shortly thereafter. He spent most of the morning reading newspapers and going over his correspondence. Lunch was usually attended with the group, with the President making his first appearance at that time. After lunch the President usually retired for a nap, and later he either went fishing in a Coast Guard patrol boat with part of the Secret Service in another boat (aft), motoring, or on occasion visiting with Belle Baruch (Mr. Baruch's daughter). The whole period of time was very pleasant, broken by occasional visitors including Mrs. Roosevelt and their daughter, Anna, Mrs. Rutherford, Miss Suckley, and various important dignitaries on urgent business. In the late afternoon and early evening the President would go over the contents of the "pouch" (brought daily from Washington by plane) and sign the necessary papers. Dinner was at 7 PM, preceded by cocktails of which the President had one or two dry martinis. Rarely did the President give the signal for rising from dinner before 8:30 or 9 PM. The conversation was animated with the President playing the dominant role. It ranged from reminiscences with Mr. Baruch over earlier contemporaries and incidents to a discussion of recent and current events.

He continued to feel well and was in good spirits. He slept soundly and ate well. However, he did complain intermittently of abdominal gas, but he had no nausea. The physical examinations were unchanged. He had no cardiac symptoms, but the blood pressure remained elevated. Accordingly, it appeared that the Thesodate treatment was not effective. It was stopped, and a saturated solution of potassium iodide, 10 drops twice a day, was administered. During the week ending April 20, 1944, a marked diurinal change in the blood pressure had been noted. The highest readings were invariably recorded in the morning, the lowest in the evening. For example, the blood pressure taken before breakfast, with the patient still in a prone position, was 230/126 mm Hg. One hour later the blood pressure was 210/106 mm Hg. The only activity during this interval was for the patient to sit up and eat his breakfast. After he was prone again the blood pressure had risen to 218/112 mm Hg. That evening it was 190/90 mm Hg. Potassium iodide treatment was stopped because of increased nasal congestion. Phenobarbital treatment, ¼ grain three times a day, was restarted. An electrocardiogram taken April 21 showed less digitalis effect, and an extra tablet (0.1g) was given then and again 4 days later.

He was asymptomatic until April 28, when late in the afternoon he began to complain of abdominal pain and tenderness associated with slight nausea. There was no radiation of the pain. Bowel movements had been regular. There were no cardiac symptoms. On physical examination the temperature was 98.6 F; pulse, 76/min; and blood pressure, 230/120 mm Hg. There was no jaundice. Heart and lungs were unchanged. The abdomen was not distended, but there was tenderness and voluntary spasm over the right upper quadrant, the lower right quadrant, and the epigastrium. There was tympany, but bowel sounds could be heard. A tentative diagnosis of acute cholecystisis was made, and he was given ½ grain codeine by hypodermic injection, with some relief. He slept well, but the next day the symptoms were still present. They apparently were not severe enough to interfere with his appetite. He had two very loose bowel movements with much gas. The abdominal tenderness appeared somewhat less pronounced on palpation. The electrocardiogram was unchanged. Temperature and pulse were normal. Blood pressure was 196/112 mm Hg. Phenobarbital treatment was discontinued, and he was put on a soft diet. By May 1 he was free of all abdominal distress, felt well, and subjectively and objectively appeared to be in good shape. Because of his apparent recovery, normal diet was resumed, but after luncheon on May 2 he had a recurrence of his abdominal distress and that evening was acutely uncomfortable. With the use of local applications of heat and codeine hypodermically he was made more comfortable and was able to have a fairly restful night. However, the blood pressure was recorded at 240/130 mm Hg, and he complained of soreness in the back of his neck and a throbbing sensation all through the body. There were no cardiac symptoms.

He was kept in bed for the next 2 days, and at the end of this period his symptoms had entirely subsided. He looked well. His lungs were entirely clear. The heart remained enlarged, with the apical impulse in the left anterior axillary line. The first sound at the apex was of relatively good tone and was followed by a soft apical systolic murmur. The second aortic sound was greater than P_2. There was some residual soreness and tenderness on palpation over the right upper quadrant and caecum. The electrocardiogram was unchanged. The blood pressure readings taken twice daily between April 9 and June 14, 1944, averaged about 196/112 mm Hg on awakening and 194/96 mm Hg in the evening.

Back in Washington

On the President's return to Washington, it was arranged to have X rays taken of this gall bladder (May 26). The X rays showed a good functional response, but there were indications of a group of cholesterol stones. He was accordingly placed on a low-fat diet of 1,800 calories in an attempt to prevent abdominal symptoms as well as to reduce his weight, which was now 188 lb. Because of the atrophy of his legs and thighs, his weight was concentrated in this chest and abdomen.

The time from the middle of May to the early part of August was without incident relative to the President's health. On July 13 he left Washington to go to Hawaii to meet with Admiral Chester Nimitz and General Douglas MacArthur to discuss the future strategy of the War in the Pacific. The trip was made by private train. The transcontinental trip was made at a leisurely pace, affording the President opportunity for rest and to work on a speech that he planned to deliver at San Diego. On this journey, as well as all others, the President was able to sleep well, always without medication. He appeared in good spirits and apparently enjoyed himself thoroughly. A stop was made in Chicago where the Democratic Presidential Convention was in progress. The President did not leave the train. He proceeded to San Diego, where on July 20, 1944, the President, speaking over the radio from the train, accepted the nomination of the Democratic Party for the fourth term as President of the United States. The speech was delivered in a special railroad car before a small group, including his sons James and John and their wives, Admiral Leahy, General Watson, Judge Samuel Rosenman, Elmer Davis, Grace Tully, Dorothy Brady, and me.

State of the War

When the President left Washington on July 13, 1944, the World War situation might be summed up as follows.

146

Normandy

In spite of the worst June weather for many years, the beachhead in Normandy had not only been firmly secured, but troops and supplies had been landed at rates that established an assured future local superiority. The harbor at Cherbourg was in our possession. Decisive superiority in the air and in motorized divisions was destroying enemy reserves more rapidly than they could be thrown into combat. We had carried out our promise to the Russians to establish a second front.

The recent visit of General de Gaulle to Washington gave some promise of better cooperation with the French Liberation Committee, although the British and American press continued to criticize our non-recognition policy. Some few individual writers were beginning to point out that General de Gaulle appeared to be more interested in his own political future than in driving the Germans out of France.

Mediterranean

Allied armies were still pursuing the retreating German armies in Northern Italy. The Germans were believed to be preparing a strong line north of Florence and Pisa for a final stand. The Prime Minister had argued strongly that we abandon the so-called ANVIL operation (an attack on the southern coast of France) so that our amphibious forces might be able to press attacks in the northern Adriatic. He had reluctantly agreed to prepare for ANVIL in compliance with our promise to the Russians at Teheran and in furtherance of the strategical ideas of General Eisenhower and our Joint Chiefs of Staff. General Wilson had been directed to make every effort to deliver ANVIL attack by mid-August.

Russia

The greatest gamble in history had been taken when President Roosevelt, Prime Minister Churchill, and their advisors decided that they could trust Stalin's promise to coordinate his attack with ours. Half-hearted support of our Normandy landing might have cost us all of the men and equipment that had been thrown into France. Some pessimists feared that the Russians might not carry out their part of the 1944 assault. Although the Russian drive began slowly in late June, by July 13 it had increased steadily in power and in effectiveness and was on that date under way along the entire front with a momentum and drive that appeared irresistible. It appeared to many, both among the Allies and among the neutrals, that the defeat of Germany was certain and that it would be accomplished within the year 1944. The much-vaunted secret robot weapon was causing distressing loss of life and property in England, but this destruction was not believed to threaten the total Allied war effort.

China, Burma, and India

The Japanese thrust at India through Burma had been blocked by the combined forces of Mountbatten. The Japanese were in full retreat, and, after having suffered severe losses there, General Stilwell's investment of Myikenia assured for the time being a continuance of our air supply into China. The Japanese effort to establish a line of supply between North and South China was meeting with very ineffective opposition by the Chinese, and all reports indicated a complete lack of cooperation between the Northern Communist Chinese and the forces of Generalissimo Chiang Kai-Shek. In a desperate effort to pull various conflicting forces of China together, President Roosevelt, on the advice of the Joint Chiefs of Staff, had urged Chiang Kai-Shek to place General Stilwell in command of all operations, political and military, in China. This recommendation had apparently been favorably received but had not as yet been put into effect.

Pacific

Except for the weakening of the Allied position on the mainland of China, our combined operations in other parts of the Pacific had proceeded with gratifying success. The capture of Saipan and Guam seemed assured. All of New Guinea had been recaptured except for isolated pockets of Japanese resistance. The bombing of the mainland of Japan from Saipan and China was already beginning. Our submarines and powerful carrier task forces were steadily destroying the Japanese Merchant Marine and such parts of her Navy as risked leaving port. The nature of further major operations against Japan was still under discussion. A meeting between the President and General MacArthur and Admiral Nimitz was therefore one of the very greatest importance. The possibility that Russia might give us the use of her Siberian ports and airfields in the near future also gave special importance to the President's visit to the Aleutians and to Alaska.

Visit to the Pacific

Departure from San Diego aboard the heavy Cruiser USS Baltimore occurred early on July 22. The 2 days spent in San Diego were busy ones for the

President. He received the various commanding officers in his private railroad car, went to lunch at his daughter-in-law's home (Mrs. John Roosevelt); had dinner with his son, Colonel James Roosevelt, at the home of Rear-Admiral Davis (Commander Training Command, amphibious Force, Pacific Fleet); inspected amphibious Training Base at Oceanside, Calif., some 40 miles from San Diego; as well as visiting the San Diego Naval Hospital at Balboa Park. Despite this round of activities, the President showed no evidence of fatigue and was intensely interested in the various aspects of the military installations visited.

The President's days aboard ship were restful. He continued to sleep well and spent most of the afternoons on the flag bridge enjoying the sun and cool breezes. On the second day out his military aide, General Edwin Watson, developed an attack of acute pulmonary edema. This was treated with morphine and digitalization. Electrocardiograms showed no evidence of recent necrosis, and his recovery was rapid. On July 26 the USS Baltimore arrived at Pearl Harbor. The crews of the ships in the harbor—and there were hundreds, including aircraft carriers, battleships, and cruisers—manned the rail in white uniforms in honor of the President's arrival. The President's flag was hoisted at the main of the Baltimore in recognition of the honors rendered. This was a violation of sound security measures in time of war, but it was found that the news of the President's visit had become common knowledge in Honolulu 2 days before. Every effort was made to localize this knowledge through strict censorship.

After the ship was moored approximately 40 flag and general officers came on board the Baltimore to call on the President. The following 3 days were spent in extensive tours of inspection of various Naval, Marine, and Army installations during the day, followed by dinners with numbers of guests in the evening. The conference between General MacArthur, Admiral Leahy, and the President was held on July 28, and the best method of conducting the Pacific campaign in the future was discussed. The President made the final decisions. Throughout this period of hectic activity the President moved without obvious fatigue or difficulty of any kind.

On the afternoon of July 29 the President's party reboarded the Baltimore and, after 4 days at sea, arrived at Adak, Alaska. The weather had changed from the semitropical temperatures of Hawaii to fog, cold, and rain, with temperatures in the range of 42 to 52 F. Again, there was a round of inspections of the Naval and Army forces and installations and receptions including a lunch with a representative group of enlisted men. On the scheduled day of departure, the Baltimore was unable to get away from the dock because of a very strong crosswind, and the available tugs were unable to unmoor her. After a second attempt was unsuccessful, the President, not to be completely undone by the weather, went forward after dinner and fished over the ship's side from the forecastle, and, using a hook and line, he caught several small Dolly Varden trout and one or two other small fish. The weather abated the next day, and the ship left Adak and arrived the next morning at Kodiak Island. The day was spent with a tour and inspection of the island. The party transferred to a destroyer that took them via the Inside Passage of southeastern Alaska to Bremerton, Wash. There the President gave a major speech to the assembled navy-yard workers and the nation over a nation-wide radio hook-up.

For the first time in many months the braces for his legs were applied and he delivered the speech while standing upright and resting his arms on the speaker's stand, which was erected on the fan-tail of the destroyer. He began his address at 5 P.M. and spoke for 35 min. During the early part of the speech the President for the first time experienced substernal oppression with radiation to both shoulders. The discomfort lasted about 15 min, gradually subsiding at the end of this period. Within an hour a white blood count was taken and an electrocardiogram tracing made. No unusual abnormalities were detected. Blood pressure levels at that time and subsequently were within the range of previous observations. A series of electrocardiograms taken over the next few days were also unchanged.

Return to Washington

The trip from Bremerton to Washington by the special train was leisurely and uneventful. On this, as well as on other trips made by the President, his food was prepared and served by a specially selected group of Filipinos. From long experience the cook was familiar with the favorite foods and types of seasoning preferred by the President. However, with the low-fat diet that had been enforced since his attack of acute cholecystitis in May and the restrictions of calories, there had been a progressive loss of weight of which the President was rather proud. He was insistent on a further loss to around 170 lb. With the weight reduction already achieved (15 lb) there had been no reduction in his vigor and feeling of well-being. But, as usually happens with weight loss of this degree, the President had lost some flesh from his face. His features had become sharpened and he looked somewhat haggard in place of his normal, robust appearance. Despite the best efforts of the cook, liberalization of calories, and much persuasion, he obstinately kept himself on his restricted diet. There were no complaints at this time, or subsequently, of any abdominal discomfort. X rays of the stomach, intestine, and colon which had been performed 4 months previously were normal.

During the five weeks of the President's absence from Washington, the following had occurred. The President was nominated on July 20, by the Democratic Party, for a fourth term with Senator Harry Truman as nominee for Vice-President. The Russians had captured Riga and invaded Warsaw. The American troops in Normandy had captured Brittany, thereby denying the Germans the use of the ports of Brest, St. Nazaire, and Lorient, while making these ports open to attack. Their use for further decentralization of American troops on French soil was of great importance to us. Capture was completed of Saipan, Tinian, and Guam with attendant destructive attacks on the Bonins.

The President was back in Washington on August 17, 1944, and on the following day he told his press conference that he expected to see Prime Minister Churchill soon. Speculation was rife in the press as to the time and place for the conference, and this was cleared when the President and Mr. Churchill arrived in Quebec, Canada, on September 11 to plan the knockout blow against Japan. The trip to Quebec was made by train and, as usual, the President enjoyed the journey. The conference with its attendant round of activities was noteworthy only in that his blood pressure tended to be higher than usual. After viewing a motion picture "Wilson" this was particularly evident, but there were no cardiac symptoms. As noted, he had been receiving 0.1g of digitalis each day with an additional 0.1 g twice a week. There was no complaint of nausea or discomfort of any kind, but he was still insistent in his desire to lose more weight. He now weighed 168 lb. Phenobarbital was increased from ¼ grain to ½ grain three times a day. Blood pressure ranged from 180/100 to 240/130 mm Hg.

Election and Inauguration

During the month of October the President was engaged in more than his usual amount of activity. Besides the duties and obligations of the Presidency, he was now involved in the election. As a result, there was a complete disregard of the rest regime, and there were periods of prolonged activity. As a concession, he delivered his speeches while sitting. It may be noted that during this period of stress he was very animated. He really enjoyed going to the "hustings," and despite this his blood pressure levels, if anything, were lower than before. He was eating somewhat better, and, despite prolonged periods of exposure, he did not contract any upper respiratory infections. The physical examination remained unchanged.

By November 18, 1944, his appetite had again become poor, and he had lost a little more weight. Additional nourishment in the form of eggnogs was taken, and all restrictions were removed from his diet. The President looked tired. His color was fair, and he had no difficulty in lying flat. The lungs were clear. The apical impulse of the heart was felt 3 to 4 cm to the left of the midclavicular line. The sounds of the heart were clear and of good quality. The first sound at the apex was followed by a soft systolic murmur. The second aortic sound was greater than P_2. There were no diastolic murmurs. Blood pressure was 210/112 mm Hg. The abdomen was soft, and the liver was not palpable.

On November 27, 1944, the President left Washington and traveled by train to Warm Spring, Ga., for a period of rest and recuperation. In this relaxed and familiar environment his appetite improved somewhat, but his weight remained unchanged at 165 lb. A lower right molar tooth had become loose and was somewhat painful. This was removed under local anesthesia, without difficult. He had very few visitors, and, except for attending to the contents of the "pouch" that arrived each day from Washington, the days were spent in reading, motoring about the Warm Spring Foundation, and in conversation with his intimates. A little after a week of his arrival, he entered the pool for the first time. The air was cool, and the water was pleasantly warm. He seemed to enjoy it and thought that some contraction of the hips had developed. Blood pressure determinations taken before and after showed an alarming rise (260/150 mm Hg). Because of this, further swimming was definitely discouraged. In order to correct the contracture of his hips, he began some exercises that consisted of lying supine on the edge of the bed and allowing his heels to touch the floor. After several days of this he felt that this had had a beneficial effect on the muscles of his thighs. His general condition remained essentially unchanged. He continued to have difficulty in eating ("can't eat—cannot taste food"), and as a result he had lost a little more weight. He was urged to eat, and its importance was stressed. An electrocardiogram (tracing) showed no change, and there was no evidence of digitalis toxicity. However, the dosage of digitalis was cut to 0.1 g each day in order to minimize any possible effect of the drug on his desire for food. With the routine of rest and relaxation being more carefully observed, the blood pressure levels tended to be a little lower. There was no change in the physical examination.

He returned to Washington on December 19 and again resumed his usual routine at the White House and began to work on his Inaugural Address. This was delivered to a relatively small group of people (several hundred) from the rear veranda of the White House—the guests assembled on the ground below. He gave it without difficulty, although he used his leg braces for the first time since August the year before. Despite the coldness of the day, he wore neither hat nor overcoat. At the reception that evening he appeared to be in excellent spirits.

Trip to Yalta

Two days later the President and his party left Washington for the Yalta Conference. Arriving at Norfolk the next day (January 23) by train, the President immediately boarded the heavy cruiser Quincy (a sister ship to Baltimore). The weather during the first 2 days at sea was poor, with rain and a rough sea, but the President was an excellent sailor and, as usual, slept well. During the latter part of the journey the President was on deck to enjoy the sun and fresh air, an hour in both the morning and afternoon. He thoroughly enjoyed the trip, resting in the afternoon and retiring early at night.

A few days before his arrival at Malta, disconcerting messages began to be received from the Prime Minister about the difficulties of reaching Yalta and the unhealthy living conditions there. "If we had spent ten years on research we could not have found a worse place in the world than Yalta. . . . It is good for typhus and deadly lice which thrive in those parts." This was followed by other messages from the Prime Minister, who reported the drive from the airfield at Saki to Yalta as being 6 hr instead of 2 hr as originally reported by Mr. Harriman; that one of his people had reported the mountain part of the drive as frightening and at times impassable; and the health conditions as wholly unsanitary, as the Germans had left the building infested with vermin. It was, therefore, a great relief upon arriving at Malta to learn from Mr. Harriman and our advance party that, although we would face a difficult drive after landing at the airport at Saki, it would not be too tiring if completed during daylight and if we had clear weather; also, that the medical officers of the USS Catoctin anchored at Sevastopol had accomplished a very effective job of debugging at Yalta.

The President arrived at Malta on the morning of February 2, 1945. The whole day was spent in meetings. Among those coming aboard the ship to greet and confer with the President were, in order, Secretary of State E. R. Stettenius, Jr.; Ambassador to Russia W. Averell Harriman; Mr. Harry Hopkins; the Governor General, Sir Edmond Schreiber of Malta; Admiral Sir John Cunningham, Allied Naval Commander-in-Chief, Mediterranean; General of the Army George C. Marshall; Fleet Admiral Ernest J. King; Admiral Harold R. Stark, Commander, U.S. Naval Forces, Europe; Vice-Admiral Hewitt; Prime Minister Churchill and his daughter, Section Officer Sarah Oliver; Anthony Eden, British Foreign Secretary; and Admiral Emory Land, Director of War Shipping Administration. After lunch the President left the ship for a 30-mile automobile drive about the Island of Malta. After he returned to the ship the United States Joint Chiefs of Staff came aboard, and the President met with them in his quarters. Present were Admirals Leahy and King and General Marshall. An hour later they were joined by Prime

Minister Churchill and the British Combined Chiefs of Staff. The Combined Chiefs of Staff had been in conference at Malta for several days before the President's arrival, and this was the first plenary meeting with the President and the Prime Minister. The meeting lasted an hour, and at 10 PM the President had dinner. He left the ship an hour later to proceed by automobile to Luqa Airfield, Malta, to enplane for the trip to Saki in the Crimea, where he arrived late the next morning, February 3, 1945, a flight of some 1,400 miles. His plane was accompanied by five fighter planes because of the nearness of German-occupied territories. The average altitude traveled was 6,000 to 8,000 ft, which did not cause the President any discomfort, but he slept rather poorly on the plane because of the noise and vibration.

The Yalta Conference

After reviewing the honor guard at the airport of Saki, the President and the members of his party left by automobile for Livadia Palace near Yalta, some 80 miles distant from Saki. The drive was over poorly paved, narrow, winding roads. The entire distance was guarded by Soviet troops. This trip took five hours, but the President appeared to take it in stride, napping at intervals.

The President slept well that night, and the conferences began the next morning, Sunday, February 4. He worked very hard, both before and during the conferences. There was a constant stream of visitors from the time he awakened in the morning until lunch, and on occasion he had no time to take his afternoon rest. For the first three or four nights he developed a paroxysmal cough that was moderately productive but would awaken him at night, after which he would go back to sleep. He denied dyspnea, orthopnea, or cardiac pain. The lungs were clear. The heart and blood pressure were unchanged, and there were no electrocardiographic changes. The nose was obstructed, and this was treated with nose drops before he retired at night. The cough disappeared with the use of terpin hydrate and codeine. He continued to eat well and had no gastric discomfort.

The formal meetings of the Crimean Conferences, which were attended by the President, Prime Minister Churchill, Premier Stalin, and their aides, were usually convened at 4 PM at the Livadia Palace and lasted three to four hours, followed an hour later by dinner. On February 8, after an especially arduous day and an emotionally disturbing conference (he was worried and upset about the trend of the discussions that day at the Conference, namely, Poland) he was obviously greatly fatigued. His color was very poor (gray), but examination showed that his lungs were clear and the heart sounds were of good quality—regular in rhythm and rate (84/min). The blood pressure, however, for the first time showed pulsus alternans. A change in his routine was enforced. His hours of activity were rigidly controlled so that he could obtain adequate rest. No visitors were allowed until noon, and at least an hour of rest was enforced in the afternoon before the Conferences.

Within two days he appeared to be much better. His mood was excellent. His appetite was excellent, and he appeared to enjoy Russian food and cooking. There was no cough and the pulsus alternans had disappeared. The weather throughout this period, February 2 to 12, was pleasant; the average temperature was 40° F.

Return Via Egypt

The Crimean Conference was formally adjourned on Sunday, February 11, 1945, at 3:45 PM. Immediately afterwards the President and his party left Livadia Palace by motor for Sevastopol, a distance of 80 miles. On this trip, General Edwin Watson, the President's Military Aide, became ill (acute congestive heart failure). The President and his party went aboard the USS Catoctin, which was anchored at Sevastopol, and spent a restful night. The next morning the party motored to the airfield at Saki, a distance of 80 miles. After a brief ceremony, the plane left for Deversoir Field, Egypt. This field was operated by the United States Air Force and was located on the shores of Great Bitter Lake, about 17 miles south of Ismalia, Egypt. The plane flew at a maximum of 9,000 ft. The President was comfortable throughout, napping at intervals. On arrival the party boarded the Quincy, which had come from Malta several days previously and had anchored in Great Bitter Lake, where the next three days were spent. The weather was mild, and the President was completely symptom-free. Physical examinations were unchanged. This interval was enlivened by the visits on successive days of King Farouk of Egypt, Haile Selassie I of Ethiopia, and Ibn Saud, King of Saudi Arabia, with their entourages. Conferences were held with each, and gifts were exchanged.

The party left Great Bitter Lake on February 14 aboard the Quincy and stopped at Alexandria the next morning. Here the President received, among others, Secretary Stettinius, who reported on meetings held in Moscow with Foreign Commissar Molotov after the Crimean Conference. Prime Minister Churchill conferred with the President approximately 3½ hr. He had come to Alexandria by air from the Crimea by way of Athens, Greece. The Quincy left for Algiers that night, arriving the morning of February 18. General Charles De Gaulle, Provisional President of France, had been invited to meet with the President but declined the invitation. The Quincy left that afternoon on schedule for Newport News. Two days later, at sea, General Watson died. He had been confined to his cabin since the onset of illness, which was complicated by a cerebral hemorrhage and right hemiplegia. Outwardly the President took the death of General Watson calmly, but it was obvious that he was deeply moved. General Watson had been a friend and companion of the President for many years, and there was a deep affection between them. Mrs. Watson had been notified two days before that the General's condition had become critical. She was immediately notified of his death, but for security reasons to insure the safety of the President's return voyage it was decided to make no public announcement until the President had safely reached the continental United States.

The President's general health remained good. His nose bothered him from time to time because of some nasal stuffiness, but he had no cough. Physical examination and electrocardiogram were unchanged. Blood pressure during these past few days had been quite variable. The return aboard ship was otherwise uneventful. The weather, for the most part, was good. The President spent an hour to two on deck practically every day, and he rested well at night. Phenobarbital treatment had been discontinued.

During the two weeks after his return from Yalta, the President again began to ignore his rest regimen. In addition to a heavy schedule during the day, he began to work much too late in the evenings. His appetite had become poor, and, although he had not been weighed, it appeared that he had lost more weight. He complained of not being able to taste his food. There was no nausea. Because of this anorexia, digitalis was withheld for several days, although no digitalis toxicity was discernible in the electrocardiogram. There was no cough or cardiac symptoms. Heart size was unchanged. The sounds were clear and of good quality. The rhythm was regular, and the apical systolic murmur had not changed. Blood pressure values were somewhat lower. Despite the withdrawal of digitalis, he was still troubled with his lack of appetite. Otherwise, he insisted that he felt well. Digitalis therapy was resumed.

Last Days at Warm Springs

By the end of March he began to look bad. His color was poor, and he appeared to be very tired, although he continued to sleep well. Heart and lungs were unchanged. A period of total rest was urged. Accordingly, on March 29 the President left Washington for Warm Springs, Ga. The weather there was ideal, and within a week there was a decided and obvious improvement in his appearance and sense of well-being. He had begun to eat with appetite, rested beautifully, and was in excellent spirits. He began to go out every afternoon for short motor trips, which he clearly enjoyed. He had given up the eggnogs in favor of a gruel between meals. The physical examination was unchanged except for the blood pressure, the level of which had become extremely wide, ranging from 170/88 to 240/130 mm Hg. There was no apparent cause and effect. By April 10 improvement had continued. His color was much better, and his appetite was very good; he asked for double helpings of food. Although he had not been weighed, it was apparent that he had begun to gain a little weight. He had been resting very well, and he began to increase his activities. He was in excellent spirits and began to plan a weekend, involving a barbecue and attendance at a minstrel show.

On April 12 I saw the President at 9:20 AM, a few minutes after he had awakened. He had slept well but complained of a slight headache and some stiffness of the neck. He ascribed this to a soreness of the muscles, and relief was experiences with slight massage.

He had a very good morning, and his guests commented on how well he looked. He was occupied during the morning going over State papers and, while doing so, was sitting in a chair, as the subject of some sketches that were being made by an artist. He suddenly complained of a terrific occipital headache. He become unconscious a minute or two later.

1:30 PM to 2:30: When I saw him 15 min later, he was pale, cold, and sweating profusely. He was totally unconscious with fairly frequent generalized titanic contractions of mild degree. Pupils of the eyes were at first equal, but in a few minutes the right pupil became widely dilated. The lungs were clear, but he was breathing stertorously but regularly. Heart sound were excellent, heart rate was 96/min. Systolic blood pressure was well over 300 mm Hg; diastolic pressure was 190 mm Hg. He had voided involuntarily.

Warmth in the form of hot water bottles and blankets was applied, and papavarine, 1 grain, was administered intravenously. Amylnitrite was also given to relieve the apparent intense vasoconstriction. Reflexes were unobtainable in the legs; right elbow was + + +.

It was apparent that the President had suffered a massive cerebral hemorrhage. I immediately called Washington on the private telephone line and contacted Dr. McIntire and informed him of the catastrophe. He told me that he would call Dr. Paullin in Atlanta immediately.

2:45 PM: Color was much improved. Breathing was a little irregular and stertorous, but deep. Blood pressure had fallen to 240/120 mm Hg. Heart sound were good—rate, 90/min.

3:15 PM: Pupils were approximately equal. Breathing had become irregular but of good amplitude.

3:31 PM: Breathing suddenly stopped and was replaced by occasional gasps. Heart sounds were not audible. Artificial respiration was begun and caffeine sodium benzoate given intramuscularly. At this moment Dr. Paullin arrived from Atlanta. Adrenalin was administered into the heart muscle.

3:35 PM: I pronounced him dead.

In Review

The diagnosis of systolic hypertension was documented in 1937; of systolic and diastolic hypertension in 1941; and followed three years later by the appearance of congestive heart failure. Subsequently, there was a single episode of coronary insufficiency without evidence of myocardial infarction. At no time was there any evidence of renal dysfunction. There was clinical and X-ray evidence of cholecystitis and cholelithiasis. Death was the result of a massive cerebral hemorrhage. An autopsy was not performed at the expressed wish of Mrs. Roosevelt (despite the urgent request of the Russian authorities who thought that the President might have met foul play).

As noted, the state of the President's health during the last years of his life was a topic of general concern. Rumor and speculation were primarily its basis, aided and abetted by the change in his appearance. With his loss of weight, initiated primarily by his medical regimen but enhanced by the development of some loss of appetite and his own desire to continue the weight-reduction program, he lost his usually robust appearance, and the loss of flesh from his face gave him a rather haggard appearance. This further increased the concern about his health and was misinterpreted by many of those who came into contact with him or who viewed his pictures in the public press.

I should also like to comment on the allegations that the President had suffered several "small strokes" before his death. Clinically, there was no evidence of strokes. His behavior toward his friends and intimates was unchanged and his speech unaltered. The latter was in question, particularly on the occasion of his last address before the Congress to report on the meeting at Yalta. It was noticed on the radio by many that his speech was at times hesitant and that he occasionally appeared to be at a loss for words. When queried about this later, he laughingly reported that while giving the speech he had spoken at intervals from memory and "off the record" and that he had then had slight difficulty in finding the proper place when returning to read the printed words of his address.

In conclusion, I should like to reiterate that this clinical record is written in the interest of accuracy and to answer some unfounded rumors. Many people rightfully attach much importance to the health records of the men who they have considered and elected to the office of President of the United States.

On joining the U.S. Naval Medical Corps in 1942 I had not the slightest inkling that I would be the attending physician to President Franklin D. Roosevelt from March 1944 to the day of his death and that I would be privileged to see him almost daily and to accompany him on all of his trips during this period. As a result of this unforgettable experience, and as a practicing physician, I have often wondered what turn the subsequent course of history might have taken if the modern methods for the control of hypertension had been available.

Appendix C
Interviews

Person	Date	Identification
Asbell, Bernard	November 17, 1994	Historian; author
Blum, Harry MD	October 26, 1994	Otolaryngologist, retired
Bookatz, Samuel	April 11, 1996	U.S. Navy artist, White House
Boring, Floyd	October 17, 1994	Secret Service 1944–1960
Breitman, Robert	August 24, 1994	Historian; Holocaust
Brownell, Herbert	April 5, 1993	Campaign manager, Governor Dewey 1944
Bruenn, Howard MD	October 2, 1993 and others	FDR's cardiologist 1944–1945
Burns, James McGregor	August 30, 1993	FDR biographer, professor of political science, Williams College
Daniels, Margaret Truman	October 21, 1999	Daughter of Harry S. Truman
Elsey, George	October 18, 1993	Map Room Office, White House

Etter, Harry MD	April 9–11, 1996	Physiatrist; Rear Admiral U.S. Navy, retired
Ferrell, Robert H.	December 3, 1994 and others	Historian; biographer of Harry S. Truman
Feinlieb, Manning MD	—	Biostatistician, National Institutes of Health (NIH)
Galbraith, John K.	January 11, 1995	Historian; government official
Gallagher, Hugh G.	November 6, 1993	Biographer of FDR
Gibson, Nina Roosevelt	March 3, 1994	Daughter of John Roosevelt; granddaughter of Eleanor and FDR
Gilbert, Robert E.	Various meetings 1994, 1995 December 30, 1999	Political scientist Northeastern University
Ginsburg, David	October 31, 1994	Attorney, colleague of Benjamin V. Cohen
Ginzberg, Eli	October 16, 1994	Economist; Special Assistant, War Department
Goodwin, Doris Kearns	October 15, 1994	Historian; biographer of FDR and Eleanor
Griffith, James	October 19, 1994	Secret Service, White House 1942–1945
Gurewitsch, Edna	September 29, 1993	Eleanor's physician
Hamby, Alonzo	February 28, 1993	Truman scholar, University of Ohio
Hannegan, William	December 8, 1993 and others	Son of Robert Hannegan; Chairman of Democratic National Committee 1944
Heller, Milton	December 15, 1994	Son-in-law; biographer of Dr. Joel Boone
Herman, Jan K.	December 15, 1994	Historian, U.S. Navy
Herzstein, Robert	October 3, 1994	Historian, Holocaust
Hiss, Tony	April 27, 1993	Son of Alger Hiss

Hopkins, Robert	September 10, 1993 September 30, 1993	Son of Harry Hopkins
Hoxie, R. Gordon	October 19, 1994; 1995; 1996	President, Center for the Study of the Presidency
Hyman, Sydney	December 10, 1993	Historian
Irwin, Barbara	June 16, 1993	Librarian, History of Medicine, New Jersey Medical School
Karski, Jan, Professor	October 19, 1994	Author
Lattimer, John MD	September 6, 1993	Urologist, authority on presidential assassination
Lasser, William	October 31, 1994	Biographer, Benjamin V. Cohen; faculty, Clemson University
Lipson, Milton	October 15, 1994	Secret Service White House 1939–1942
MacArthur II, Douglas	September 24, 1993	Nephew of General Douglas McArthur; government official
Mikesh, Robert	November 15, 1994	Pilot for FDR, World War II
Minnich, Caroline	October, 1994	Daughter of Dr. James Paullin
Pehle, John W.	January 11, 1995	Director, War Refugee Board, 1944
Raper, Mrs. H.S.	October 26, 1994	Physiotherapist at Warm Springs
Roosevelt, Eleanor	March 31, 1994	Niece of Eleanor and FDR
Roosevelt, Mrs. Franklin Jr.		Daughter-in-law of FDR
Roosevelt, James Jr.	April 11, 1996	Grandson of FDR
Schmidt, Ivan MD	March 1994	Staff, Lahey Clinic
Seagraves, Eleanor	September 26, 1993	Granddaughter of FDR

Smith, Elmer	November 15, 1994	Pilot for FDR, World War II
Stassen, Harold	November 11, 1993	Governor of Minnesota; U.N. Delegate
Stuart, Robert Jr.	October 17, 1993	Staff member, American Embassy, Paris 1944
Swanson, Mrs. Homer	November 16, 1994	Widow of Dr. Homer Swanson, neurosurgeon
Trohan, Walter	October 10, 1994	Reporter, *Chicago Tribune*
Ward, Geoffrey	November 6, 1993 August 1, 1994	Biographer of FDR
Weaver, Robert	November 1, 1993	Sub-cabinet officer in Roosevelt Administration
Weisse, Allen MD	1993, 1994	Cardiologist, New Jersey Medical School
Welles, Benjamin	December 10, 1993	Son of Sumner Welles

Appendix D
Wartime Conferences

Casablanca Conference occurred between January 12–14, 1943. The principals were Roosevelt, Britain's Prime Minister Winston Churchill, and representing France, General Henry Giraud and General Charles de Gaulle. The demand for unconditional surrender as a condition for peace was agreed upon by the Allies. Political problems between factions in the French government were addressed, the invasion of Sicily planned, and invasion of France postponed for one year.

Cairo-Teheran Conference between Roosevelt, Prime Minister Churchill, and Chinese Nationalist leader General Chiang Kai-shek was held from November 22–26, 1943. From November 28 to December 1, Roosevelt and Churchill met with Soviet Premier Joseph Stalin. The latter meeting led to plans for D-Day with the selection of General Dwight D. Eisenhower as supreme commander. There was initial discussion of Roosevelt's proposal for the United Nations organization by the "Big Three."

Hawaii Conference was held July 26–28, 1944. Attending were Roosevelt and three U.S. military commanders: General Douglas MacArthur, Admiral Nimitz and Admiral Leahy. They were there to discuss Pacific strategy.

Quebec Conference, (first) (August 17–24, 1943) with code name Trident. Subjects included Italian operations, planning for operation Overlord (cross channel invasion of France), agreement on sharing of information about atomic energy, among others.

Quebec Conference, (second) (September 10–17, 1944) (code name Octagon) included Roosevelt, Churchill, Canadian Prime Minister MacKenzie King, Foreign Minister Anthony Eden, military leaders, Secretary Morgenthau (Treasury). Noted for presentation of Morgenthau Plan for post-war Germany. It was a draconian plan for eliminating industry and converting Germany into a pastoral, agricultural nation. Initially signed by both Churchill and Roosevelt, it was later abandoned following widespread criticism. Other subjects were Lend-Lease continuation, and division of Germany into zones of occupation.

Yalta Conference (also known as the Crimean Conference) included the "Big Three" from the Cairo-Teheran Conference and was held from February 4–11, 1945. Planning for the founding conference of the United Nations, disposition of nations liberated from German occupation, and accommodation of Soviet requirements to enter the war against Japan were the main topics.

Notes

Preface

1. *Newsweek*, April 30, 1945, 45.

Introduction

1. In an interview with the author, October 1994, Dr. Howard G. Bruenn noted that he had not discussed the severity of the hypertension with Roosevelt since he never asked.

2. The certified copy of Franklin Delano Roosevelt's Certificate of Death, issued by the State of Georgia, Department of Public Health, stated the "primary cause of death" as cerebral hemorrhage with no mention of hypertension (Appendix A).

3. Jan K. Herman, "The President's Cardiologist," *Navy Medicine*, 8.2 (March–April 1990): 8, Dr. Howard G. Bruenn, a cardiologist stationed at Bethesda Naval Hospital noted that when he was called to examine the president in March 1944, "He (the president) was in heart failure," and that the condition was attributed to "high blood pressure.... From what I remember from his chart, it was first detected at least several years before I saw him."

4. Reporting the death of Roosevelt, in an article datelined Washington, April 12, the *New York Times* noted in its opening sentence that "Franklin Delano Roosevelt . . . died suddenly and unexpectedly at 4:35 P.M. today at Warm Springs, Georgia. . . ."

5. Bruenn writes in "Clinical Notes on the Illness and Death of President Franklin D. Roosevelt" (*Annals of Internal Medicine* 72, no. 4 [April 1970]: 597), that ". . . rumors about the state of his health began to be bruited about as early as 1936, 9 years before his death. . . . These speculations continued throughout the remainder of his life and rose to a crescendo of debate and uncertainty after his death."

6. See Dr. Ross T. McIntire, *White House Physician* (New York: G.P. Putnam's Sons, 1946).

7. "Longevity of Presidents, Vice Presidents and Unsuccessful Candidates for President," *Statistical Bulletin* 80: 4 (July–September 1980): 2; Longevity of Presidents of the United States, *Statistical Bulletin* (March 1976): 2.

8. Bruenn in "Clinical Notes" compiles a chronology of the time he spent as FDR's cardiologist.

9. Author's telephone interview with Douglas MacArthur II, September 24, 1993; comments by Professor Richard Newstadt, Douglas Dillon Professor of Government emeritus, Harvard University, Cambridge, MA. Following author's presentation at Emory University, Atlanta, GA, January 26–28, 1995.

10. Bob Woodward, *Shadow: Five Presidents and the Legacy of Watergate* (New York: Simon & Schuster, 1999), xx, 1–2.

11. Ibid., iii.

12. Ibid., 514–517.

Chapter 1. The Twentieth-Century Presidency: A High-Risk Occupation

1. Wartime leadership responsibilities and preparation for peace in the future, with the accompanying goal of preventing future conflagrations, understandably posed especially onerous and difficult burdens on presidents Woodrow Wilson, Franklin D. Roosevelt, Lyndon B. Johnson, and Richard Nixon.

2. George Bush suffered from atrial fibrillation secondary to hyperthyroidism. Treatment for hyperthyroidism may have led to hypothyroidism (deficient activity of the thyroid gland) and a slowing of the mental process and depression, which may have been present in the 1992 campaign.

3. W.A. DeGregorio, *The Complete Book of U.S. Presidents, from George Washington to George Bush*, 3rd ed (New York: Wings Book, 1991).

4. "Longevity of Presidents, Vice Presidents, and Unsuccessful Candidates for the Presidency," *Statistical Bulletin.* 80, no. 4 (July–September 1980): 3–8.

5. Ibid., 1. "In contrast to current life tables, which customarily show death rates at each age for a group of persons living at the same time, cohort life tables trace the mortality experience of a group of persons born at the same time and subject to the same general conditions during their lifetime."

6. This earlier analysis of the Metropolitan Life Insurance Co. will be modified depending on the ultimate longevity of the four current ex-presidents (Carter, Ford, Reagan, Bush). However, the decreased longevity in deceased presidents is shown by comparison with the three control populations and may be confirmed since some appointees as early as the mid-1960s are also still alive.

7. Only two of forty-two presidents were less than forty-five years of age when inaugurated. The Republic was 110 years old before there would be a president less than age forty-five—Theodore Roosevelt was the youngest at forty-two following McKinley's assassination, September 1901. Another sixty years would pass before there would be a second president younger than forty-five—John F. Kennedy was elected at age forty-three.

8. F. Russell, *The Shadow of Blooming Grove; Warren G. Harding in His Times* (New York: McGraw Hill, 1968), 80.

9. Arthur M. Schlesinger Jr., ed., *The Almanac of American History* (New York: Barnes and Noble, 1993), 440.

10. E.A. Weinstein, *Woodrow Wilson: A Medical and Psychological Biography* (Princeton, NJ: Princeton University Press, 1981), 14, 15, 16.

11. C.G., Lasky, *Eisenhower's Heart Attack* (Lawrence, KS: University Press of Kansas), 19–56.

12. Addison's disease has potentially serious implications for two reasons: It requires life-long treatment with steroids, agents that have physical and psychological side effects. Also, the disease itself is associated with various systemic problems and risk of lethal infection unless appropriately treated. According to Theodore Sorenson, *Kennedy* (New

York: Harper & Row, 1965), 38–42, Kennedy preferred not to use "Addison's disease" because it had a frightening sound to most laymen. He referred to his ailment as "adrenal insufficiency." There may be a technical rationalization for abiding the term Addison's disease since the original cases were usually associated with tuberculosis of the adrenal glands.

13. Jerrold M. Post and Robert S. Robins, *When Illness Strikes the Leader* (New Haven, CT: Yale University Press, 1993), 52.

14. An article by J.J. Brooks et al., "The Final Diagnosis of President Cleveland's Lesion," *Transactions and Studies of the College of Physicians of Philadelphia*, 2 vol. (1980), 1–26.

15. Post and Robins, *When Illness Strikes the Leader*, 7–9.

16. R.E. Gilbert, "The Political Effects of Presidential Illness: The Case of Lyndon B. Johnson," *Political Psychology* 16, no. 4 (1995): 769.

17. Dr. Howard G. Bruenn, Roosevelt's cardiologist, in an interview in *Navy Medicine* (March–April 1990), 8–9, stated that "He never asked me a question about the medications I was giving him, what his blood pressure was, nothing. . . . He was not interested. . . . He had a job to do and the hell with everything else."

18. Frances Russell, *The Shadow of Blooming Grove* (New York: McGraw Hill, 1968) 669.

19. Hoover quote in J.T. Barber, *The Presidential Character: Predicting Performance in the White House* (Englewood Cliffs, NJ: Prentice-Hall, 1977), 48.

20. Ibid., 271.

21. Post and Robbins, *When Illness Strikes the Leader*, 88.

22. Robert E. Gilbert, *The Mortal Presidency: Illness and Anguish in the White House* (New York: Fordham University Press, 1998), 18.

Chapter 2: Pre-Presidential Years: The Defining Experiences

1. Oral Interview with Olin Dows, by Emily Williams, August 8, 1978. Transcript in Oral History Collection, Franklin D. Roosevelt Library, Hyde Park, New York.

2. Geoffrey C. Ward, *A First Class Temperament: The Emergence of Franklin Roosevelt* (New York: Harper & Row, 1989), xiii.

3. Jerrold M. Post and Robert S. Robins, *When Illness Strikes the Leader* (New Haven, CT: Yale University Press, 1993), 25.

4. Hugh Gregory Gallagher, *FDR's Splendid Deception* (Arlington, VA: Vandamere Press: Dodd, Mead, 1989), xiv.

5. Will of James Roosevelt, *Roosevelt Family Papers*, Franklin D. Roosevelt Library.

6. F. Kennon Moody, "F.D.R. and His Neighbors: A Study of the Relationship Between Franklin Delano Roosevelt and the Residents of Dutchess County." Ph.D. diss., State University of New York at Albany, 1981.

7. Ward, *A First Class Temperament*, 18.

8. Ted Morgan, *F.D.R.: A Biography* (New York: Simon & Schuster, 1985), 206–211.

9. Interview with Robert Hopkins, at his home on 48th Street in Washington, D.C., September 20, 1993. Mr. Hopkins is the son of Harry Hopkins, a principal Roosevelt aide and confidant. He was also the official Signal Corps photographer at all of the international conferences from Casablanca through Cairo, Teheran, and Yalta.

10. Geoffrey C. Ward, *Before the Trumpet: Young Franklin Roosevelt 1882–1905* (New York: Harper & Row, 1986), 124.

11. Elliott Roosevelt, ed., *FDR: His Personal Letters, 1905–1928* (New York: Duell, Sloan and Pearce, 1948), 155.

12. Ward, *Before the Trumpet*, 199.

13. Elliott Roosevelt, *FDR: His Personal Letters, 1905–1928*, 205.
14. Ibid., 279.
15. Ibid., 301.
16. Ibid., 357.
17. Ibid., 441.
18. Ibid., 315.
19. Ibid.; the use of I.P for infantile paralysis (Roosevelt's own acronym) is typical of Roosevelt's coping style using bantering humor to reduce the inevitable anxiety.
20. Ibid., 334.
21. Ward, *Before the Trumpet*, 119.
22. Elliott Roosevelt, *FDR: His Personal Letters*, Eleanor Roosevelt to James Roosevelt Roosevelt, August 18, 1921.
23. Ibid., Eleanor Roosevelt to Sara Delano Roosevelt, August 27, 1921.
24. Ward, *A First Class Temperament*, 575, notes that when he left the Boy Scout Camp at Bear Mountain, "With him went a mysterious virus, perhaps incubated somewhere among the Boy Scouts, inhaled or ingested at some point during the hot, hectic day, too small for any microscope to detect, but already moving through his bloodstream, multiplying as it moved."
25. Noah B. Fabricant, "Franklin D. Roosevelt's Tonsillectomy and Poliomyelitis," *The Eye, Ear, Nose, and Throat Monthly* XXXVI (June 1957).
26. Eleanor Roosevelt to James Roosevelt Roosevelt, August 14, 1921, in Elliott Roosevelt, *FDR: His Personal Letters*, 523.
27. Ward, *A First Class Temperament*, 572.
28. Ibid., 525.
29. Roosevelt to Sara Delano Roosevelt, October 1924, *Roosevelt Family Papers*, Franklin D. Roosevelt Library.
30. Roosevelt to Eleanor Roosevelt, October 1924, *Roosevelt Family Papers*, Franklin D. Roosevelt Library.
31. Roosevelt to James Roosevelt Roosevelt, April 28, 1925, *Family Business and Personal Papers*, Franklin D. Roosevelt Library.
32. Roosevelt to Sara Delano Roosevelt, Autumn, 1924, *Roosevelt Family Papers*, Franklin D. Roosevelt Library.
33. Eleanor Roosevelt, *This I Remember* (New York: Harper & Brothers, 1949).
34. Elliott Roosevelt, *FDR: His Personal Letters*, 635.
35. Gallagher, *FDR's Splendid Deception*, 94, describes the situation as "a unspoken code" that agreed not to show the president in a wheelchair or being transferred to or from automobiles. He also quoted the Roosevelt biographer John Gunther as saying ". . . the fact that he used a wheelchair was never printed at all." However, *Time* magazine made several references to his wheelchair in reporting the 1944 campaign.

Chapter 3. Presidential Years 1933–1943: The Picture of Health

1. Letter April 29, 1931, Franklin D. Roosevelt Library.
2. Medical Examiner's Report, The Equitable Life Assurance Society of the United States, October 3, 1930, PPF, Franklin D. Roosevelt Library, Hyde Park, NY.
3. See *Liberty Magazine* July 15, 1931. This incident is discussed in Betty Houchin Winfield, *FDR and the News Media* (Urbana: University of Illinois Press, 1990), 20, and Frank Freidel, *The Triumph* (Boston: Little, Brown), 211.
4. *Compiled Presidential Press Conferences of Franklin D. Roosevelt*, Vol. 22, July 1943–December 1943 (New York: DaCapo Press).

5. Fireside Chat, March 12, 1933. *Official File*, Franklin D. Roosevelt Library.

6. Fireside Chat, May 7, 1933.

7. *Compiled Press Conferences of Franklin D. Roosevelt*, Vol. 22, July 1943–December 1943.

8. Ibid., xx.

9. Ibid.

10. Winfield, *FDR and the News Media*, 127–128.

11. *Compiled Press Conferences of Franklin D. Roosevelt*, Vol. 22, July 1943–December 1943.

12. Inaugural Address of Franklin D. Roosevelt, President of the United States. January 20, 1937 (Washington, D.C.: United States Government Printing Office, 1937) vii.

13. Although awakened several times from sleep in the early morning of Monday, September 2, with the news of the German invasion of Poland, thus starting World War II, Roosevelt appeared alert, clear, and quite active at his 10 A.M. press conference. K.S. Davis, *FDR: Into the Storm, 1937–1940* (New York: Random House), 487.

14. Winfield, *FDR and the News Media*, 140.

15. Ibid., 140.

16. Fireside Chat, December 28, 1940.

17. *Compiled Press Conferences of Franklin D. Roosevelt*, Vol. 22, July 1943–December 1943.

18. James McGregor Burns, *Roosevelt: The Soldier of Freedom 1940–1945* (New York: Harcourt, Brace, and Jovanovich, 1970), 145–146.

19. Vice Admiral Ross T. McIntire, *White House Physician* (New York: G.P. Putnam's Sons, 1946), 12.

20. Hugh Gregory Gallagher, *FDR's Splendid Deception* (New York: Dodd Mead, 1985), 170.

21. John Tebbel and Sarah Miles Watts, *The Press and the Presidency: From George Washington to Ronald Reagan* (New York: Oxford University Press, 1985), 441.

22. Winfield, *FDR and the News Media*, 94. See Chapter Five, "The New Deal Publicity System."

23. Winfield, *FDR and the News Media*, 107, and Grace Tully, *F.D.R., My Boss* (New York: Charles Scribner's Sons, 1949), 100. In addition to Roosevelt's ability to articulate his beliefs and visions, he also was conscious of the manner in which those words were heard. Winfield relates the story first told by Grace Tully that Roosevelt added a false tooth before each radio broadcast to prevent whistling on certain words.

24. Winfield, *FDR and the News Media*, 98, notes that Early's instructions are to be found in various memos (examples dated January 30, February 2 and 8, May 15, 1934) in the Official Files, Box #36, Franklin D. Roosevelt Library.

25. William Leuchtenburg, *F.D.R. and the New Deal* (New York: Harper & Brothers, 1963), 169.

26. J.B. West, *Upstairs at the White House* (New York: Coward, McCann & Georghehan, 1937), 7.

27. In the early 1980s, a complication was recognized in survivors of polio. Termed "post-polio syndrome" it usually occurs thirty years after the initial episode and includes new joint and muscle pain, new muscular weakness, new respiratory deficiencies, cold intolerance, and unaccustomed fatigue. Roosevelt sustained only the latter and this symptom is too vague and solitary to ascribe it to the post-polio syndrome.

28. Gallagher, *F.D.R.'s Splendid Deception*, 95.

29. Elliott Roosevelt, "They're Lying About F.D.R.'s Health," *Liberty Magazine*, May 1949, 18, 73–76. Anna Roosevelt, "My Life With F.D.R.," *The Woman's Digest*, XXII

(May 1949): 6–13, 112–113, also refutes Dr. Wold's assertions. She uses basically the same proof that Elliot used—"I was there" and know that things happened differently than Dr. Wold asserts. She also quotes a letter from Dr. Ross T. McIntire, personal physician to the president, stating that "One can say that Dr. Wold has no basis for any of his arguments." In his rebuttal, Elliott claims that when he talked with Wold the doctor acknowledged that he was not a staff member of two hospitals in St. Paul as the article had mentioned. Dr. Wold's article appeared in the February 15, 1949 issue of *Look* magazine.

30. Frederick A. Storm, "How is President Roosevelt's Health Today?" *Liberty*, vol. 14, no. 22, May 29, 1937.

31. "The News of the Week in Review," *New York Times*, Section Four, Sunday, July 15, 1937, 3, col. 2.

32. *New York Times*, July 26, 1935, 26, col. 4, Senator Joseph T. Robinson "assailed the foes of FDR." On August 2, 1935, 2, col. 2, proclaimed "Roosevelt is Vigorous in Mind and Body."

33. *New York Times*, August 8, 1935, 10, col. 5, notes that Edwin P. Cramer of West Plainfield, New Jersey, had appeared before the Senate Lobby Investigation Committee and acknowledged starting the campaign.

34. *New York Times*, December 1, 1937, 1, col. 4; December 4, 1, col. 7; December 1, 6, col. 7; December 8, 1, col. 5.

35. Arthur Krock, *New York Times*, February 17, 1939, 18, col. 5.

36. *New York Times*, February 18, 1939, 1, col. 8.

37. Howard C. Bruenn, "Clinical Notes on the Illness and Death of President Franklin D. Roosevelt," *Annals of Internal Medicine* 72 (1970): 579–591.

38. *New York Times*, May 7, 1941, 1, col. 2. and May 8, 1941, 24, col. 3.

39. *New York Times*, May 9, 1941, 6, col. 4.

40. *New York Times*, December 10, 1941, 8, col. 5.

41. *New York Times*, February 21, 1942, 8, col. 2; February 22, 1942, 15, col. 1; April 9, 6, col. 6; December 6, 1942, 22, col. 3.

42. One clear example of omission is the momentous visit of Dr. Alexander Sachs (representing Professor Albert Einstein), which led to the Manhattan Project, a $2 billion gamble with cosmic consequences. This occurred on October 11, 1939 (and may have had a follow-up on October 12, 1939), but is omitted from the Usher's Diaries.

43. See James A. Farley, *James A. Farley's Story : The Roosevelt Years* (New York: McGraw-Hill, 1948).

44. William C. Bullitt, *For the President: Personal and Secret Correspondence between Franklin D. Roosevelt and William C. Bullit* (Boston: Houghton, Mifflin, 1972), 383.

45. No verification or mention in the Usher's Diaries, and the fact that this anecdote was published twenty-seven years after Roosevelt's death, makes its validity doubtful.

46. These tracings were reviewed by cardiologist Howard Bruenn in March 1944.

47. Doris Kearns Goodwin, *No Ordinary Time* (New York: Simon & Schuster, 1994), 235.

48. Bruenn, "Clinical Notes," 579–591.

49. Stool examination for ova and parasites were negative in March 1940 and May 1944. The water in the White House was tested bacteriologically in July 1944; one showed *E. Coli* and the other was sterile. These tests were "routine" according to Dr. Bruenn.

50. Blood pressure elevations are considered mild (140/90), moderate (160/100), severe (180/110) and very severe (210/120) according to the National Heart, Lung and Blood Institute, National Institutes of Health, *Fifth Report of the Joint National Committee, 1993* and *The Sixth Report in the Archives of Internal Medicine*. 157:2413–2445, 1997.

51. These findings were provided from file notes of Dr. Bruenn.

52. Anna Roosevelt Halstead, Oral History, Columbia University, 1973, 39: "None of

us knew exactly what was wrong with Father. . . . We knew he had high blood pressure, and that's all. I never heard him (Dr. Bruenn) discuss Father's health at all, so that I had absolutely no idea."

53. Anna Roosevelt Halsted, Oral History, Columbia University, 1973, 36.

54. Interview with Dr. Harry Blum, October 26, 1994. Retired otolaryngologist (ENT specialist) in his mid-90s who practiced this specialty and used these medications in the 1940s.

55. McIntire, *White House Physician*, 76.

56. A. Merriman Smith, *Thank You, Mr. President* (New York: Harper and Brothers, 1946), 184.

57. A.M. Fishberg, *Hypertension and Nephritis* (Philadelphia: Lea and Febiger, 1939), 609.

58. F.H. McDowell and F. Plum, "Arterial Hypertension Associated with Acute Anterior Poliomyelitis." *New England Journal of Medicine* 245:241–245, 1951.

59. L. Weinstein "Cardiovascular Disturbances in Poliomyelitis" *Circulation* 15:741–742, 1957.

60. Joel T. Boone Collection, Library of Congress, Box 32, F.D. Roosevelt.

61. Ibid.

62. McIntire, *White House Physician*, 55.

63. He related to President Hoover that Roosevelt assured him that he would be asked to stay on as presidential physician, but was dismissed with loss of rank and salary. When he confronted Roosevelt he was told evasively that they wanted him stay. Roosevelt, however, may have merely, with typical courtesy, suggested "we will see a lot of you" without a definite offer. Dr. Boone met President-elect Roosevelt during a courtesy call on President Hoover. He showed him the medical facilities at the White House and was invited to visit the Center at Warm Springs. Dr. Boone had met Roosevelt in 1918 when the then Assistant Secretary awarded him a Croix de Guerre. The magnitude of Roosevelt's paralysis and its effect on this previously vigorous man was shocking to Dr. Boone. The interaction with the new president was limited. He reported to the White House medical office daily in March, 1933, but not thereafter. Mrs. Roosevelt and several of the staff were treated by him. The only medical interaction with Roosevelt was the new president's comment on his chronic nasal and sinus condition. At no time did Dr. Boone provide Roosevelt with medical care.

64. Jerrold M. Post and Robert S. Robins, *When Illness Strikes the Leader: The Dilemma of the Captive King* (New Haven, CT: Yale University Press, 1993), 90.

65. Bruenn, "Clinical Notes," 579 and interview with author.

66. In a telephone conversation in September, 1993 with Mrs. Eleanor Seagraves (daughter of Roosevelt's daughter Anna), Seagraves indicated to the author that "the family had the highest regard for Dr. Howard Bruenn, who they felt was an extremely competent and conscientious young internist/cardiologist." On the other hand, she does feel also that there was some concern about the professional capabilities of Vice Admiral Ross T. McIntire.

67. Bruenn, "Clinical Notes," 579.

Chapter 4. Presidential Years 1943–1944: Decline and Deception

1. Jeffrey B. Morris and Richard B. Morris, eds., *Encyclopedia of American History* (New York: Harper Collins, 1996), 431.

2. James McGregor Burns, *Roosevelt: The Soldier of Freedom 1940–1945* (New York: Harcourt, Brace and Jovanovich, 1970), 409.

3. Robert E. Gilbert, *The Mortal Presidency: Illness and Anguish in the White House* (New York: Fordham University Press, 1998), 54.

4. Eleanor Roosevelt, *The Autobiography of Eleanor Roosevelt* (New York: DaCapo Press, 1972), 263.

5. Ibid., 327.

6. Grace Tully, *FDR: My Boss* (New York: Charles Scribner's Sons, 1949), 273.

7. Ross T. McIntire, *White House Physician* (New York: G.P. Putnam and Sons, 1946), 183.

8. William D. Hassett, *Off the Record with FDR, 1942–45* (New Brunswick, NJ: Rutgers University Press, 1958), 292.

9. Anna Roosevelt Halsted, Oral History Project, Columbia University, 1973.

10. Merriman Smith, *Thank You Mr. President* (New York: Harper, 1946), 25, 135.

11. Burns, *Roosevelt: The Soldier of Freedom*, 409.

12. Howard G. Bruenn, interviews with author.

13. Harold Smith, Director of the Budget, Notes on Meetings with President, Franklin D. Roosevelt Library.

14. Eleanor Roosevelt, *The Autobiography of Eleanor Roosevelt*, 268.

15. Writing in *Annals of Internal Medicine* 72 (1970): 579–591, Dr. Bruenn states that the examination took place on March 27, 1944. However, Roosevelt had just returned from a weekend trip to Hyde Park that afternoon, hence Tuesday morning, March 28, is the correct date.

16. Robert Sherwood, Roosevelt's speech writer and biographer, made reference in *Roosevelt and Hopkins* (New York: Harper and Brothers, 1948), to the president's "bad heart"—commenting that in January 1943 during his flight to Casablanca, the plane could not fly above 8,000 feet due to the president's heart condition. No documentation is provided by Sherwood, nor is there documentation of general medical care provided by any physician or cardiologist. The plane, a C54 named the *Dixie Clipper*, was in fact designed for altitudes of less than 10,000 feet for all passengers and crew regardless of health status per interview with the pilots of the *Sacred Cow*, Elmer Smith and Robert Mikesh, April 15, 1994. They were unaware of any of Roosevelt's medical problems. There were oxygen cylinders aboard as a precaution but not for a specific medical problem. Descriptions of the *Dixie Clipper* (flew to Casablanca, January 14, 1943 and returned to Liberia and Brazil with Roosevelt and used a second time on last leg of trip to Teheran, November 1943) and the *Sacred Cow* (used for the trip from Malta, February 3, 1945 to Yalta) are found in the *American Aviation Historical Society Journal* 8, no. 2 (Summer 1963).

17. Dr. James E. Paullin, president of the American Medical Association, and Dr. Frank Lahey, founder of the Lahey Clinic, had occasion to examine Roosevelt on March 31. Caroline Minnich, Paullin's daughter, in a telephone interview in October 1991 recalled Admiral McIntire as "FDR's friend" and Dr. Bruenn as "the real doctor."

18. Jan Herman, "The President's Cardiologist," *Navy Medicine* (March–April 1990): 6. In this interview, Dr. Bruenn credits Anna Roosevelt with pressuring Admiral McIntire to schedule the examination.

19. Howard G. Bruenn, "Clinical Notes on the Illness and Death of President Franklin D. Roosevelt, *Annals of Internal Medicine* 72, no. 4 (April 1970), 579–591.

20. Ibid., 580.

21. Bruenn, interview with author.

22. "Blood Pressure Level and Mortality among Men." *Statistical Bulletin* of the Metropolitan Insurance Company 41: 1–4 (June 1960).

23. Herman, "The President's Cardiologist," 8.

24. Jim Bishop, *FDR's Last Year*, April 1944–1945 (New York: William Morrow, 1974), 383, claims Dr. Robert Duncan examined the president again in December 1944 in the presence of Dr. Bruenn. Bruenn denies this and describes Duncan, who appears in several places in Bishop's book, as an administrator and not an active clinician.

25. Bruenn, "Clinical Notes," 581.

26. One of the current speculations deals with a privately held, unpublished, hand-written letter by Dr. Frank Lahey. Dr. Bruenn is aware of such a letter and had no idea of its contents. He recalls that Dr. Lahey had only one or two direct medical interactions with the president. In later meetings with the Board of Consultants he "threw up his hands," and indicated that the problems were nonsurgical and therefore "signed-off" on the case.

27. Robert H. Ferrell, *The Dying President* (Columbia: University of Missouri Press, 1998), 41.

28. Quoted in Ferrell, *The Dying President*, 45.

29. Bruenn, several interviews with the author .

30. Ibid.

31. Ibid., Burns, *Roosevelt: The Soldier of Freedom*, 411.

32. *White House Usher's Diary*, Official File, Franklin D. Roosevelt Library, Hyde Park.

33. *New York Times*, May 18, 1933, 1, col. 2.

34. *New York Times*, March 3, 1934, 1, col. 6.

35. Ibid.

36. *New York Times*, November 12, 1935, 21, col. 7.

37. *New York Times*, September 6, 1936, 18, col. 4

38. *New York Times*, January 1, 1937, 4, col. 5.

39. *New York Times*, August 11, 1938, 1, col. 1, and 2, col. 4.

40. Bruenn, interviews with author.

41. *New York Times*, January 1, 1944, 1, col. 2.

42. *New York Times*, January 2, 1944, 20, col. 1.

43. *New York Times*, January 4, 1944, 19, col. 4.

44. *New York Times*, January 29, 1944, 15, col. 2.

45. *New York Times*, February 26, 1944, 8, col. 1.

46. *New York Times*, March 2, 1944, 34, col. 8.

47. *New York Times*, March 22, 1944, 1, col. 2. ·

48. *New York Times*, March 24, 1944, 17, col. 7.

49. *New York Times*, March 25, 1944, 17, col. 6.

50. *New York Times*, March 26, 1944, 35, col. 3.

51. Francis L. Loewenheim, Harold D. Langley, and Manfred Jonas, eds. *Roosevelt and Churchill, Their Secret Wartime Correspondence* (New York: Dutton, 1975), 410–483.

52. Ibid., 403–409 (A Polish exile and eyewitness to the Holocaust.)

53. Mr. Jan Karski met with Roosevelt on July 28, 1943, to discuss the Polish under-ground and the Holocaust. He also met with members of the War Cabinet in London. In an interview with the author, on October 19, 1994, Mr. Karski believed that singling out of Jews by Roosevelt would have been counterproductive by demoralizing others who suffered. He felt that the president was not insensitive to the humanitarian issues involved and indicated that Roosevelt's role as international leader was most important. He noted that Roosevelt was alert, well-informed, and showed no signs of ill health in a lengthy interview about a tragic situation. Professor Karski's role in alerting world leaders to the Holocaust was based on his eye-witness account of concentration camps. His heroic efforts are described at length in the Holocaust Museum, Washington, D.C. He was Professor of International Relations at Georgetown, and died in July 2000.

54. Bruenn, "Clinical Notes," 580.

55. *New York Times*, March 29, 1994, 1, col. 6.

56. Ibid., 1, col. 6.

57. *New York Times*, March 31, 1944, 23, col. 7.

58. *New York, Times,* April 1, 1944, 9, col. 1.
59. *New York Times,* April 3, 1944, 23, col. 7.
60. *New York Times,* March 31, 1944, 23, col. 7.
61. *New York Times,* April 5, 1944, 1, col. 2.
62. Ibid.
63. Eleanor Roosevelt, *The Autobiography of Eleanor Roosevelt,* 268.
64. *New York Times,* May 8, 1, col. 1.
65. Ibid.
66. *Time,* May 22, 1944, 28.
67. Dr. Harry Etter, interview with author, April 9–11, 1996.
68. *New York Times,* June 9, 1944, 7, col. 6.
69. Bruenn, "Clinical Notes," 584.
70. *New York Times,* June 9, 1944.
71. *New York Times,* June 14, 1944, 22, col. 1.
72. Bruenn, "Clinical Notes," 579.
73. Bruenn, interview with author.
74. Herman, "The President's Cardiologist," 11.
75. Caroline Minnich, daughter of Dr. James Paulling, telephone interview with author, October, 1944.
76. McIntire, *White House Physician,* 186.
77. Bruenn, "Clinical Notes," 146.
78. Jan Herman, "The President's Cardiologist," 10.
79. Jonathan Daniels, *White House Witness* (Garden City, NY: Doubleday, 1975), 3.
80. Bruenn, interview with author.
81. Anna Roosevelt Halsted, Oral History Project, Columbia University, New York, 35.
82. Bruenn, interview with author.
83. In an article in *Look* magazine, February 15, 1949, Dr. Karl Wold described Roosevelt's four strokes: (1) summer of 1938 while visiting his son James at the Mayo Clinic; (2) after the Teheran Conference in December 1943; (3) Palm Sunday, March 25, 1945; (4) the fatal episode April 12, 1945. Anna Roosevelt disputes these allegations in "My Life with FDR." *The Woman's Digest* XXII (May 1949): 7–12, 112–113.

Chapter 5. Presidential Years 1944–1945: The Last Campaign

1. *New York Times,* June 9, 1944, 7, col. 6.
2. *New York Times,* June 14, 1944, 22, col. 1.
3. Roosevelt to Robert E. Hannegan, July 10, 1944, *Papers of Robert E. Hannegan,* Harry S. Truman Library.
4. Ibid.
5. Ibid.
6. Kenneth S. Davis, *FDR: The Beckoning of Destiny 1882–1928* (New York: G.P. Putnam's Sons, 1972), 153.
7. Ibid., 164. Ted Morgan, *FDR: A Biography* (New York: Simon & Schuster, 1985), 87, also covers the comparison problem.
8. Peter Collier, *The Roosevelts: An American Saga* (New York: Simon & Schuster, 1994) describes in detail "a state of civil war between them [the two families]." He concludes with a description of the families coming together again in 1989.
9. Jan K. Herman, "The President's Cardiologist," *Navy Medicine* (March–April): 9.
10. Dr. Howard Bruenn, interview with author.
11. Jim Bishop, *FDR's Last Year April 1944–April 1945* (New York: William Morrow, 1974), 22–23. David Ginsburg, a New Deal staff member, interviewed by the author on

October 31, 1994, was a close friend of Cohen's. He commented that Cohen had led him to believe that Roosevelt would not survive the term.

12. Harold L. Ickes, *Diary*, Sunday, June 4, 1944, Manuscript Division, Library of Congress.

13. Ibid., Saturday, May 13, 1944.

14. Frances Perkins, *The Roosevelt I Knew* (New York: Viking Press, 1946), 388.

15. Samuel I. Rosenman, *Working With Roosevelt* (New York: DaCapo Press, 1952), 438.

16. Ross T. McIntire, *White House Physician* (New York: G. P. Putnam and Sons, 1946), 194.

17. Bishop, *FDR's Last Year*, 72.

18. Bruenn, interview with author.

19. Anna Roosevelt Halsted, *Oral History Project*, Columbia University, New York.

20. Robert Ferrell, *The Dying President: Franklin D. Roosevelt, 1944–1945* (Columbia: University of Missouri Press, 1998), 76.

21. James Roosevelt, *Affectionately, F.D.R.: A Son's Story of a Lonely Man* (New York: Harcourt, Brace, 1959), 350.

22. Bishop, *FDR's Last Year*, 109.

23. James Farley, *New York Times*, July 22, 1944, 1, col. 2.

24. Edward J. Flynn, *You're the Boss* (New York: Viking, 1947), 155.

25. Edward Pauley, memorandum to Jonathan Daniels, Robert Hannegan Papers, White House Central Files, Harry S. Truman Library, n.d (probably 1950).

26. Ibid.

27. David McCullough, *Truman* (New York: Touchstone, 1993), 295.

28. "Democrats: The Struggle," *Time*, July 24, 1944, 1.

29. Society of Actuaries, *Build and Blood Pressure Study* (Schaumburg, IL: Society of Actuaries, 1959), vol. 2, 255 ff.

30. Ibid.

31. Ibid.

32. Cerebrovascular accident, or stroke, is due to bleeding (hemorrhage) into the brain, which, in fact, occurred on April 12, 1945, or a blockage (thrombosis) of a blood vessel.

33. These calculations were done using tables provided by the *Statistical Bulletin* of the Metropolitan Life Insurance Company, using the cumulative probability method (June 1960).

34. Ho, K.K.L., et al. "The Epidemiology of Heart Failure: The Framingham Study," *Journal of American College of Cardiology* 22, Supplement A (October 1993): 6A-13A.

35. Actuarial calculations are the courtesy of William Woodman, Cos Cob, Connecticut, a member of the New York Life Underwriting Actuary Committee.

36. W. B. Kannel, et al. "Epidemiologic Assessment of the Role of Blood Pressure in Stroke," *Journal of the American Medical Association* 214, no. 2 (October 12, 1970): 301–310.

37. James Roosevelt, *Affectionately, F.D.R.*, 351.

38. Howard G. Bruenn, "Clinical Notes on the Illness and Death of President Franklin D. Roosevelt," *Annals of Internal Medicine* 72, no. 4 (April 1970): 586.

39. James Roosevelt, *Affectionately, F.D.R.*, 355.

40. James Roosevelt, *My Parents: A Differing View* (Chicago: The Playboy Press, 1976), 278–279.

41. Ibid, 285.

42. R.M. Daley, H.E. Ungerleider, and R.S. Gubner, "Prognosis in Hypertension," *Journal of the American Medical Association* 121 (February 6, 1943): 385.

43. Rosenman, *Working with Roosevelt* (New York: 1972), 439.

44. Ibid.

45. James Farley, Letter to the Editor, *New York Times*, March 5, 1951.

46. Joseph P. Kennedy's diaries bluntly forecast Roosevelt's imminent demise based on both his own meeting in 1944 with the president and the reported views of Senator Truman, as vice presidential candidate, and Democratic National Committee Chairman Robert Hannegan. The references are clearly bitter due to Kennedy's estrangement from Roosevelt and the recent loss of his oldest son, Joseph P. Kennedy, Jr., in a bombing mission. Crude anti-Semitic references abound. He clearly anticipates that Truman, as president, will "Kick out all these incompetents and Jews . . . and ask fellows like myself and others to come back and run the government." Amanda Smith, ed., *Hostage to Fortune: The Letters of Joseph P. Kennedy* (New York: Viking, 2001), 607–612.

47. Michael R. Beschloss, *Kennedy and Roosevelt: The Uneasy Alliance* (New York: W.W. Norton, 1980), 255.

48. Roosevelt to Robert E. Hannegan, July 10, 1944 (See Note 3.)

49. Doris Kearns Goodwin, *No Ordinary Time* (New York: Simon & Schuster, 1994), 526–527.

50. William Hannegan, telephone interview with author, December 8, 1994, noted that the call by Roosevelt to the party leaders was planned to insure Senator Truman's acceptance and break a seemingly deadlocked convention. After Truman's acceptance, he led on the second ballot.

51. Robert G. Nixon, oral history interview with Jerry Hess, October 9, 16, 19, 20, 21, 22, 23, 28 , 29, 30; November 4, 5, 6, 20, 23, 1970, pp. 66–67. Harry S. Truman Library, Independence, Missouri.

52. John K. Galbraith, telephone interview with author, January 11, 1995.

53. Margaret Truman Daniel, telephone interview with author, October 21, 1999.

54. Ibid. When asked specifically whether this opinion, namely that Roosevelt would complete the fourth term, continued during the 1944 campaign, post-election, at the inaugural and after Roosevelt's March 1, 1944, Address to Congress, she was emphatic in denying any thought of succession.

55. In an interview with the author, Mrs. Daniel expressed doubts about the validity of references ascribed to her father, of any anxiety, nightmares, or any other concerns regarding Roosevelt's likelihood of dying.

56. Harry S. Truman, *Draft Copy of Memoirs*, 1, Truman Post-Presidential Files, Memoirs Files, Box 16, Harry S. Truman Library.

57. William Hannegan, telephone interview with author, December 8, 1993.

58. "The Presidency: The Waikiki Conference," *Time*, August 21, 1944, 21.

59. Ibid.

60. Rosenman, *Working with Roosevelt*, 462.

61. Ibid. When Robert Nixon's supervisor in New York saw the San Diego photograph, he called Nixon and asked: "My god, that photograph, is Roosevelt dying?" Nixon described the picture much as had Rosenman—his jaw was slack, his mouth was open, his face drawn and pallid. Robert Nixon, oral history interview, Harry S. Truman Library, Independence, Missouri.

62. George Elsey, telephone interview with author, October 18, 1993.

63. Bruenn, "Clinical Notes,"586.

64. "Roosevelt Asserts We Need Bases Nearer Japan," *Chicago Daily Tribune*, August 13, 1944, 1, col. 1.

65. "The Presidency: The President's Week," *Time*, August 28, 1944, 16.

66. "The Presidency: After Due Consideration," *Time*, September 4, 1944, 20.

67. MacKenzie King, *Diary*, entry for September 11, 1944.

68. Ibid.

69. Bruenn, "Clinical Notes," 587.

70. Franklin D. Roosevelt, Speech File, Franklin D. Roosevelt Library, Hyde Park, NY.

71. "The Campaign: The Old Magic," *Time*, October 2, 1944, 21.

72. "The President's Week," *Time*, October 9, 1944.

73. "The Presidency: Hannegan's Enthusiasm," *Time*, October 16, 1944, 1.

74. Ibid.

75. "The Presidency: He's Perfectly O.K.," *Time*, October 16, 1944, 17.

76. Ibid.

77. "The President's Health," *Newsweek*, October 23, 1944, 40.

78. "Truman Can't Picture Dewey as President," *Chicago Daily Tribune*, October 17, 1944, 9, col. 2.

79. Editorial, "Mr. Roosevelt's Health," *Chicago Daily Tribune*, October 17, 1944, 14.

80. Ibid.

81. "Pennsylvania Is Key to Victory," *Chicago Daily Tribune*, October 20, 1944, 11, col. 1.

82. "Mr. Truman is Well," *Chicago Daily Tribune*, October 24, 1944, 10, col. 1.

83. "A Vote for F.D.R. May be a Vote for Truman," *Chicago Daily Tribune*, October 28, 1944, 10, col. 1.

84. A similar description of McIntire was printed in Jeanne Perkins, "The President's Doctor," *Life*, July 31, 1944, 4. She also describes the size of duties, noting that under his leadership the medical forces of the Navy had increased from 11,000 to 140,00.

85. *Time*, October 23, 1944, 17.

86. Bruenn, "Clinical Notes," 587.

87. "Ovation in the Rain," *Time*, October 29, 1944, 1.

88. *New York Times*, October 22, 1944, 1:1–2.

89. "President All Right After Ride in Rain," *New York Times*, October 24, 1944, 1, col. 2.

90. Ibid., 2.

91. *New York Times*, October 22, 1944, 36, col. 3–4.

92. Ted Morgan, *F.D.R., A Biography*, (New York: Simon & Schuster, 1985), 738.

93. "The Strangest Campaign," *Time*, November 6, 1944, 2, col. 2.

94. Shortly after the election, Roosevelt returned to Washington driving to the White House with both Vice President Henry A. Wallace and Vice President-elect Harry S. Truman. He assured the crowd that he was not planning to make Washington his permanent home. At his first press conference following the election, Frank Kent of the *Baltimore Sun* asked Roosevelt about his plans for a fifth term to a roar of laughter led by the president. The issue of a fifth term was raised by Robert Hannegan in preempting Roosevelt in April 1944 and proclaiming him the party's choice was only for a fourth term, but if there were an emergency, for a fifth term as well. Hence, the illusion of a life span not only of four years, itself a virtual impossibility, but even eight years.

95. *Life*, July 31, 1944.

96. *Life*, October 9, 1944.

97. *Life*, November 6, 1944.

98. Because of Roosevelt's paralysis, weights were only approximate. Two or more attendants would hold him upright on the scale. Interview with Dr. Bruenn.

99. Bruenn, "Clinical Notes," 587.

100. Amos Perlmutter, *FDR and Stalin: A Not So Grand Alliance* (Columbia: University of Missouri Press, 1984). Even at a political level the Perlmutter thesis is dubious. Perlmutter's belief that "It is possible that Roosevelt might have been more insistent in his courtship of Stalin had he been in good health," p. 181, is problematic. The same study faults Roosevelt for his failure to protect the non-Communist London government-in-exile against the Lublin Poles who were supported by Stalin.

101. Robert Ferrell, *Choosing Truman: The Democratic Convention of 1944* (Columbia: University of Missouri Press, 1994).

102. Ibid., 3.

103. Amos Perlmutter, *FDR and Stalin: A Not So Grand Alliance*, 179–181. It is interesting to note that in the communications, the Soviet Minister of Foreign Affairs Vyacheslav M. Molotov and Ambassador Adrei Gromyko make no mention of Roosevelt's health. They looked forward to his election for a fourth term in 1944. In their view, the election of Thomas Dewey would be a strong blow to Soviet-American relations. They both possessed an accurate, detailed knowledge of domestic American politics. However, there is not a hint of succession to the presidency except by election in 1948.

104. Author interviews with Dr. Bruenn.

105. Roosevelt's will, Vertical File, Roosevelt Papers, Roosevelt Library.

106. James Roosevelt, *Affectionately, F.D.R.*, 347–248.

107. This is one of three paradoxical mortality sequences involving presidents, or presidential candidates in the twentieth century. Former President Woodrow Wilson survived his younger, presumably healthier successor, Warren G. Harding. Ambassador to the United Nations and former presidential candidate, Governor Adlai Stevenson (1952, 1956) died in July 1965, age 65. His life span was less than that of his opponent, President Dwight D. Eisenhower by more than a decade, even though Governor Stevenson had forecast Eisenhower's demise in the 1956 campaign.

108. Correspondence and notes, Harold G. Smith, Budget Director, Roosevelt Library.

109. Editorial, *New York Times*, January 21, 1945.

110. Robert Ferrell, *The Dying President*, 102, suggests that perhaps one must doubt if the episode between James and his father just prior to the inauguration actually happened.

111. John Gunther, *Roosevelt in Restrospect: A Profile in History* (New York: Harper, 1950), 28.

112. Frances Perkins, *The Roosevelt I Knew* (New York: Viking Press, 1946), 391.

113. George Martin, *Madam Secretary: Frances Perkins* (Boston: Houghton Mifflin, 1976), 461.

114. Samuel Bookatz, personal interview with author, April 11, 1996, at Bethesda Naval Hospital.

115. Storm Whaley, personal interview with author, April 12, 1996, Bethesda, MD.

116. Bruenn, "Clinical Notes,"588.

117. "Roosevelt Health Fine, Says Doctor," *New York Times*, 21 January 1945, 26, col. 7.

118. John Crider, "A Grim Roosevelt Begins New Term," *New York Times*, January 21, 1945.

119. Editorial, *New York Times*, January 21, 1945.

120. *New York Times*, "News of the Week in Review," January 21, 1945.

121. William M. Rigdon, *White House Sailor* (Garden City, NY: Doubleday, 1962), 139.

122. Douglas MacArthur II, telephone interview with author, September 24, 1993. Author's note: The meeting in question with Roosevelt took place at 11:00 a.m., and I asked MacArthur about this because of the diurnal variation which Roosevelt had exhibited to a number of observers. He was usually more alert in the morning. Perhaps the only explanation was that Roosevelt was under increased stress. Harry Hopkins had left to return to the Mayo Clinic. Judge Rosenman had been called, but had not yet arrived from London. Major General Watson was terminally ill at this time.

123. Robert A. Stuart, Jr., telephone interview with author, October 17, 1993.

124. Tony Hiss, telephone interview with author, April 27, 1993.

125. Bruenn, "Clinical Notes," 589. It should be noted that this was not discussed until twenty-five years later when he published his notes.

126. Robert Hopkins, telephone interview with author, September 10, 1993, and a personal interview on September 20, 1993, at his home in Washington, D.C.

127. Edward R. Stettinius, Jr., *Roosevelt and the Russians: The Yalta Conference* (Garden City, NY: Doubleday, 1949), 72.

128. Charles E. Bohlen, *Witness to History 1929–1969* (New York: W.W. Norton, 1973), 172.

129. James F. Byrnes, *Speaking Frankly* (New York: Harper, 1947), 12.

130. McIntire, *White House Physician*, 217.

131. Rosenman, *Working with the President*, 522.

132. Perkins, *The Roosevelt I Knew*, 395.

133. Editorial, *Life*, February 26, 1945, 24.

134. Editorial, *Life*, September 6, 1948, 24. Quoted in Edward R. Stettinius' book *Roosevelt and the Russians: The Yalta Conference* (Garden City, New York: Country Life Press, 1949).

135. Lord Moran, (Charles Wilson): taken from the *Diaries of Lord Moran: The Struggle for Survival, 1940–1965* (Boston: Houghton Mifflin, 1966), 242.

136. Eleanor Roosevelt, *Autobiography of Eleanor Roosevelt* (New York: DaCapo Press, 1972), 275.

137. Rosenman, *Working With Roosevelt*, 527.

138. Eli Ginzberg, telephone interview with author, October 16, 1994.

139. Editorial, *New York Times*, March 2, 1945.

140. "FDR Rambles in Talk; Discern DeGaulle Slap," *New York Times*, March 2, 1945, 9, col. 1.

141. Walter Trohan, telephone interview with author, October 10, 1994, contends that Harry S. Truman, Eleanor Roosevelt, Anna Roosevelt, and "everyone at the National Convention in July knew that the president was dying." The preponderance of evidence from other sources would suggest that this was not true.

142. "President Returns Home in 'Great Health' . . . Secretary Reports," *New York Times*, March 1, 1945, 13, col. 1–2.

143. Howard Bruenn, telephone interview with author, January 7, 1995, expressed more open disappointment with Dr. McIntire.

144. MacKenzie King, *Diary*, entry for March 10, 1945.

145. MacKenzie King, *Diary*, entry for March, 13, 1945. At dinner in the White House on this evening were Anna and her husband Col. Boetigger, and an additional guest, Mrs. Rutherfurd, whom the president introduced as "another relative."

146. Six months earlier, King's unpublished diaries described Roosevelt as distinctly older, worn, much thinner in face and body at the second Quebec Conference, September 10–17, 1944, so much so that King was shocked, feeling that the president had "failed very much." The loss of his usual ebullience, "his old hearty self and his laugh," and his strength were apparent. Surprisingly, McIntire was observed as "really concerned" in contrast to his continuous bland, categorical reassurances to the press. King referred to Roosevelt perspiring and on the last day (September 17) looking "so frail—his face and body visibly reduced in size.

147. *New York Times*, March 23, 1945, 3, col. 1.

148. Francis L. Loewenheim, Harold D. Langley, and Manfred Jones, editors, *Roosevelt and Churchill: Their Secret Wartime Correspondence* (New York: E.P. Dutton & Co., 1975) 661.

149. Ibid., 674.

150. Edwin H. Friedman, *A Failure of Nerve: Leadership in the Age of the Quick Fix* (Bethesda, MD: The Edwin Friedman Estate/Trust, 1999), 277.

151. Ibid., 279.

152. "Pope Blessed President in Message of Week Ago," *New York Times*, April 13, 1945, 2, col. 2.

153. Eleanor Roosevelt, *This I Remember*, 342–343.

154. Robert Sherwood, *Roosevelt and Hopkins*, 527–528.

155. Bishop, J. *FDR's Last Year, April 1944–April 1945* (New York, William Morrow & Co., Inc., 1974) 480. William D. Hassett, *Off the Record with FDR* (New Brunswick, NJ, 1958), 318. Rosenman, see Note 133.

Chapter 6. "The Day of the Lord, April 12, 1945"

1. Bernard Asbell, *When F.D.R. Died* (New York: Holt, Rinehart and Winston, 1961), 21.

2. Edward R. Stettinius, Jr., *Roosevelt and the Russians* (Garden City, NY: The Country Life Press), 1949, 310–313.

3. James McGregor Burns, *Roosevelt: The Soldier of Freedom* (New York: Harcourt, Brace and Jovanovich, 1970), 583.

4. Ibid., 584.

5. Ibid., 762. Burns notes that on Roosevelt's last day in Washington he spoke with Anne O'Hare McCormick of the *New York Times*, and told her he no longer believed what he had told Congress about his confidence in Stalin. Averell Harriman also noted in a private memorandum that Roosevelt no longer believed the Russians; Harriman Papers, Franklin D. Roosevelt Library.

6. Howard G. Bruenn, "Clinical Notes on the Illness and Death of President Franklin D. Roosevelt," *Annals of Internal Medicine* 72, no. 4 (April 1970): 690.

7. Ross T. McIntire, *White House Physician* (New York: G.P. Putnam and Sons, 1946), 238.

8. William Hassett, *Off the Record with FDR* (New Brunswick, NJ, 1958), 327. (The title of this chapter, "The Day of the Lord, April 12, 1945," is adapted from Hassett, p. 133.)

9. Ted Morgan, *FDR: A Biography* (New York: Simon & Schuster, 1985), 761.

10. Quoted in Burns, *Roosevelt: The Soldier of Freedom*, 587.

11. *Churchill and Roosevelt: The Complete Correspondance* ed. by Warren F. Kimball. Volume III. Alliance Declining (Princeton, NJ: Princeton University Press, 1984), 63.

12. Hassett, *Off the Record with FDR*, 333.

13. Robert Sherwood, *Roosevelt and Hopkins* (New York: Harper and Brothers, 1948) 882, expresses that optimism: ". . . although crippled physically and prey to various infections, he was spiritually the healthiest man I have ever known. He was gloriously and happily free of the various forms of psychic maladjustment which are called by such names as inhibition, complex phobia. His mind, if not always orderly, bore no traces of paralysis and neither did his emotional constitution."

14. Ted Morgan, *FDR*, 762.

15. This telephone call was reported by Jim Bishop, *FDR's Last Year* (New York: William Morrow, 1974), 573. However, it is not mentioned in any of Bruenn's writings. Bishop further notes that McIntire would write that Bruenn's report "was most optimistic . . . and that every cause for anxiety seemed to have lifted," 573.

16. William Hassett, *Off the Record*, 336, mentions the two men carrying Roosevelt from his chair to his bedroom. Bruenn, "The President's Cardiologist," 13, notes that he and Prettyman carried the president to his bedroom where Bruenn began treatment.

17. Jan K. Herman, "The President's Cardiologist," *Navy Medicine* (March–April 1990): 13. Mrs. Howard Bruenn was at home in Rockville, Maryland that afternoon with her two young children. There news of FDR's death came as a complete shock to Mrs. Bruenn as it did to many others. She had been a nurse at Presbyterian Hospital in New York, and had considerable clinical experience. She recalls seeing Roosevelt as a guest at the fourth inauguration, and having felt as did the *New York Times*, that the president, although tired, was doing reasonably well.

18. "Oral History Interview with James J. Rowley," September 20, 1988, by Niel M. Johnson, Harry S. Truman Library, 15.

19. Telephone interview with James A. Griffith, October 19, 1994.

20. The medical events here can be found in Bruenn's, "Clinical Notes," 590. The exact wording can be found in Appendix B.

21. McIntire, *White House Physician*, 243.

22. Interview with Dr. Bruenn.

23. Telephone interview with H. Stuart Raper, M.D., October 26, 1994. He expressed concern that no calls were made to any of the physicians who worked in Warm Springs. Since Roosevelt had very little medical work at Warm Springs, mainly orthopedic or related to his braces, Raper's acquaintance with Roosevelt was mostly social at picnics, cocktail parties, and other events. In a telephone conversation with the author, November 15, 1994, Mrs. Raper remembered that Roosevelt "looked dreadful" during these days in April, but she did not think of him as being critically ill.

24. McIntire, *White House Physician*, 241.

25. Telephone interview with Dr. H. Stuart Raper, October 26, 1994.

26. Telephone interview with Mrs. H. Stuart Raper, November 15, 1994.

27. Telephone interview with Mrs. Homer Swanson, November 16, 1994. Her account does differ slightly from Dr. Raper's because she noted that Dr. Swanson drove to the outskirts of Atlanta where he was met by an escort (possibly a state trooper) who told him it was too late and that Roosevelt had died. This varies from Dr. Raper's account in which Swanson accompanied Paullin to Warm Springs.

28. Bernard Asbell, *When F.D.R. Died* (New York: Holt, Rinehart & Winston, 1961), 63–67. Source for the clock times included.

29. Harry S. Truman, Letter to Mrs. George P. Wallace, April 12, 1945, Harry S. Truman Library.

30. Asbell, *When F.D.R. Died*, 109.

31. Correspondence and notes of Harold G. Smith, Director of the Budget, Franklin D. Roosevelt Library.

32. Roosevelt's approach to dropping the atomic bomb was guided by military realities. Meeting with General Leslie R. Groves and Secretary of War Henry L. Stimson, Roosevelt asked if the bomb was available for tactical use against the Germans who had just launched the Ardennes offensive two days earlier (December 16, 1944), but was told that it was still experimental and would not be ready until August 1945. General Groves left the meeting with the impression that Roosevelt had no reservations about its use against the Nazis if the war in Europe had continued to that time. Eisenhower, J.S.D. *The Bitter Woods* (New York: G.P. Putnam and Sons, 1969).

33. Samuel I. Rosenman, *Working with Roosevelt* (New York: DaCapo Press, 1952), 467–469.

34. *New York Times*, April 13, 1945, 1, col. 5 and 6.

35. David Selin, interview, September 4, 2000, Palm Beach, Florida.

36. *New York Times*, editorial page, April 13, 1945.

37. Ibid.

38. Bishop, *FDR's Last Year, April 1944–April 1945* (New York: William Morrow, 1974) 585.

39. *New York Times*, "Even His Family Unaware of Condition as Cerebral Stroke Brings Death," April 13, 1945, 1, col. 5 and 6.

40. *New York Times*, "Roosevelt Health Long Under Doubt," April 13, 1945, 9, col. 6.

41. *Life*, April 23, 1945, 30.

42. Telephone interview with Harold Stassen, November 16, 1993.

43. Telephone interview with Robert Weaver, November 1, 1993.

44. *Life*, April 23, 1945, 32.

45. Ibid.

46. Francis Russell, *The Shadow of Blooming Grove* (New York: McGraw Hill, 1968), 594.

47. Sigmund Freud, "Thought for the Times on War and Death," in *Collected Papers* (London: International Psychoanalytical Press, 1925), vol. IV, 305.

48. Asbell, *When F.D.R. Died*, 149.

49. *Life*, April 23, 1945, 30.

50. Harold Orlansky, "Reactions to the Death of President Roosevelt," *The Journal of Social Psychology* 26 (1947): 235–266.

51. P. Schilder, *Goals and Desires of Man* (New York: Columbia University Press, 1942), 110, provides the explanation of death as accident: "We are . . . not very far away from the point of view of children who consider death not as the natural end of life but as the result of violence inflicted upon an individual. . . . Because of the independence of the outer world which influences the individual, our life is partially determined by occurrences (accident) over which we do not have power. . . . According to this formulation, death is an accident, like a flood or an avalanche."

52. Orlansky, "Reactions to the Death of President Roosevelt," 235–266.

53. Ibid.

54. Hassett, *Off the Record*, 327–328.

55. *Time*, April 23, 1945.

56. Telephone interviews with Agent Floyd Boring, October 17, 1994; Agent James Griffith, October 19, 1994; Agent James T. Crowley, September 20, 1998.

57. The Secret Service protection given to Vice President Truman in March was justified by the need to protect him from crowds at various gatherings. It was agreed to by Secretary of Treasury Henry Morgenthau at the insistence of General Harry Vaughn, Truman's aide, but was not in anticipation of succession. Vaughn makes no reference to the possibility of succession in his oral history at the Harry S. Truman Library (January 14, 1963). None of the three agents (Milton Lipson, Floyd Boring, and James Griffith) I interviewed attach much significance to the protection provided Truman as vice president. His predecessor, Henry A. Wallace, also had Secret Service protection assigned, at least selectively. The agents were part of the White House detail detached as needed for the vice president and not specifically in anticipation of succession.

58. Telephone interview with George Elsey, October 19, 1993.

59. Merriman Smith, *Thank You, Mr. President: A White House Notebook* (New York: Harper, 1946).

60. "Oral History Interview with Judge Marvin Jones," April 3, 20, 24, 1970 and May 8, 14, 1970, Harry S. Truman Library, Independence, Missouri.

61. Bruenn, "Clinical Notes," 591, also notes that such an autopsy was not performed at the expressed wish of Mrs. Roosevelt.

62. "Oral History Interview with Harry Easley," August 24, 1967 by J.R. Fuchs, 99, Harry S. Truman Library.

63. Harry S. Truman, "Memoirs First Draft," Truman Post Presidential Files, Memoirs File, Box 16, Harry S. Truman Library.

64. Ibid., and Harry S. Truman, *Memoirs: Year of Decision* (Garden City, NY: Doubleday, 1955), 1.

65. Ibid., 2.

66. "Roosevelt, Franklin D., re Illness and Death of," Memoirs File, Truman Post Presidential Papers, Box 645, Harry S. Truman Library.

67. Richard L. Miller, *Truman the Rise to Power* (New York: McGraw Hill, 1986), 394.

68. "Oral History Interview with Harry Easley," August 24, 1967, by J.R. Fuchs, 99, Harry S. Truman Library.

69. Margaret Truman, *Harry S. Truman* (New York: Morrow, 1972), 205.

70. Harold Ickes, Diary, February 25, 1945, 9574, Reel 7, Manuscript Division, Library of Congress.

71. Alonzo Fields, *My 24 Years in the White House* (New York: Coward-McCann, 1960), 114.

72. "Oral History Interview with George Elsey," no date, 259, Harry S. Truman Library.

73. Interview with Bruenn.

74. Ickes, Diary.

75. McIntire, *White House Physician.*

76. Geoffrey C. Ward, ed., *Closest Companion: The Unknown Story of the Intimate Friendship Between Franklin D. Roosevelt and Margaret Suckley* (New York: Houghton Mifflin, 1995).

Chapter 7. Lessons for the Twenty-First Century

1. Quoted from Hugh Gallagher, *FDR's Splendid Deception* (New York: Dodd Mead, 1985), 214.

2. Howard Bruenn, "Clinical Notes on the Illness and Death of President Franklin D. Roosevelt," *Annals of Internal Medicine* 72: 579–591, 1970.

3. Interviews with Bruenn. Bruenn also was aware of a surgical approach (a splanch-nicectomy), but had not considered it in Roosevelt's case. On other medical issues, Bruenn was unaware of the occurrence of a penicillin rash, indicated by Jim Bishop in *FDR's Last Year April 1944–April 1945* (New York: William Morrow, 1974), experienced by Roosevelt on his trip to Yalta. In fact, he was not aware that Roosevelt even received penicillin. Bishop, *FDR's Last Year*, 211, also refers to Dr. Robert Duncan as a chest specialist sent by McIntire to "supplement Bruenn's cardiological examination." The examination of Roosevelt by Duncan is said by Bishop to have occurred in December 1944 in the presence of Bruenn, who has described Duncan as an administrator primarily and not an active clinician at that time. Duncan had no clinical role, according to Bruenn, who also denies that the president underwent surgery for removal of a nevus (possibly a melanoma) over the left eyebrow or for any other reasons. A surgeon, Dr. Harry Goldsmith, raised the issue of a metastatic lesion to the brain many years after Roosevelt's death (Cf. Harry Goldsmith, "Unanswered Mysteries in the Death of Franklin D. Roosevelt," *Journal of Surgery, Gynecology and Obstetrics*, vol. 149, December 1979). Bruenn denies that Roosevelt had any other malignancy or that he was admitted to any hospital under his own or another name. He does not know why the White House water was tested bacteriologically, except as a routine precaution.

4. Telephone interview with Walter Trohan. Trohan was a well-known journalist with he *Chicago Tribune*, who reported in his book, *Political Animals* (Garden City, NY: Doubleday, 1975), that he had made a specific forecast of Roosevelt's death. He also identified two physicians whose roles are unknown, but who may have been called in to deal with serious matters—Dr. Wallace Mason Yater ("a leading Georgetown University Medical School diagnostician," was physician to Harry Hopkins, Roosevelt's adviser, but did not treat the president) and another Washington surgeon, Dr. William Calhoun "Pete" Sterling. The latter is said to have suggested an operation in the winter of 1942–1943, but felt a more senior man should be considered. Dr. Frank Lahey is said to have initially recommended surgery, but reversed himself after Roosevelt's return from Teheran when his decline became quite noticeable. Trohan is not sure what surgery was recommended, possibly for carcinoma of the prostate or colon. Trohan insists that Bruenn was from Boston and that he was inducted into the Navy specifically "to look after the President's

health." He further errs in saying that Bruenn was not present "at the President's side when death came."

Yater's daughter, Millicent Yater Fuller, notes her late father's concern for Roosevelt's health as early as 1940. In a privately published memoir, Dr. Yater is quoted as advising Hopkins that a third term might prove fatal to Roosevelt. This was based on casual, social observation of Roosevelt since Yater at no time examined the president.

Sterling's alleged recommendation of a surgical procedure, perhaps a prostatectomy, was the subject of Washington gossip and duly noted by the FBI. It is discussed in detail in K.R. Crispell and C.F. Gomez, *Hidden Illness in the White House* (Durham, NC: Duke University Press, 1988), 115–117.

5. The medical personnel who gathered on March 29, 1944 to discuss the results of Roosevelt's physical examination were all military: Dr. Ross T. McIntire (Vice Admiral and Surgeon General, U.S. Navy and President's physician); Captain John Harper (Officer in Command, Naval Hospital); Captain Robert Duncan (Executive Officer at the Naval Hospital); Captain Charles Behrens (Officer in Command, Radiology Department of the Naval Hospital); Dr. Paul Dickens; Dr. Howard Bruenn. Cf. Bruenn, "Clinical Notes," 581.

6. Hugh Gregory Gallagher, *FDR's Splendid Deception* (New York: Dodd Mead, 1985), 183.

7. Ibid., 178–191. In a chapter entitled "Depression," Gallagher sets forth the argument that for the last sixteen months of his life, Roosevelt suffered from "depressive neurosis," although he understands that it is "notoriously unwise to diagnose the mental state of persons one has never known, who are long since dead."

8. Sherman Adams, *Firsthand Report* (New York: Harper, 1961), reports on this meeting.

9. Robert E. Gilbert, *The Mortal Presidency* (New York: Basic Books, 1992), 103.

10. *New York Times*, November 6, 1956, 1, col. 5.

11. Jeffrey B. Morris and Richard B. Morris, *Encyclopedia of American History* (New York: Harper Collins, 1996), 458.

12. Telephone interview with Herbert Brownell, August 24, 1994.

13. Major party candidates for president have uniformly been white males and Protestant (except for Governor Alfred E. Smith, 1928, and Senator John Kennedy, 1960) throughout the nation's history. If current health and future survival prospects were a key requirement, qualified women candidates would be preferred because of their greater life expectation at any attained age.

14. C.G. Lasby, *Eisenhower's Heart Attack* (Lawrence: University Press of Kansas, 1997), 155–199.

15. An additional level of complexity would be posed, even in the healthy, stable president or candidate. The impact of psychological or physical illness in spouse or children, or of particularly tense and difficult family relationships, might erode executive effectiveness. The wives of Presidents Lincoln, McKinley, and Harding sustained serious illnesses, and a son of President Lincoln and of President Coolidge sustained fatal infections, namely, typhoid fever and sepsis, respectively.

16. Jeffrey B. Morris and Richard B. Morris, *Encyclopedia of American History* (New York: Harper Collins, 1996), 141.

17. Ibid., 290.

18. *New York Times*, April 13, 1945.

19. Ross T. McIntire, *White House Physician* (New York: G.P. Putnam and Sons, 1946), 67.

20. C. Moran, *Churchill Taken from the Diaries of Lord Moran: The Struggle for Survival* (Boston: Houghton Mifflin, 1966), 218, 223, 236.

21. Quoted in Jerrold M. Post and Robert S. Robins, *When Illness Strikes the Leader* (New Haven, CT: Yale University Press, 1993), 26.

22. Robert Joynt, "Who Is Minding the World?" *Journal of the American Medical Association* 272, no. 21 (December 7, 1994): 1699.

23. Arthur S. Link and James F. Toole, "Presidential Disability and the Twenty-fifth Amendment," *Journal of the American Medical Association* 272, no. 21 (December 7, 1994): 1694.

24. Cited in Richard Hansen, *The Year We Had No President* (Lincoln: University of Nebraska Press, 1962), 121.

25. Ibid. Link and Toole note that determination of disability is a medical function, but that during the hearings on drafting the Twenty-fifth Amendment only one physician, but not a single neurologist, psychiatrist, or any representative of a major organization of the medical community, was asked for opinions.

26. Jimmy Carter, "Presidential Disability and the Twenty-fifth Amendment," *Journal of the American Medical Association* 272, no. 21 (December 7, 1994): 1698.

27. Ted Morgan, *FDR: A Biography* (New York: Simon & Schuster, 1985), 517–518, illustrates the relationship conflict of Garner and Roosevelt as Roosevelt considered a third term with a quote from the *Congressional Digest:* "It is a case of Franklin D. Roosevelt, epitome of the New Deal . . . against John Nance Garner, to whom much of the New Deal is anathema."

28. Post and Robins, *When Illness Strikes the Leader*, 113.

29. Jan K. Herman, "The President's Cardiologist," *Navy Medicine*, March–April 1990, 8.

30. Robert Gilbert, *The Mortal Presidency*, 187–188.

31. *Disability in U.S. Presidents: Report, Recommendations and Commentaries* by *The Working Group* (Winston-Salem, NC: Bowman Gray Scientific Press, 1997).

Bibliography

Articles

Bateman, Herman. "Observations on President Roosevelt's Health During World War II." *Mississippi Valley Historical Review* XLIII:82–101, June 1956 to March 1957.

Boyer, N.H. "The Treatment of Hypertension." *Medical Clinics of North America* 27: 1421–1437, 1942.

Brooks, J.J. et al. "The Final Diagnosis of President Cleveland's Lesion." *Transactions and Studies of the College of Physicians.* 2:1–26, 1980.

Bruenn, Howard G. "Clinical Notes on the Illness and Death of President Franklin D. Roosevelt." *Annals of Internal Medicine* 72, no 4: 579–591, 1970.

Carter, James. "Presidential Disability and the Twenty-fifth Amendment." *Journal of the American Medical Association* 272:1698, 1994.

Daley, R.M., Ungerleider, H.E., and Gubner, R.S. "Prognosis in Hypertension." *Journal of the American Medical Association* 121:383–389, 1943.

Fabricant, Noah B. "Franklin D. Roosevelt's Tonsillectomy and Poliomyelitis." *The Eye, Ear, Nose and Throat Monthly,* vol. XXXVI, June 1957.

Gilbert, Robert E. "The Political Effects of President Illness: The Case of Lyndon B. Johnson." *Political Psychology,* vol. 16, no. 4, 1995.

Hamberger, W.W. "The Treatment of Hypertension." *Medical Clinics of North America* 25:129–145, 1941.

Herman, Jan K. "The President's Cardiologist." *Navy Medicine,* March–April 1990.

Ho, K.K.L, et al. "The Epidemiology of Heart Failure: The Framingham Study." *Journal American College of Cardiology* 22:6A-13A, 1993.

Joynt, Robert J. "Who is Minding the World?" *Journal of the American Medical Association* 272:1699–1700, 1994.

Kagen, A., et al. "Blood Pressure and Its Relation to Coronary Heart Disease in the Framingham Study." *Hypertension* 81:53–81, 1959.

Kannel, W.B., et al. "Role of Blood Pressure in the Development of Congestive Heart Failure: The Framingham Study." *The New England Journal of Medicine* 287:781–787, 1972.

Link, Arthur S., and Toole, J.F. "Presidential Disability and the Twenty-fifth Amendment." *Journal of the American Medical Association* 272:1694–1697, 1994.

"Longevity of Presidents, Vice Presidents and Unsuccessful Candidates for President." *Statistical Bulletin,* July–September 1980.

Orlansky, H. "Reactions to the Death of President Roosevelt." *Journal of Social Psychology* 26:235–266, 1947.

Perkin, Jeanne. "The President's Doctor." *Life,* July 31, 1944.

Roosevelt, Anna. "My Life With FDR." *The Woman's Digest,* vol. XXII, May 1948.

Roosevelt, Elliott. "They're Lying about FDR's Health." *Liberty Magazine,* May 1949.

Storm, Fred A. "How is President Roosevelt's Health Today?" *Liberty Magazine,* vol. 14, November 22, 1937.

Books

Abbott, T.P. *The Exemplary President.* Amherst: University of Massachusetts Press, 1990.

Abrams, H.L. *The President Has Been Shot.* New York: W.W. Norton, 1992.

Abramson, R. *The Life of Averell Harriman 1891–1986: Spanning the Century.* New York: William Morrow, 1991.

Adams, Sherman. *Firsthand Report.* New York: Harper & Row, 1961.

Albert, M. *Winston S. Churchill: Road to Victory 1941–45.* Boston: Houghton Mifflin, 1986.

Asbell, Bernard. *When FDR Died.* New York: Holt, Rinehart and Winston, 1961.

————. *The FDR Memoirs.* Garden City, NY: Doubleday, 1973.

Barber, J.T. *The Presidential Character: Predicting Performance in the White House.* Englewood Cliffs, NJ: Prentice-Hall, 1977.

Batchelor, John C. *Father's Day: A Novel.* New York: Henry Holt, 1994.

Beschloss, Michael R. *Kennedy and Roosevelt: The Uneasy Alliance.* New York: W.W. Norton, 1980.

Bishop, Jim. *FDR's Last Year, April 1944–April 1945.* New York: William Morrow, 1974.

Boettiger, James R. *A Love in Shadow.* New York: W.W. Norton, 1978.

Bohlen, Charles E. *Witness to History 1926–1969.* New York: W.W. Norton, 1973.

Brinkley, David. *Washington Goes to War.* New York: Ballantine Books, 1988.

Bullitt, O.H., ed. *For the President: Personal and Secret Correspondence Between Franklin D. Roosevelt and William C. Bullitt.* Boston: Hougton Mifflin, 1972.

Burns, James McGregor. *Roosevelt: The Soldier of Freedom 1940–1945.* New York: Harcourt, Brace, Jovanovich, 1970.

Churchill, A. *The Roosevelts: American Aristocrats.* New York: Harper and Row, 1965.

Churchill, Winston S. *The Second World War: Triumph and Tragedy.* Boston: Houghton Mifflin, 1953.

Ciechanowski, Jan. *Defeat in Victory.* Garden City, NY: Doubleday, 1947.

Collier, Peter, with Horowitz, D. *The Roosevelts.* New York: Simon & Schuster, 1994.

Crispell, K.R., and Gomez, C.Z. *Hidden Illness in the White House.* Durham, NC: Duke University Press, 1988.

Dall, C.B. *FDR: My Exploited Father-in-Law.* Tulsa, OK: Christian Crusade Publications, 1968.

Daniels, Jonathan. *White House Witness 1942–45.* Garden City, NY: Doubleday, 1975.

Davis, Kenneth S. *FDR: The New Deal Years 1933–37.* New York: Random House, 1979.

————. *The Beckoning of Destiny 1882–1928.* New York: G.P. Putnam and Sons, 1972.

————. *FDR: Into the Storm.* New York: Random House, 1993.

DeGregorio, W.A. *The Complete Book of U.S. Presidents from George Washington to George Bush.* New York: Wings Book, 1991.

Donovan, R.J. *Tumultuous Years: The Presidency of Harry Truman 1949–53.* New York: W.W. Norton, 1982.

Eisenhower, J.S.D. *The Bitter Wood.* New York, G.P. Putnam and Sons, 1969.

Emmet, John Hughes. *The Living Presidency.* New York: Coward, McCann and Geoghegan, 1973.

Farley, James A. *Jim Farley's Story: The Roosevelt Years.* New York: McGraw-Hill, 1948.

Farr, F. *FDR.* New Rochelle, NY: Arlington House, 1972.

Feerick, J.D. *From Failing Hands: The Story of Presidential Succession.* New York: Fordham University Press, 1965.

————. *The Twenty-fifth Amendment.* New York: Fordham University Press, 1976.

Feingold, H.L. *The Politics of Rescue.* New York: Holocaust Library, 1970.

Ferrell, Robert H. *Choosing Truman.* Columbia: University of Missouri Press, 1994.

————. *The Dying President: Franklin D. Roosevelt, 1944–1945.* Columbia: University of Missouri Press, 1998.

————. *Truman: A Centenary Remembrance.* New York: Viking Press, 1984.

————, ed. *Dear Bess: The Letters from Harry to Bess Truman 1910–1959.* New York: W.W. Norton. 1983.

————. *Harry S. Truman: A Life.* Columbia: University of Missouri Press, 1994.

Fishberg, A.M. *Hypertension and Nephritis.* Philadelphia: Lea and Febiger, 1939.

Flynn, Edward J. *You're the Boss.* New York: Viking, 1947.

Freidel, Frank. *Franklin D. Roosevelt. A Rendezvous With Destiny.* Boston: Little, Brown, 1990.

Friedman, Edwin H. *A Failure of Nerve: Leadership in the Age of the Quick Fix.* Bethesda, MD: Edwin H Friedman Estate/Trust, 1999.

Gallagher, Hugh Gregory. *FDR's Splendid Deception.* New York: Dodd Mead, 1985.

Geddes, D.P. *Franklin Delano Roosevelt—A Memorial.* New York: Dial Press, 1945.

Gilbert, Robert E. *Mortal Presidency. Illness and Anguish in the White House.* New York: Basic Books, 1992.

————. *Mortal Presidency. Illness and Anquish in the White House,* 2nd. ed. New York: Fordham University Press, 1998.

Goodwin, Doris Kearns. *No Ordinary Time.* New York: Simon & Schuster, 1994.

Graham Jr., O.L., and Wander, M.R. eds. *Franklin D. Roosevelt: His Life and Time: An Encyclopedic View.* Boston: G.K. Hall, 1985.

Gross, Michael B., and Kumar, Martha Joynt. *Portraying the President: The White House and the News Media.* Baltimore: Johns Hopkins University Press, 1981.

Gunther, John. *Roosevelt in Retrospect: A Profile in History.* New York: Harper, 1952.

Halasz, N. *Roosevelt Through Foreign Eyes.* Princeton, NJ: D. Van Nostrand, 1961.

Harmon, Richard. *The Year We Had No President.* Lincoln: University of Nebraska Press, 1962.

Harriman, W.A., and Abel, E. *Special Envoy to Churchill and Stalin 1941–46.* New York: Random House, 1975.

Hassett, William D. *Off the Record with FDR 1942–45.* New Brunswick, NJ: Rutgers University Press, 1958.

Hiss, Alger. *Recollections of a Life.* New York: Seaver Books/Henry Holt, 1988.

Hoover, H. *The Ordeal of Woodrow Wilson.* New York: McGraw Hill, 1958.

————. *The Memoirs of Herbert Hoover.* New York: Macmillan, 1952.

Hughes, E.J. *The Living Presidency.* New York: Coward, McCann and Geoghan, 1972.

Karski, J. *Story of a Secret State.* Boston: Houghton Mifflin, 1944.

Lasby, C.G. *Eisenhower's Heart Attack.* Lawrence: University Press of Kansas, 1997.

Lash, Joseph. *A World of Love, Eleanor Roosevelt and Her Friends 1943–62.* Garden City, NY: Doubleday, 1984.

Leuchtenberg, W.E. *In the Shadow of FDR: From Harry Truman to Bill Clinton.* Ithaca, NY: Cornell University Press, 1993.

Lippman Jr., T. *The Squire of Warm Springs: FDR in Georgia, 1924–45.* Chicago: Playboy Press, 1977.

Lowenheim, Harold; Langley, Harold D., and Jonas, Manfred, eds. *Roosevelt and Churchill: Their Secret Wartime Correspondence.* New York: Dutton, 1975.

McCullough, David. *Truman*. New York: Touchstone, 1993.

McIntire, Ross T. *White House Physician*. New York: G.P. Putnam and Sons, 1946.

Miller, Nathan. *FDR: An Intimate History*. Garden City, NY: Doubleday, 1983.

Lord Moran (Charles Wilson). *Churchill: Taken from the Diaries of Lord Moran*. Boston: Houghton Mifflin, 1966.

Morgan, Ted. *FDR: A Biography*. New York: Simon & Schuster, 1985.

Morris, Jeffrey B. and Morris, Richard B. *Encyclopedia of American History*. New York: Harper Collins, 1996.

Park, B.E. *The Impact of Illness on World Leaders*. Philadelphia: University of Pennsylvania Press, 1986.

———. *Ailing, Aging, Addicted: Studies of Compromised Leadership*. Lexington: University Press of Kentucky, 1993.

Perkins, Frances. *The Roosevelt I Knew*. New York: Viking Press, 1946.

Perlmutter, Amos. *FDR and Stalin*. Columbia: University of Missouri Press, 1993.

Pfiffner, J.P., and Hoxie, R.G. *The Presidency in Transition*. New York: Center for the Study of the Presidency, 1989.

Post, Jerrold M., and Robins, Robert S. *When Illness Strikes the Leader*. New Haven, CT: Yale University Press, 1993.

Reedy, George. *The Twilight of the Presidency*. New York: World Publishing Company, 1970.

Reilly, M.F. *Reilly of the White House*. New York: Simon & Schuster, 1947.

Reeves, Richard. *President Kennedy: Profile of Power*. New York: Simon & Schuster, 1993.

Rigdon, William M. *White House Sailor*. Garden City, NY: Doubleday, 1962.

Roosevelt, Eleanor. *The Autobiography of Eleanor Roosevelt*. New York: Da Capo Press, 1972.

———. *This I Remember*. New York: Harper & Brothers, 1949.

Roosevelt, Elliott, ed. *FDR: His Personal Letters* (Volumes 1 and 2). New York: Duell, Sloan and Pearce, 1948.

Roosevelt, James. *Affectionately F.D.R., A Son's Story of a Lonely Man*. New York: Harcourt Brace, 1959.

———. *My Parents: A Differing View*. Chicago: Playboy Press, 1976.

Rosenman, Samuel I. *Working with Roosevelt*. New York: Harper & Row, 1951.

Russell, F. *The Shadow of Blooming Grove: Warren G. Harding and His Times*. New York: McGraw Hill, 1968.

Savage, S.J. *Roosevelt, the Party Leader 1932–45*. Lexington: University Press of Kentucky, 1991.

Schilder, P. *Goals and Desires of Man*. New York: Columbia University Press, 1942.

Schlesinger Jr., A.M. *The Age of Roosevelt: The Crisis of the Old Order 1919–33*. Boston: Houghton Mifflin, 1957.

———. *The Coming of the New Deal*. Boston: Houghton Mifflin, 1959.

———, ed. *The Almanac of American History*. New York: Barnes & Noble, 1993.

Sherwood, Robert *Roosevelt and Hopkins*. New York: Harper, 1948.

Smith, Merriman. *A White House Memoir*. New York: W.W. Norton, 1972.

———. *Thank you Mr. President*. New York: Harper, 1946.

Smith, R.N. *Dewey and His Times*. New York: Simon & Schuster, 1982.

Society of Actuaries. *Build and Blood Pressure Study*. Schaumburg, IL: Society of Actuaries, 1959.

Sorenson, Theodore. *Kennedy*. New York: Harper & Row, 1965.

Starling, E.W. *Starling of the White House*. New York: Simon & Schuster, 1984.

Stettinius Jr., Edward R. *Roosevelt and the Russians: The Yalta Conference*. Garden City, NY: The Country Life Press, 1949.

Tebbel, J., and Watts, S.M. *The Press and the Presidency*. New York: Oxford University Press, 1985.

Trohan, William T. *Political Animals*. Garden City, NY: Doubleday, 1975.

Truman, Harry S. *Memoirs: Year of Decisions.* Garden City, New York: Doubleday and Company, 1955.

Truman, Margaret. *Harry S. Truman.* New York: William Morrow, 1973.

Tully, Grace. *FDR—My Boss.* New York: Charles Scribner's Sons, 1949.

Wann, A.J. *The President as Chief Administrator: A Study of Franklin D. Roosevelt.* Washington, DC: Public Affairs Press, 1968.

Ward, Geoffrey. *Before the Trumpet, Young Franklin Roosevelt 1882–1905.* New York: Harper & Row, 1986.

Ward, Geoffrey C., ed. *Closest Companion: The Unknown Story of the Intimate Friendship Between Franklin D. Roosevelt and Margaret Suckley.* New York: Houghton Mifflin, 1995.

————. *A First Class Temperament: The Emergence of Franklin Roosevelt.* New York: Harper & Row, 1989.

Weinstein, E.A. *Woodrow Wilson: A Medical and Psychological Biography.* Princeton, NJ: Princeton University Press, 1981.

West, J.B. *Upstairs at the White House.* New York: Coward, McCann and Georghan, 1937.

Wilson, Robert A., ed. *Character Above All: Ten Presidents from FDR to George Bush.* New York: Simon & Schuster, 1995.

Winfield, Betty Houchin. *FDR and the News Media.* Urbana: University of Illinois Press, 1990.

Woodward, Robert. *Shadows—Five Presidents and the Legacy of Watergate.* New York: Simon & Schuster, 1999.

Compiled Presidential Press Conferences of Franklin D. Roosevelt. New York: De Capo Press, July, 1943–December, 1943.

Manuscripts

Bruenn, Howard. G. Diary. Franklin D. Roosevelt Library.

Hannegan, Robert E. Papers. Harry S. Truman Library.

Ickes, Harold. L. Diary. Library of Congress.

King, MacKenzie. Diary. Library of Congress.

Pauley, Ed. "Memorandum to Jonathan Daniels." White House Office Files. Harry S. Truman Library.

Roosevelt, Franklin D. Family Papers. Franklin D. Roosevelt Library.

Roosevelt, Franklin D. Official File. Franklin D. Roosevelt Library.

Roosevelt, Franklin D. Speech File. Franklin D. Roosevelt Library.

Smith, Harold D. Diary. Franklin D. Roosevelt Library.

Truman, Harry S. Papers. Harry S. Truman Library.

Truman, Harry S. "Letters Related to Roosevelt's Health." Harry S. Truman Library.

Oral Histories

Easley, Harry, by J.R. Fuchs. Harry S. Truman Library, August 24, 1967.

Elsey, George M., by Jerry Hess. Harry S. Truman Library, 1969–1970.

Graham, Wallace, by Niel M. Johnson. Harry S. Truman Library, March 30, 1989.

Halsted, Anna Roosevelt, by James E. Sargent. Columbia University Oral History Project, 1973.

Nixon, Robert G., by Jerry N. Hess. Harry S. Truman Library, 1970.

Rowley, James J., by Niel M. Johnson. Harry S. Truman Library, September 20, 1988.

Index

A

Abrams, Herbert, xi
age (*see* longevity, presidential)
Agnew, Spiro, 127
airplane, use while campaigning, 31–32
alcohol consumption, 38–39
Allen, George, 66, 71
Ambrose, Stephen, xi
Annals of Internal Medicine, 91
appendicitis, 17
Arthur, Chester A., *107*
Asbell, Bernard, 159
assassination attempts, presidential, 3
atomic bombs, 102–3
audiotape analysis, 93–95

B

Barkley, Alben, 71, 72, 103
Baruch, Bernard, xiv, 56, 64, 114, 144
Behrens, Charles, 46
Bennett, Edward, 19
Bennett, Robert, 101
Beschloss, Michael R., 71
Bethesda Naval Hospital, 58
Biddle, Frances, *12*
birth of Roosevelt, 16
Bishop, Jim, 104
Black, Hugo, 33

blood pressure (*see* hypertension)
Blum, Harry, 159
Board of Medical Consultants, 47, 48
Boettiger, Anna Roosevelt (daughter of
    FDR)
  Harold Ickes' concerns voiced to, 115
  information withheld from, 104
  limited understanding of father's health
      problems, 60, 65
  longevity of, *40*
  on stress in White House, 38
Boettiger, John (son-in-law of FDR), 71,
    111–12
Bohlen, Charles E. (Chip), 88
Bookatz, Samuel, 85, 159
Boone, Joel, 41–42
Boring, Floyd, 109, 159
Brazil, response to Roosevelt's death, 106
Breitman, Robert, 159
Bremerton speech, 74–75, 115
Brinkley, David, 102
bronchitis, 54–55, 60, 79
Brownell, Herbert, 123, 126, 159
Bruenn, Howard G.
  comments of
      on Board of Medical Consultants,
          47
      on Bremerton speech, 75
      on FDR at Warm Springs, 97,
          97–98

Bruenn, Howard G.
  comments of *(continued)*
    on FDR's attitude toward his
      health, 61, 63
    on FDR's fourth inauguration, 85
    on FDR's last day, 99, 100, 101
    on jeopardized Yalta efforts, 97
    on McIntire's cover-ups, 60, 91
    on missing medical records, 58,
      59
    on Mrs. Roosevelt's viewpoint of
      husband, 64
    on newspapers' daily causality
      lists, 52
    on not hospitalizing FDR, 48
    on Quebec meeting, 76
    on Yalta Conference, 87–88
  examinations of FDR, 45–46, 47, 56
  interview date, 159
  medical recommendations by, 61,
    119–20, 131–32
  (see also Clinical Notes on the Illness
    and Death of President Franklin D.
    Roosevelt [Bruenn])
bulbar polio, 39
Bullitt, William C., 37, 89, 128
Burma, during World War II, 148
Burns, James MacGregor, 97, 159, xi
Bush, George H., 4, *9*, 10
Byrnes, James F., 71, 72, 88, 115

C

Cabinet members
  dismissal of, 131
  longevity of, 4–5, *12*
Caffery, Jefferson, 87
Cairo-Teheran Conference, 163
Camp, Lawrence, 50
campaigning, for fourth term, 62–95
  airplane use, 31–32
  announcement to run, 62
  family's feelings about, 64–65
  FDR's feelings about, 63
  motivation for running, 62–63, 71
  New York City tour, 80–81
  political figures' feelings about, 65–66,
    72–73
  Roosevelt's advisors on, 63–64
  running mate/successor, 72–73
  wheelchair use, 78

Carter, James (Jimmy), *9*, 10, 129–30
Casablanca Conference, 163
cerebral hemorrhage, 100, 105, 157
Cermak, Anton J., 26
Chiang Kai-shek, *12*, 43, 163
Chicago Daily Tribune (newspaper)
  attitude toward McIntire, 91
  on FDR's health, 78
  on no coverage of Bremerton speech,
    75
  on Truman as president, 79
  on Yalta address to Congress, 90
childhood of Roosevelt, 15–17
China, during World War II, 148
Choosing Truman (Ferrell), 83
Churchill, Winston
  conference involvement, 43, 86, 151,
    163, 164
  conflicts with Stalin, 92–93, 98
  longevity of, *12*
  on Roosevelt's death, 107
Civilian Conservation Corps, 28
Cleveland, Grover, 10–11
Clinical Notes on the Illness and Death of
  President Franklin D. Roosevelt
  (Bruenn), 58, 138–58
  election and inauguration, 151–52
  last days at Warm Springs, 156–57
  March 1994 examination
    diagnosis and recommendations,
      139–40
    further observations, 140–41
    group consultation, 141–43
    physical examination, 138–39
    South Carolina stay, 143–46
  return to Washington, 150–51
  State of the War, 146–50
  Yalta Conference, 154–55
    return via Egypt, 155–56
    trip to, 153–54
Clinton, William (Bill), xvi, 8, *9*, 118
Closest Companion, 116–17
Cohen, Benjamin V., 63–64
Collier, P., *40*
conferences
  Hawaii Conference, 163
  Quebec Conference, 163–64
  Teheran Conference, 43
  wartime, 163–64
  Yalta Conference, 86–90
    agreements of in danger, 96–97

conferences
  Yalta Conference *(continued)*
    Bruenn's clinical notes regarding, 153–56
    overview, 164
  (see also press conferences)
confidence, FDR's, 14–15
congestive heart failure
  documentation of, 157
  failure to report, 60
  survival probability, 67
congressmen, length of terms, 8
conservation, of natural resources, 28
Constitution *(see* Twenty-fifth Amendment)
Coolidge, Calvin, *9, 107*
Corcoran, Thomas, 114
coronary problems *(see* congestive heart failure; hypertension)
Crider, John, 86
Crimea Conference *(see* Yalta Conference)
Cummings, Homer C., *12*
current/future issues, 133–34

D

Daniels, Jonathan, 60, 91
Daniels, Josephus, 18
Daniels, Margaret Truman (daughter of Harry Truman), 159
Day FDR Died, The (Bishop), 104
de Gaulle, Charles, *12,* 147, 155, 163
death of FDR, 98–100
  days prior to, 109–10
    Dorothy Suckley's comments on, 116–17
    Harold Ickes' comments on, 113–16
  medical action just before, 100, 101–2
  passing of power following, 102
  reactions to
    denial and deception, 108–12
    initial, 102–7
    Truman's, 102
Declaration of Cairo, 43
Deegan, Nancy, xi
Delano, Laura, 116
dementia, Twenty-fifth Amendment's provisions for, 128–29
deMille, Cecil B., 55

Democratic National Committee, 65–66
depression, 128–29, 131
Dewey, Thomas E., 81, 103, 123
Dickens, Paul, 47
digitalization, 46–47, 156
disability, presidential
  Twenty-fifth Amendment's provisions for, 127–32
  (see also poliomyelitis)
doctor-patient metaphor
  and World War II, 29–31
  and Great Depression, 25, 27–29
doctors' examinations *(see* examinations, physical)
Dolphin, The (yacht), 18
Douglas, William O., 71, 72
Dr. New Deal, 27–28, 108
Dr. Win-the-War, 29–31
Dulles, Allen, 98
Duncan, Robert, 46, 59, 83
Dying President, The: Franklin D. Roosevelt, 1944–1945 (Ferrell), 47, 90, 103

E

Eagleton, Thomas, 10
Early, Steven T.
  on FDR's health, 52, 53, 80
  role of with journalists, 32
  role of with photographers, 33
Easley, Harry, 110, 111
economic problems, national, 25
Eden, Anthony, 164
Edison, Charles, *12*
Eisenhower, Dwight D., 8, 9, *9,* 122–23
election, presidential *(see* campaigning, for fourth term)
Elsey, George, 75, 109, 112, 159
emotional health, 18, 92–93
Esperancilla, Irineo, 100
Etter, Harry, 57, 160
Evans, Ruth, xii
examinations, physical
  failure to perform rectal examination, 47
  by Harry Etter, 57
  March 1994 examination, 138–41
  pre-presidential, 26–27
  revealing hypertension, 45–46, 54, 56

F

Fabricant, Noah, 20–21
Fala speech, 76
Farley, James F., *12*, 37, 65, 71
FDR and Stalin (Perlmutter), 83
fear
  after FDR's death, 106
  FDR's comment on, 118
Federal Aid system, 28
Feinlieb, Manning, 160
Ferrell, Robert H., 47, 83, 90, 103,
  160
Field, Alonzo, 112
Filmore, Millard, *107*
fire, FDR's fear of, 18
Fireside Chats
  1933, 28
  1940, 30
  1943, 44
  1945, 94–95
Fitzpatrick, Paul F., 81
Flynn, Edward J., 65, 66, 71
Ford, Gerald R., 3, *9*, 10, 127
Forrestal, James V., *12*, 64, 114, 131
Fox, George, 70
Framingham Study, 69
*Franklin D. Roosevelt, His Life and
  Times: An Encyclopedic View*
  (Graham and Wander), *12*
Franklin D. Roosevelt Library (New
  York), 58, xi
Freud, Sigmund, 107
Friedman, Edwin H., xi, 92–93
future/current issues, 133–34

G

Galbraith, John K., 72, 160
Gallagher, Hugh G., 31, 33–34, 160
Garfield, James, *107*
Garner, John, *12*, 130
Gibson, Nina Roosevelt (granddaughter
  of FDR), 160
Gilbert, Robert E., xi, 11, 132, 160
Ginzberg, Eli, 90, 160
Giraud, Henry, 163
Goodwin, Doris Kearns, xi, 160
Graebner, Walter, 106
Graham, O.L., Jr., *12*
Grayson, Cary, 41, 121

Great Britain, response to FDR's death,
  106
Great Depression, 25
Griffith, James, 100, 109, 160
Gromyko, Andrei A., 103
Gunther, John, 85
Gurewitsch, Edna, 160

H

Halsted, James, 65
Hamby, Alonzo, 160
handicap, FDR's (*see* poliomyelitis)
Hannegan, Robert, 56–57, 62, 77, 80
Hannegan, William, 72, 74, 160
Harding, William G.
  age at death, *107*
  Americans' feelings upon death of,
    106–7
  doctor's diagnosis of, 42
  health record, *9*
  pre-presidential health problems, 8–9
  on stress of presidential office, 11
  successor of, *107*
Harper, John, 46, 59
Harrison, William H., *107*
Harry S. Truman Library (Independence,
  Missouri), xi
Hassett, William D., 52, 97–98, 98–99,
  109
Hawaii Conference, 163
health problems, FDR's
  cerebral hemorrhage, 100, 105, 157
  congestive heart failure
    documentation of, 157
    failure to report, 60
    survival probability, 67
health risks of presidency, 3–13
  assassination attempts, 3
  factors contributing to
    disparity between presidential
      responsibility and authority,
      7
    expectations of public, 8
    politically determined health
      care, 10–11
    pre-presidential, 8–9, 10
    probing by media, 7–8
    stress of office, 11–12
    time frame of presidency, 8
  presidential longevity, 4–6

heart problems (*see* congestive heart failure; hypertension)
Heller, Milton, 160
hemorrhage, cerebral, 100, 105, 157
Herman, Jan K., xi, 59, 160
Herzstein, Robert, 160
Hibbs, Russell A., 26
high blood pressure (*see* hypertension)
Hiroshima, Japan, 102
Hiss, Alger, 87
Hiss, Tony, 87, 160
Hobcaw estate, 56, 64, 114, 143–46
Holocaust, 54
Hoover, Herbert, 4, 5, *9*, 11, 23
Hopkins, Harry L., *12*, 44, 103
Hopkins, Robert, 88, 161
Howe, Louis, 32
Hoxie, R. Gordon, 161
Hull, Cordell, *12*
Hurd, Charles, 57
Hyman, Sydney, 161
hypertension
  and chest pains, 69–70
  and decision not to hospitalize, 48
  disability probability, 69
  documentation of, 157
  early recordings of, 37–39
  effect of running for third/fourth term on, 39–40
  examination revealing, 45–46, 54, 56, 139–40
  failure to report, 60, 61
  FDR's awareness of, 83, 84, 116, 117
  just after election, 82
  McIntire's denial of, 97
  meeting regarding, 141–43
  not listed as cause of death, 101
  possible causes of, 38–39
  statistics on, *40*
  survival probability, 66–68, 70
  treatment for, 47
  visible effects of, 43–44, 53
  at Warm Springs in 1945, 97–98

I

Ickes, Harold L., 64
  knowledge/lack of knowledge of FDR's health, 111–12, 113–16

Ickes, Harold L. *(continued)*
  longevity of, *12*
  reaction to FDR's death, 103
impairment, presidential (*see* disability, presidential)
inauguration, fourth, 84–86, 152
India, during World War II, 148
infantile paralysis (*see* poliomyelitis)
interviews, 159–62
invincibility, aura of, 32, 72, 108
Irwin, Barbara, 161
Irwin, Edwin, 101
isolationism, 30

J

Jackson, Graham, 99
Jackson, Mrs. Robert, 110
Japan, during World War II, 148
Jefferson, Thomas, 125
Johnson, Andrew, *107*
Johnson, Lyndon B., 3, 4, 9, 11, 132
Jones, Jesse, *12*, 103
Jonse, Marvin, 110
Journal of the American Medical Association, 128–29, 129–30
Joynt, Robert, 128–29
justices, 5–6, 8

K

Kaiser, Henry J., 103, 116
Karski, Jan, 161
Keen, W.W., 19
Kelly, Edward, 71
Kennedy, Foster, 26
Kennedy, John F., 3, *9*, 132
Kennedy, Joseph, 71
King, McKenzie, 75, 91–92, 164
Klein, Arthur G., 53
Knox, Frank, *12*
Krock, Arthur, 35, 105

L

Lahey, Frank, 47, 141
Lambert, Samuel W., 26
Lasser, William, 161
Lattimer, John, 161
legislators, length of terms, 8
LeHand, Marguerite, 37, 69, 83

Liberty Magazine, 27, 34
Life (magazine), 56, 82
  on Americans' dependence on FDR,
    106
  on Truman's presidential appointment,
    102
  on Yalta address to Congress, 90
  on Yalta Conference, 89
lifespan, presidential, 4–6
Lincoln, Abraham, *107*
Link, Arthur S., 129
Lippman, Walter, 89
longevity, presidential, 4–6
Look (magazine), 34
Looker, Earle, 27
Lovett, Robert A., 19

M

MacArthur, Douglas, 87, 163
MacKenzie, Eileen, 106
marriage, FDR's
  effect of poliomyelitis on, 21
  (*see also* Roosevelt, Eleanor)
Mayo Clinic, 33–34
McCormack, Robert, 78
McGovern, George, 10
McIntire, Ross T.
  Board of Medical Consultants recom-
    mendations to, 47
  comments of
      to American Medical Society,
       58
      on Bruenn's recommendations,
       131–32
      day of fourth inauguration, 86
      direct misstatements, 56, 59
      on FDR's death, 41, 97, 100,
       105, 112, 115–16
      in *Liberty Magazine*, 34
      in *New York Times*, 49–50, 51,
       52, 55–56, 62
      orders to Bruenn, 45, 46
      on Roosevelt's running for fourth
       term, 64
      on Tehran trip, 57–58
      in *Time* magazine, 79
      at Yalta Conference, 88–89
  cover-up of hemorrhage, 104
  during FDR's last moments, 101
  feelings of others toward, 42, 55, 91

McIntire, Ross T. *(continued)*
  motivation for clinical judgments, 121
  political role, 113
McKellar, Kenneth, 125
McKinley, William, 3, *9*, *107*
McNary, Charles, 84
media
  effect on presidential health, 7–8
  misinformation campaign with, 59–61
  Roosevelt's control of, 32–42
      during Hugo Black nomination,
       33
      photographs, 33, 60
      via public information officers,
       32–33
  rumors circulated by, 33–36
    (*see also Chicago Daily Tribune*;
      Fireside Chats; *New York Times*;
      press conferences)
medical screening, 121–25
Mediterranean area, during World War II,
  147
Mercer, Lucy, 16, 17, 92
Metropolitan Life Insurance Company
  studies, 6, 7, 46
Mikesh, Robert, 161
Miller, Richard L., 111
Milton, Lipson, 161
Minnich, Caroline, 59, 161
Moody, F. Kennon, xi
Morgenthau, Henry, 99
Morgenthau, Henry J., Jr., *12*, 125, 164
Mortal Presidency, The (Gilbert), 12
Moses, John, 161
Murphy, Frank, *12*
Mutual Life Insurance Company, 26

N

Nagasaki, Japan, 102
National Youth Administration, 28
natural resource conservation, 28
naval training stations, Senate Naval
  Affairs Committee inquiry regard-
  ing, 20, 21–22
Neustadt, Richard, xv
New Deal, 27–28, 108
New York City tour, 80–81
New York Daily News (newspaper),
  77–78
New York Sun (newspaper), 77

New York Times (newspaper), 34, 35–36, 62–95
  about Stettinius in line of succession, 125
  attitude toward McIntire, 91
  comments after FDR's death, 104
  on Eisenhower-Stevenson race, 122
  on FDR's death, 103, 105
  on inaugural address, fourth, 84–85, 86
  McIntire's reassurances on FDR's health, 49–50, 51, 52, 55–56, 62
  on New York tour, 80
  on Pope's message to FDR, 93
  on Yalta address to Congress, 90
news media (*see* media)
newsreel analysis, 93–95
nightmares, FDR's, 117
Nixon, Richard M., xvi, 3, *9*
Nixon, Robert G., 72
Normandy, France, 147
Noyes, Daniel, 73–74, 111

O

O'Donnell, John, 77–78
Office of the Secretary of the Navy, 20, 21–22
O'Reilly, Robert, 10–11
Orlansky, Harold, 108
Osmena, Sergio, 99

P

paralysis (*see* poliomyelitis)
parents of presidents, longevity of, 4, *5*
Parker, Edward, 16
Parkinson's disease, 42
Pauley, Edward, 72
Pauley, Edwin, 66
Paullin, James A., 47, 59, 100, 101, 141
Pearl Harbor attack, 29–31
Pearson, Drew, 115
Pehle, John W., 161
Peluso, Pat, xi
Pendergast, Thomas J., 78
periotonsillar abscess, 17
Perkins, Frances, *12*, 64, 85, 89
Perlmutter, Amos, 83
photographs, in media
  Roosevelt's control of, 33
  selecting and editing of, 60

photographs, of FDR
  "haggard" appearance in, 158
  last one, 99
  at Yalta Conference, 88, 89
physical examinations (*see* examinations, physical)
physicians, White House
  appropriate role of, 120–21
  (*see also* Boone, Joel; McIntire, Ross T.)
pneumonia, 17
poliomyelitis
  coping skills, 24
  diagnosis of, 19
  effect on marriage, 21
  effect on political career, 21–24
  emotional effect, 21
  FDR's support of victims of, 24
  and FDR's use of doctor-patient metaphor, 25
  and hypertension, 39
  initial onset, 19
  late onset of, 20
  and media, 24–25, 33
  as motivation for others, 31
  and physical appearance, 24
  and risk of death, 67
  spread of, 17–18
  susceptibility to, 20–21
  treatment for, 19–20, 22
Pomper, Gerald, xi
Pons, Lily, 55
Pope Pius XII, 93
Post, Jerrold, xi, 15, 131
pre-presidential years, FDR's, 14–25
  dispelling stigmatization of disability, 15
  emotional health, 18
  illness during, 16–18
  influence of mother on, 15–16
  self-confidence, factors affecting, 14–15
presidential longevity, 4–6
presidential scandals, xvi
Presidential Succession Act, 125, 133
Press and the Presidency, The (Tebbel and Watts), 32
press conferences
  December 28, 1943, 28, 29
  frequency of, 36
press conferences, FDR's
  comments about health at, 54–55

press conferences, FDR's *(continiued)*
  control of, 32–33
  health problems visible at, 53, 86
pressure of presidential office, 11, 20, 92–93
Prettyman, Arthur, 100
probability of disability, 69
probability of survival, 66–68, 70
public information officers, 32
public opinion
  of diseased leaders, 10
  effect on presidential health, 7–8
  of Roosevelt's health, 33–34
Public Works Administration (PWA), 28

Q

Quebec Conferences, 75–76, 163–64

R

radio broadcasts, Roosevelt's *(see* Fireside Chats)
Radio Correspondent's Dinner, 85
Raper, H. Stewart, 101
Raper, Mrs. H.S., 161
Rayburn, Sam, 101, 103
Reagan, Ronald, xvi, 8
Reilly, Mike, 100
Republican party, 23
responsibility, presidential, 7
Rigdon, William R., 86–87
Robins, Robert, 131
Rockefeller, Nelson A., 127
Roosevelt, Anna (daughter of FDR) *(see* Boettiger, Anna Roosevelt)
Roosevelt, Eleanor (niece of Eleanor and FDR), 161
Roosevelt, Eleanor (wife of FDR)
  on FDR's Hobcaw stay, 56
  and FDR's illness, 19–20, 21, 22–23, 43, 45
  on FDR's report to Congress, 90
  influence of mother-in-law on, 16
Roosevelt, Elliot (son of FDR), 34, *40*
Roosevelt, Isaac, *40*
Roosevelt, Jacobus, *40*
Roosevelt, James (son of FDR), 15, *40*

Roosevelt, James *(continued)*
  on FDR's chest pains, 69, 70
  on FDR's running for fourth term, 65, 83
Roosevelt, James, Jr. (grandson of FDR), 161
Roosevelt, John (son of FDR), *40*
Roosevelt, Mrs. Franklin J. (daughter-in-law of FDR), 161
Roosevelt, Nicholas, *40*
Roosevelt, Sara Delano (mother of FDR), 15–16
Roosevelt, Theodore, 3, *9*, 63, *107*
Roosevelts, The (Collier), *40*
Roper, Daniel C., *12*
Rosenman, Samuel
  on Bremerton speech, 74–75
  on FDR's appearance after Yalta, 89
  on FDR's concern with party unity, 71
  on FDR's report to Congress, 90
  on FDR's running for fourth term, 64
  on FDR's secrecy, 103
Roukema, Marge, 58–59
Rowley, James R., 100
rumors, regarding Roosevelt's health, 33–37
Russia *(see* Union of Soviet Socialist Republics)
Russell, Frances, 106–7
Rutherford, Lucy *(see* Mercer, Lucy)

S

scandals, presidential, xvi
schedule, FDR's, 36, 48–49, 93
Schmidt, Ivan, 161
screening, medical, 121–25
Seagraves, Eleanor (granddaughter of FDR), 42, 103, 161
Secret Service agents, 109
self-confidence, FDR's, 14–15
Selin, David, 104
Senate Naval Affairs Committee, 20, 21–22
Senate, president pro tempore of, 124, 125
senators, length of terms, 8
Shannon, Neil, 109
Sherwood, Robert, 72, 93
Shoumatoff, Elizabeth, 99
Smith, Alfred E., 23

Smith, Elmer, 162
Smith, Harold G., 44, 84
Smith, Merriman, 38, 44, 109–10
Smith, Walter Bedell, 87
smoking, effect on FDR, 38
Society of Actuaries, 66
Soviet Union (*see* Union of Soviet
    Socialist Republics)
Speaker of the House, 124
Stalin, Joseph
  conference involvement, 163
  conflicts with Churchill, 92–93
  on FDR's death, 110
  longevity of, *12*
  relationship with FDR, 97, 98
  at Teheran Conference, 43
  at Yalta Conference, 86
Stassen, Harold, 106, 162
State of the Union Address, 44
Stettinius, Edward R., Jr., *12*, 88, 102,
    103, 125
Stevenson, Adlai, 122
Stimson, Henry, 36, 125
stock market crash, 25
Storm, Frederick A., 34
stress of presidential office, 11, 20,
    92–93
strokes
  no evidence of in FDR, 158
  probability of, 69
Stuart, Robert A., Jr., 87, 162
succession, presidential (*see*
    Twenty-fifth Amendment)
Suckley, Dorothy, 116–17
Suckley, Margaret, 100
Supreme Court justices, 5–6
survival probability, 66–68, 70
Swanson, Claude A., *12*
Swanson, Homer, 101
Swanson, Mrs. Homer, 162

T

Tarchiani, Alberto, 103
Taylor, Zachary, *107*
Tebbel, John, 32
Teheran Conference, 43
terms, length of, 8
Textbook of Medicine (Cecil), 47
Third Neutrality Act, 30
Thomas A. Edison Industries, 35

Thompson, Craig, 106
throat infections, 17
Time (magazine)
  on FDR's health, 74, 75, 76, 77, 79
  on FDR's running for fourth term,
    66, 81
"togetherness position," 92–93
tonsillectomy, 21
Toole, James, 129
travel of Roosevelt, 31–32, 33
Trohan, Walter, 91, 162
Trout, Bob, 108
Truman, Harry S.
  appointed as president, 102, *107*
  Chicago Daily Tribune's comments
    on, 79
  concern on assuming presidency,
    73–74
  and FDR's death, 101–2
  on FDR's health, 78
  on FDR's nearing death, 110–11
  health record, *9*
  longevity of, *12*
  no initial thoughts on succession,
    73
  not prepared by FDR, 83
  on own qualifications for presidency,
    79
  on presidential disability, 129
  Robert McCormack's comments on,
    78
  vice-presidential nomination, 72,
    115
Truman, Margaret, *73*, 111
Twenty-fifth Amendment
  declaration of presidential disability,
    129
  if available during FDR's presidency,
    130–31
  overview, 125
  text of, 126–27
  use of, 127
  weaknesses of, 127–30
Tyler, John, *107*
typhoid fever, 17

U

Union of Soviet Socialist Republics
    (USSR)
  interest in FDR's health, 92–93

Union of Soviet Socialist Republics (USSR) *(continued)*
    part in 1944 assault, 147–48
    response to FDR's death, 106
    and Yalta agreements, 96–98
United Nations, 63, 96
U.S. Naval Hospital (Bethesda, Maryland), 58
Usher's Diaries, 37, 48, 93
USS Quincy (ship), 86–87, 153, 155
USSR *(see* Union of Soviet Socialist Republics)

V

Vandenberg, Arthur, 103
vice presidents, longevity of, *12*

W

Walker, Frank, *12*, 71
Wallace, David W., 74
Wallace, Henry A., *12*, 66, 71, 72
Wander, M.R., *12*
Ward, Geoffrey, xi, 17, 18
Watson, Edwin, 155–56
Watts, Sarah, 32
Weaver, Robert, 106, 162
weight loss, 150, 151, 152, 158
Weisse, Allen, 162
Welles, Benjamin, 162
Whaley, Storm, 85
wheelchair use, 78
When Illness Strikes the Leader: The Dilemma of the Captive King (Post and Robins), 42
White House Physician (McIntire), 59, 112
White, Theodore, 106

Wickard, Claude R., *12*
wife, FDR's *(see* Roosevelt, Eleanor)
Williams, Aubrey, 53, 54
Willkie, Wendell, 83–84
Wilson, Woodrow, 3, 4
    dismissal of Cabinet member, 131
    effect of stroke, 121, 129
    health record, *9*
    length of presidency, 8
    pre-presidential health problems, 9
    on stress of presidential office, 11
Wold, Karl C., 34
Woodin, William H., *12*
Works Progress Administration (WPA), 28
World War II
    Burma during, 148
    China during, 148
    and doctor-patient metaphor, 29–31
    events in 1944, 53–54
    and FDR's decision to run for fourth term, 39–40, 63
    Holocaust, 54
    India during, 148
    initial U.S. neutrality, 30
    Japan during, 148
    Mediterranean area, 147
    news coverage concentration on, 51–52
    Normandy, 147
    Pacific during, 148–50
    Russian drive, 147–48

Y

Yalta Conference, 86–90
    broken agreements of, 96–97
    Bruenn's clinical notes regarding, 153–56
    overview, 164

About the Author

Hugh E. Evans, M.D., is Professor and former Chairman of Pediatrics, Professor of Prevention Medicine and Community Health, New Jersey Medical School. He is a clinician, educator, researcher, and administrator with a career that spans more than forty years.

He graduated from Columbia College, State University of New York Health Science Center, and had his postdoctoral training at Johns Hopkins Hospital and the National Institutes of Health. He has written more than one hundred papers, as well as numerous abstracts and presentations. He has been active in a number of local, regional, and national medical organizations and served on The Working Group on Disability in United States Presidents.